Paul Porter and his Brothers. [A tale.] By the Author of "Merry and Grave; or, What's in a Name?" [P. A. Blyth.]

Paul Porter, P. A. Blyth

Paul Porter and his Brothers. [A tale.] By the Author of "Merry and Grave; or, What's in a Name?" [P. A. Blyth.]
Porter, Paul
British Library, Historical Print Editions
British Library
Blyth, P. A.
1881].
374 p. ; 8°.
012641.i.30.

The BiblioLife Network

This project was made possible in part by the BiblioLife Network (BLN), a project aimed at addressing some of the huge challenges facing book preservationists around the world. The BLN includes libraries, library networks, archives, subject matter experts, online communities and library service providers. We believe every book ever published should be available as a high-quality print reproduction; printed on- demand anywhere in the world. This insures the ongoing accessibility of the content and helps generate sustainable revenue for the libraries and organizations that work to preserve these important materials.

The following book is in the "public domain" and represents an authentic reproduction of the text as printed by the original publisher. While we have attempted to accurately maintain the integrity of the original work, there are sometimes problems with the original book or micro-film from which the books were digitized. This can result in minor errors in reproduction. Possible imperfections include missing and blurred pages, poor pictures, markings and other reproduction issues beyond our control. Because this work is culturally important, we have made it available as part of our commitment to protecting, preserving, and promoting the world's literature.

GUIDE TO FOLD-OUTS, MAPS and OVERSIZED IMAGES

In an online database, page images do not need to conform to the size restrictions found in a printed book. When converting these images back into a printed bound book, the page sizes are standardized in ways that maintain the detail of the original. For large images, such as fold-out maps, the original page image is split into two or more pages.

Guidelines used to determine the split of oversize pages:

• Some images are split vertically; large images require vertical and horizontal splits.
• For horizontal splits, the content is split left to right.
• For vertical splits, the content is split from top to bottom.
• For both vertical and horizontal splits, the image is processed from top left to bottom right.

PAUL PORTER

AND HIS BROTHERS.

"There, my little fellow," he said, "I hope the worst of your troubles are over now." *Page* 30.

PAUL PORTER

AND HIS BROTHERS.

BY THE AUTHOR OF
"MERRY AND GRAVE; OR, WHAT'S IN A NAME?"

London:

JARROLD & SONS, 3, PATERNOSTER BUILDINGS.

PREFACE.

———— ❖ ————

DESPITE life's strange vicissitudes, its dizzy heights and far-sounding depths, much of even tenor pervades human existence. And while ever and anon exalted, illustrious lives flash with meteoric brilliancy before our dazzled vision, startling us into wondering admiration, thrilling us with intense ardour and delight—yet they are the dear, long-familiar, much-loved faces, the sweet, every-day commonplaces which give to life truest solace and tenderest charm. And if in the story of "Paul Porter and his Brothers" I have not striven after impossible circumstances, or too exalted models of perfection, I have endeavoured to speak of life much as it generally is, conscious that true nobility is most frequently developed under humble guise, and the simple deeds and daily duties are those which make the largest share of that last final account which every responsible human soul must eventually render.

CONTENTS.

CONTENTS.

PAUL PORTER & HIS BROTHERS.

CHAPTER I.

CHOOSING THE NAMES.

PAUL PORTER, that was his name; not much of a name for a hero, perhaps, but then the circumstances to which he owed his name were peculiar—I will try and explain them.

To begin with, Paul was the fifth child in the family; that it should make any difference whether a child is first or fifth seems unreasonable, for a baby is a baby, whether it be first or last in the family records; still, that being fifth child did seriously affect Paul, so far as his name was concerned, remains an undisputed fact. Yet it was not so much his being the fifth child, as being the fifth boy, that proved the exasperating part of the business. For while we meet with some parents who, with a sort of passive content, will tell you that as to their children being boys or girls, they never had a wish either way, there are others who have not only a wish, but a very earnest desire about the matter. Proud parents ardently desiring an heir to wide lands, may find their wedded life crowned only by a succession of daughters; while a large family of boys will speak with something akin to reverence, of the little sister who for a few years blossomed in their midst, and then sickened, faded and died. And they will tell you in hushed tones of a little grave in the churchyard, and that father and mother always like to go home from church that way, for the sake of just passing by that little grave. Such was the case with Paul's father, Mr. William Porter. He could boast a whole band of stalwart brothers, but his only remembrance of a sister, was of a wee, pretty little maiden who gladdened their home for eight short years, and then died, leaving them almost broken-hearted at her loss. And if Mr. Porter indulged in the depths of his soul a secret wish, a fluttering hope, it was that a little daughter might fill the place of the dead Selina, the little sister whose memory was still green in the heart of her faithful brother. Not that in contemplation of the advent of his first-born, hardly to himself did he express the desire; but then the first child in itself is a source of such mysterious delight, that unless the case be urgent indeed, few will stay to cavil at its sex. Only once did the latent wish manifest itself.

One winter's night, as he and his wife sat lingering over their fire, with her hand in his, she said,

"Don't you think Oliver Ernest a pretty name, love?"

Mr. Porter answered that he did think it a pretty name. In fact, he thought but little about it; beyond a sort of instinctive feeling that the two names sounded well together, he had no particular opinion, good or bad, on the subject. But when his wife was about to propose a feminine name of equal beauty, he suddenly interrupted her.

"If we should ever have a daughter, my dear, we will call her Selina."

"Selina!" almost shrieked Mrs. Porter; "oh! I don't like that name."

Mr. Porter made no answer in words; he only gave a dry cough, and taking the poker, quietly stirred the fire. His wife supposed her spirited opposition had settled the matter. Had she lived with her husband so many years instead of months, she might have felt less certain of the result, and might probably have detected in the quiet face and manner, a very considerable degree of obstinate determination. However, there was never any real cause for altercation on the point: the baby, when he arrived, was accommodating enough to prove a boy, and the parents in their joy and pride called him Oliver Ernest accordingly.

Then when in process of time it became probable that Oliver Ernest would have a little playfellow,—or as his nurse maliciously suggested, a slit in his nose,—again a throb of the old desire woke up in the father's heart. But the hope was not to be fulfilled; the playfellow came, but, alas! he came only in the form of a brother, and Mr. Porter had really a good mind to be disappointed. And when his wife—not sharing at all in these sentiments, and who looked on another son only as another honour—formally consulted him upon the child's name, (that point being previously settled in her own mind,) he treated the matter almost with indifference, and so the second hope of the family, according to his mother's desire, was named Sydney Herbert. The two children grew and throve, and if Mr. Porter was not proud of such a pair of healthy, blooming boys, he certainly ought to have been.

And then a third link in the family chain arrived; but he, contrary to secret anticipation, also proved a boy. Still in some respects this child differed somewhat from his brothers. In the first place he did not owe his name to any ingenious arrangement on the part of his mother; for about the time of his birth, a bachelor uncle returned from abroad, and this gentleman, who bore the name of Thomas Samuel Porter, desired that the baby should be named after him, intimating that if the request was complied with, the said Thomas Samuel Porter, jun., would one day be the possessor of a very fair inheritance. So his mother comforted herself with the thought, that if he had but a plain name, he had brilliant prospects. Even Mr. Porter himself found in this circumstance some consolation for the fact of his not being the now earnestly longed-for Selina.

But when a fourth child arrived on the scene, the words, "A boy—a very fine boy, sir," fell heavy as lead on Mr. Porter's now thoroughly-disappointed soul; and when his friends pressed round him with congratulations upon being the happy father of four sons, he had to bear it all with the best grace he could. But whether children were becoming more common-place occurrences, or whether it was owing to domestic troubles which preceded his arrival—the children having all been ill with some of the sicknesses so attendant on early childhood,—certain it is that no name had been definitely fixed upon for this fourth baby. But the matter did not remain long in doubt: Mr. Porter coming in one day found his wife and the nurse engaged in an animated discussion, and upon his enquiring the cause, he was triumphantly asked if he did not consider Theodore Eustace a sweet name.

Mr. Porter winced; to tell the truth, he had been slightly twitted by some of his friends upon the rather flowing names of his children: but he had enough of the man in him to understand that just then was a time of his wife's entire supremacy, so he merely asked very mildly, by way of suggestion, if she didn't consider it rather unnecessary to have two such grand names together—rather a waste of names, in fact. But upon his wife rising up on her couch, and declaring that she could name a hundred children right off, and give them two names each, all of that description, Mr. Porter, who did not for a moment doubt her capabilities in that line, prudently dropped the subject; and Mrs. Porter, meeting with no further opposition, named him as she desired, Theodore Eustace.

So time passed, and then appeared the fifth and last of that little family circle. Another boy truly, but this time a somewhat puny, delicate one; just such a baby, that had he been a wonderful first-born, or a long-coveted heir, his days and nights would have been watched with keen solicitude. As it was, however, soon after his birth, Mrs. Porter fell ill, so dangerously ill that for a time her life was despaired of; and during this period, beside just supplying to the baby common necessities, no one seemed to make much note of his existence. Certainly Miss Dorothy Fairfield, Mrs. Porter's aunt, who came in this crisis of events to help nurse the sick wife, and superintend the household—she being a tender-hearted, gentle woman, would sometimes peer lovingly into the cradle where the baby lay; but as for naming him, no one gave a thought in that direction. His mother for the most part was delirious, and when she escaped from imminent danger, lay weak herself as a baby, and was in no state certainly to think upon the matter; and so baby seemed as if he might have been called "baby" all his life through, when one day no other than the registrar himself appeared, and formally demanded the name of the child. Miss Dorothy herself encountered him, and was struck dumb by the question: in dismay she fled to Mr. Porter for help.

"The registrar is come to register the child; what name is he to be called?"

"Call him just what you like," was the indifferent answer.

"But I don't know a name," said Miss Dorothy hopelessly. "If it had been a girl, now!"

The words, innocent in themselves, proved very irritating to Mr. Porter.

"But it is not a girl," he said, so fiercely as almost to startle Miss Dorothy.

"Well, you must name him," she said; "I can't think of anything, I'm sure."

"Then," said Mr. Porter, meditatively stroking his chin, "I suppose I must; and I'll—yes—I'll call him Paul."

"Paul! but you never had anyone in the family that name?"

"Yes, I had an uncle Paul: one of the best fellows that ever walked, was my uncle Paul. I'll call the child after him: I wonder I never thought of it for one of the others."

Having thus settled the question, he walked away with a resolute determination, and Miss Dorothy quietly went back to the sick chamber.

Soon afterwards she heard Mr. Porter's steps ascending the stairs; her patient had just then fallen into a light slumber, so as he reached the threshold of the door, she held up her finger as a signal for him to stop, and noiselessly crossed the room to where he stood.

"Well," she said, "what have you called him?"

"Paul."

"Only Paul?"

"Only Paul, of course. What does he want two names for? one name is enough for any child."

"Paul—Porter," said Miss Dorothy slowly.

A startled look crept into Mr. Porter's face. For the first time the truth flashed into his mind, that the uncle he had named the child after was his mother's brother, and therefore his surname was Munro. Now Paul Munro and Paul Porter sounded two very different things.

"Paul Porter," repeated Miss Dorothy again, looking almost apprehensively at the bed as she spoke. Mr. Porter followed the direction of her gaze, which said almost as plainly as words, "I wonder what *she'll* say to it."

But the thing was done and must be made the best of; so, putting a bold face on it, he said, "Yes, that's his name; and for all I can see, as good a name as he can want. Is all going on right?" he added, by way of diverting the subject.

"Yes, quite right; she is sleeping nicely."

"Then I'll come in another time;" so saying, Mr.

Porter went downstairs, and Miss Dorothy once more sat down by her sick niece. But, like a person trying to fit together two things that will not match, she repeated over slowly to herself, "Paul—Porter; Paul—Porter."

"Paul Porter!" said the sick woman dreamily; "who's he?"

The question seemed particularly to agitate Miss Dorothy.

"Oh nothing—I mean—not anyone at all," she said hurriedly. Then fancying her niece's eyes were still bent on her with a searching expression, she seemed suddenly impressed with the notion that her presence was imperatively demanded elsewhere: "I really think I can smell something boiling over in the kitchen. I left your broth by the fire; I'll just go and see; I shall be back in five minutes," she said.

The sick woman turned over with an uneasy moan, and Miss Dorothy, after dropping her work, and making altogether a clatter quite unlike her usual quiet movements, hurried from the room. When she came back, she was greatly relieved to find her niece again fallen asleep; and was still further secretly rejoiced, that on her waking she did not again inquire as to the identity of Paul Porter.

But though the name was thus given to the child, no one seemed in any hurry to apply it to him. Even the two most capable of doing so, joined with the others in a sort of mock, innocent way, and still called him "baby," as though that formidable visit of the registrar had never taken place. But there comes a time for all things, good or bad, to be brought to light; and so when Mrs. Porter became strong enough to be moved from her bed to the couch, one afternoon when her husband and aunt were both present, looking down at the innocent, sleeping child, she said, "And now it is certainly time we should think of a name for the baby."

Miss Dorothy fairly turned her back; Mr. Porter coughed and looked out of the window.

"What do you think about it?" said Mrs. Porter, looking in his direction.

"The truth is, my dear, the child is already named," he answered blandly.

Mrs. Porter's eyes, as they fixed themselves on her husband, grew wide open with astonishment. The thought that anyone had really taken the momentous affair in hand of naming the child, had never once arisen in her mind.

"But who named him?" she asked.

"Well, I did, my dear," replied her husband.

"And what have you called him?"

"I called—I called him Paul."

"You and I can think of something prettier than that, can't we, Aunt Dorothy?"

Again Mr. Porter coughed; it was of no use telling only half the truth. Again he summoned his blandest tones,—

"But, my dear, I don't think it is any use thinking of anything different; you see, the child is registered."

"But who registered him?"

"I did; the man came, and so I registered him Paul. You see, my dear, you were ill in bed at the time, and couldn't of course think about it, therefore I had to do it for you; so I did what I could—at any rate I did for the best."

B

"If you were forced to name him, couldn't you think of something different to Paul? What made you choose that name in particular?"

Mr. Porter's face visibly brightened; if he had done wrong, he had at least a valid reason for his wrong-doing, so he answered promptly,

"Why, my dear, I should have told you. I named him Paul after an uncle I had of that name; he and I were more like brothers when we were boys, for he was only two years older than I was, though he was my uncle. He was one of the best young fellows that ever lived; if the baby only takes like him, I shall be satisfied."

"But I don't know I ever heard you speak of this uncle before. Who was he? what did he do?"

"I don't know that he did anything in particular. He was a sailor, and while a very young man went to sea and got drowned." Mr. Porter paused suddenly, his uncle's early fate did not sound a very fortunate argument. Then he added abruptly, "But there, after all, I don't see what is amiss with the name; for my own part, I must say I like it."

"And you only gave him that one name?"

"One name I thought was enough, my dear."

"Yes, but think how it sounds—Paul Porter; and Paul is *such* a name. Some names you can nickname and make them sound prettier, but you can't even nick-name Paul. Don't you think Paul Porter sounds badly, Aunt Dorothy?" she added, turning to Miss Fairfield.

Miss Dorothy admitted that she did think so; "But," she said, "as he has got the name, I suppose he must keep it."

"Well," Mr. Porter said, "he is Paul Porter, and Paul Porter he will be for the rest of his life:" but, as though to modify the remark, he bent down and kissed his wife, and then hurriedly made his exit from the room.

CHAPTER II.

A LONG TRIAL.

DOUBTLESS Mr. Porter was right in the statement, that the name would last the child his lifetime; but it seemed at first as if that lifetime would be but of short duration; for while his brothers had all more or less been healthy and strong, Paul was delicate and feeble, and the spark of life appeared sometimes to flicker as though it would speedily go out. But, however, Paul survived the assaults that beset his infancy, and at six years of age had attained to some measure of health and strength. Mrs. Porter declared he was the plainest of all her children; certainly he had not Oliver's bright blue eyes, nor soft, dark eyes like Sydney; he had not Thomas's handsome face, and lithe, graceful figure; nor was he robust and stalwart like Theodore. Still there was a considerable degree of beauty in his soft, dark, grey eyes, full of such wistful truth and earnestness, and the curl of soft, almost chestnut brown hair fell over a broad and open brow. Then when Paul was six years old, an event occurred which threatened to mar all his future life. Owing to his delicate health he had never been subject to much restriction, and was allowed to ramble about the house at his pleasure. At the back of the house leading to the kitchen was a steep staircase, dangerous for young and heedless steps, and towards this staircase Paul one day coming with flying feet, just at the top lost his balance, and fell helplessly to the bottom. The fall in itself was a terrible one, though possibly, owing to the elasticity of childhood, he might have escaped any serious injury, but half-way down the stairs stood a pail of boiling-hot water, carelessly left there by a servant a few minutes before, and Paul striking against this, he, the pail, and the hot water, all made a tumultuous descent together.

At first it seemed doubtful what injuries had been received. The doctor shook his head and looked grave. One hip was seriously injured, and what with the scalds, the pain, and the shock the whole system had sustained, he very much doubted in his own mind if his little patient would recover. Recover, however, he did, as far as life was concerned; but no skill seemed to avail to subdue the swellings that attacked the injured limb, and there was every reason to fear that Paul would be a cripple, and that the trial, like his name, would be life-long. But in unconscious childhood and buoyant youth, the words, "a life-long trial," are but little understood; and when once the little sufferer lost his immediate pains, no shadow of a darkened future clouded his innocent soul. And when one day his mother sat grieving about having a crippled child, at sight of her tears his little heart only filled with chivalrous desire to comfort her, and laying his head down softly on her hand he said,

"I don't feel the pain so much now, so don't cry any more, mother."

A sad contrast to the other boys, so full of life and spirit, was the helpless child lying on his little couch, his face pale and wan with recent suffering. They were good lads on the whole; Oliver, who was now fifteen years old, was tall, manly, and keen of perception beyond his years, and gave promise of soon being his father's right hand in all things. Perhaps he could not think so deeply, or soar so high in imagination as Sydney; but what he did think was always clear, practical, and to the point.

Soon after Paul's accident they all were at home for the Christmas holidays, and each of them was anxious to soothe or alleviate their little brother's sufferings. But the best hand at amusing or cheering was Thomas; as he grew older he only seemed to grow more handsome and attractive, and at ten years old was one of the merriest, liveliest boys you well could find. He could sing any new song, dance any new dance, or think of a hundred comical things that would divert Paul from his pain. But the worst of Thomas was, he would do these things only how and at the time he pleased: did anything else more attractive come in the way, then Paul must wait. Thomas took care the discipline of waiting did not come to his own share. He always as much as possible chose the honied side of life, and could be very entertaining to the other happy sharers of the honey; but he had no sense of responsibility, and a continual feeling of self-esteem and approval kept all serious thoughts or reflections at bay. And so when he chose, no one could make Paul laugh so readily as Thomas, but when he did not choose, Paul must bide his time.

But if Thomas was uncertain and fickle, Theodore, the next brother, was constant and persevering; stalwart, strong in mind and body, in the sturdy little frame lay a considerable degree of latent power, and beneath the solid exterior beat a quick, warm, generous heart. If he was not so merry as Thomas, he was far more patient and kind, and so it happened that he became Paul's most chosen companion, and a strong bond of sympathy sprang up between them—the strength of the one and the weakness of the other only cementing the union closer; and not till the holidays were over and the boys gone back to school, did Paul fully realize all his little brother and companion had been to him. But he solaced himself with the thought, that when the long summer holidays came he would be better, and able perhaps to run about again. And the summer days came, and with them the summer holidays, but Paul was still a weary prisoner; with the aid of a stick or a helping hand he could walk a little, but he made slow progress; and perhaps the first shadow of pain and disappointment crept into his thoughtful grey eyes, as from his couch he lay and watched his brothers at the sports in which he now began to fully realize his inability to join.

One morning Theodore was describing to him the pleasures of a boating expedition he and his brothers had been to with some friends the evening before. He had brought some water-lilies as trophies for Paul. They had been up the river to a piece of water called the Mere: deep, silent, like a lake, encircled round with trees whose green branches seemed to shut it in from the outer world, white water-lilies growing round its shores, the Mere was a spot of peculiar beauty; and as

Theodore in boyish fashion dwelt upon the scene, Paul's eyes grew full of wistful longing as he said,

"Oh, Theo! couldn't I go too?"

Theodore shook his head doubtfully.

"I don't know," he said; "it is a long way by the road, and then we should have to go through some fields before we could get to the Mere, and I couldn't get your carriage over the gates, you know, Paul."

Paul's countenance clouded.

"Wouldn't one of the others go too and help, Theo? I would try and walk all I could."

"Oliver and Sydney are going out with father this afternoon," said Theodore; "but Thomas might go."

At that moment the person in question entered the room.

"You are just the one we want, Thomas," said Theodore. "Will you help Paul to go to the Mere this afternoon?"

"Paul can't go there, Theo: we have no boat, you know."

"No, we should drag him in his carriage."

"The carriage can't get over gates," said Thomas, lazily throwing himself into an easy chair.

"No; but we could leave the carriage somewhere, perhaps, and you and I could help lift him along."

"Well, I can't go, at any rate," said Thomas in an indifferent tone.

"Why not?" asked Theodore.

"Oh, I am going round to uncle's this afternoon (the uncle thus alluded to, being the rich bachelor uncle before mentioned); I met him in the town just now, and he says I may go and look at a new pony he has bought, and his man Jenkins will let me have a ride round the meadow on it, if uncle is not at home. So I am going round to ask Phil Carter to go with me this afternoon."

"Wouldn't to-morrow do?" asked Theodore, seeing Paul's disappointed look.

"No, I shall go to-day; to-morrow will do just as well for Paul to go to the Mere, or any other day. I'm going round to see Phil, now," he added, rising.

Tears stood in Paul's eyes as he watched Thomas's retreating figure; he already began to realize the helplessness of being dependent on others for the pleasures of life, and a look of weary pain settled on his face.

"Never mind, Paul," said Theodore kindly; "perhaps we can go another day."

"It is so hot lying here," said Paul wearily, "I should so like to go and see the cool water, and the lilies, and the trees; and to-morrow may be wet, or something else happen; and some days I could not go so far: when the pain comes bad I can hardly walk at all;" and Paul hid his face, wet with tears, on the sofa cushion.

"Don't cry, Paul," said Theodore; "wait just a minute," and he hurried out after Thomas.

"Thomas," he said, as he came panting up, "did uncle ask you particularly to go this afternoon?"

"No; he said any day I liked."

"And you have not asked Phil yet?"

"No, I am now going there."

"Then put it off one day, and go with Paul to the Mere; you can go to uncle's to-morrow."

"And Paul can go to the Mere to-morrow."

"Perhaps he won't be well enough then; and he is so disappointed," urged Theodore.

Thomas's bright face grew almost impatient as he said,

"I tell you, Theodore, I can't come; and it is all nonsense Paul wanting to go to the Mere at all. What can a lame boy do there?"

"Then you won't come?"

"I tell you no," and Thomas walked abruptly away.

As Theodore went back to the house he resolved the matter in his mind, and came to the determination that rather than disappoint Paul, he would take the whole undertaking upon himself. Paul did not want any persuading; Theodore always seemed to him such a tower of strength, that he would have undertaken exploits much more difficult than a visit to the Mere, with Theodore as his protector and companion. Besides, physically he felt stronger that morning than usual, and so consequently his spirit, though he could not have assigned the cause, was more buoyant and enterprising.

So, the matter settled, the two set off that afternoon on their expedition. It was a long way, as Theodore had said, and the roads were hot and dusty; but Theodore's brave little heart never failed him. At last they came to a great gate leading into a field, down which Theodore believed lay the path to the Mere; but the gate was high and heavy, and required all his ingenuity and strength to open it: that at length accomplished, he wheeled Paul in triumph inside. Down that field the path was easy, but at the bottom of it came a decided barrier, in the shape of a high, awkward stile. That the carriage could not be got over was plain, and difficult was the task of getting Paul over; but at last the exploit was successfully accomplished, and leaning heavily on Theodore, Paul slowly pursued his way. The path led now down a green, pleasant lane, at the end of which was a very low stile, which was mounted with less difficulty, and then only one meadow lay between them and the longed-for Mere. They soon gained the river's side, and then following its course came to the entrance to the Mere, and Paul with a sense of inexpressible delight, threw his weary little form on the green, cool grass, and taking off his hat, let the pure breeze blow on his hot brow.

Before them lay the Mere with its silent depths, and round its edges the fair lilies and the sheltering trees, among the boughs of which the wind made a soft, continual murmur. As Paul looked, deep into his soul sank the beauty of the scene before him.

"Oh, Theo! isn't it lovely?" he said, turning his rapt, eager face to his brother; and Theodore, watching his little brother's delight, felt amply repaid for any trouble the expedition had cost him.

For some time the two boys lay there on the cool grass, when suddenly the sunlight seemed dying out of the sky, and portentous shadows crept silently over the Mere. Theodore, who to the most romantic scene on earth could always have found a practical bearing, looked up immediately for the cause, and saw just behind them, over the way they had come, a dark, heavy, threatening cloud; at the same moment a low rumbling of thunder fell on his ear. Springing hurriedly to his feet,—

"Paul," he said, "we had better be going home."

"Didn't it thunder?" asked Paul nervously.

"Yes," said Theodore; "let me help you up, Paul."

The help was by no means unneeded. With the

prospect of the Mere before him, Paul had not been conscious what his exertions had cost him; but now after, his rest, as he tried to rise, he felt only conscious of pain and utter helplessness.

"You must try and walk," urged Theodore, glancing again at the angry sky. "If you can only get to your carriage, you will be all right."

Paul did try, but his steps were slow and weary; and they had got only half-way across the meadow, when the lightning, flashing full in his face, seemed to deprive him of strength altogether.

A desperate sort of fear, and Theodore's pleading voice sustained him, but it was difficult work getting over the stile; and they had gone only a few yards up the lane, when there came a vivid flash of lightning, swiftly followed by a loud, rattling peal of thunder, and Paul, slipping away from Theodore's arm, fell prostrate on the ground. In intense anguish Theodore hung over him.

"Paul! Paul!" he said tenderly.

After a minute Paul looked up.

"I can't get up, Theodore: I can't go any further."

"Oh, Paul, do try," said Theodore, with something like a quiver in his voice. "You are always such a good, brave boy; do try again, Paul."

Theodore was right; Paul was brave. Those who had witnessed his bodily sufferings had wondered at the brave patience with which he bore them; but Theodore forgot that physically he was weak, and his nerves shattered and tried by the shock of pain and suffering he had undergone. But the words put a little more strength into Paul. Feebly he tried to rise, but it was of no use, the trembling limbs bent and tottered under him : then a last despairing thought arose in Theodore's mind.

"If you cannot walk, I must try and carry you, Paul," he said.

So saying, with effort he lifted his brother in his arms ; but strong and valiant of heart though he was, the task was beyond him, and his walk degenerated into a downright stagger, till in despair he sank down with Paul on the grassy bank by the lane's side. At the same instant a pelting torrent of rain poured down. Seating Paul beside him, he pulled off his own jacket and tried to wrap it round the trembling child, who at another brilliant flash and crashing peal of thunder, clung to Theodore in mute agony.

"Hide your face on my shoulder ; you won't see the lightning then, Paul," said Theodore.

Paul did as he was told, and in that quiet spot they formed a curious picture. The trembling child clinging to his brother, and Theodore vainly striving to keep brave, though his face was full of anguish and fear, and the fear and anguish were almost solely on account of the helpless little form at his side.

A young man a few minutes later coming up the lane certainly thought them a curious picture, and stopping before them he said,

"So you are caught in the storm too, my little fellows."

Looking up, Theodore recognized Mr. Blake, the new curate, who had not long been in the neighbourhood ; and the sight of a human face, and the sound of a human voice, sent fresh courage into his soul. Even Paul's little white face, as he glanced up from Theodore's shoulder, gathered a gleam of hope. And it was a hope-inspiring face he looked into, with its open brow, soft, earnest, brown eyes, and sweet, though firm, mouth. The fair complexion and delicate turn of the features, might not indicate much physical strength, but on every line of the expressive face, truth, purity, and goodness were indelibly written. Theodore was not the first who, looking into that kindly, genuine face, had gathered confidence and strength. Theodore felt at once that friendly help had arrived.

"Oh, sir!" he said, "can you help us? can you help Paul?"

"Who is Paul?"

"This is Paul, sir; he is my little brother. He is a cripple and cannot walk, and the fright has nearly killed him."

"Poor little fellow," said Mr. Blake; "let me see what I can do for you;" and stooping down he gently lifted Paul in his arms. As he did so, Theodore's coat fell from him.

"I put that on him to try and shelter him," said Theodore.

Mr. Blake looked at him with kindly approval.

"Put it on now yourself, my little man," he said; "you must be wet through. I will see to your little brother."

Then with Theodore walking close by his side, he carried Paul till they came to the spot where they had left the carriage. Mr. Blake gently placed Paul in it.

"There, my little fellow," he said, "I hope the worst of your troubles are over now."

"Yes, sir," said Paul; "I didn't feel so much afraid when you came and carried me."

"But you were no safer really in my arms than on the bank with your brother."

"I felt so, sir," said Paul.

Mr. Blake smiled.

"It was your Heavenly Father, my child, who shielded you from harm. It was no power of mine." Then turning to Theodore he said, "Now you will have to direct me which way to go: how far are you from home?"

Theodore's face grew somewhat rueful.

"It is more than two miles, sir," he said.

Then as he described where they lived, Mr. Blake looking closer at him, said,

"I think then you must be Mr. Porter's little sons: I have seen you in church on a Sunday, but I have not been here long enough to recognize you separately. Which are you?"

"I am Theodore, and Paul is the youngest."

Then Theodore advancing to the carriage, laid his hand on the handle. Mr. Blake gently put him aside:

"I think you have had work enough for one day," he said; "you must let me take my turn now." Then as he gently wheeled Paul along: "Do you often bring your little brother so far away from home?" he asked.

"No, sir; but he wanted so much to see the Mere; that is why we came here this afternoon."

And then ashamed that Mr. Blake should have all the trouble, Theodore resolutely placed one hand on Paul's carriage as he walked along by Mr. Blake's side. The lightning and thunder had ceased, but a steady rain continued to fall, and it was well for Theodore that a

stronger, abler arm than his own was there to assist in
the homeward journey. At last they reached the boy's
home.

"Won't you come in, sir?" asked Theodore.

"No, thank you. You see, like you, I am very wet;
but I will come and see you all the first day I can. Do
you like reading, Paul?"

"Yes, sir," said Paul, with a suddenly brightening face.

"Then I will bring you some books I think you will
like. Good-bye, my little friends; I hope you will
neither of you take any harm," he added, as he turned
away. And then Theodore hastened in with his little
charge.

During the boys' prolonged absence, Mrs. Porter had
fallen into a state of exaggerated alarm and excitement;
and as soon as they reached home, naturally her maternal
reproaches fell upon Theodore, till Paul interposing,
said gently,

"Don't blame Theodore, mother; I wanted so to go
to the Mere, and it is not his fault."

Theodore bore up patiently, and at last, arrayed in
clean, dry clothes, he sat down by Paul's side, while his
mother administered to the weary child some suitable
nourishment. Then large tears gathered in Theodore's
eyes; tears born of weariness of body and sorrow of
mind, and Paul, at sight of his distress, took one of his
hands, and laying his cheek down upon it, kissed and
caressed it tenderly.

"Mother is worried and troubled," he said; "you must
not mind it, Theodore."

"But perhaps you will really take harm, Paul."

"I don't think I shall," replied Paul gravely; "and

after all, Theo, I do feel glad I have seen the Mere. I shall often lie and think about the cool water, the lilies, and the beautiful green trees."

At this Theodore's face somewhat brightened, and after a minute's pause, Paul said,

"You and I will always love one another, won't we, Theo?"

"Of course we shall," replied Theodore, to whom the question appeared a somewhat unnecessary one.

"Yes—but," said Paul, "I mean we will never quarrel like some boys do. Now the other day, Oliver and Thomas quarrelled dreadfully; we will never do like that, Theo, but we will always love each other, and think just the same about everything, won't we?"

Theodore had not sentiment enough in his composition to answer in suitable words, but in the genuine tenderness of his heart he stooped and kissed the earnest, up-turned face of his little brother; and Paul, to whom the mute act sealed the compact more eloquently than words, with a look of quiet peace lay back silently upon his pillows.

About an hour later, Thomas suddenly made his appearance.

"Where is mother?" he asked, as he hurriedly entered the room.

Theodore replied that he did not know.

"Just tell her," said Thomas, "that I am going home with Phil Carter."

The young gentleman thus designated, who had followed Thomas as far as the door, was a boy about his own height, though a year or two older, but without any of his beauty of face or grace of figure. His

C

countenance gave you rather the idea of shrewdness than intellect. The features were sharply marked, the keen dark eyes in rather close proximity, and he had straight brown hair, the forelock of which seemed to have a peculiar propensity to fall over his somewhat retreating forehead. He took no notice of Paul or Theodore, but stood softly whistling to himself in the doorway.

Theodore promised to explain Thomas's absence, and the two friends then speedily disappeared. It was getting quite late in the evening before Thomas returned.

"You have had a long evening with your friend, my boy," said Mr. Porter as Thomas entered.

"Yes; he wanted me to stay as long as I could."

"Did you see the pony?" said Sydney, looking up from the book he was reading.

"Yes; and isn't it just a beauty!" said Thomas. "Uncle was not at home, but Jenkins got it out for us, and Phil and I had a famous ride round the meadow. Do you know, Phil says he believes uncle has bought that pony on purpose for me. He said so before Jenkins, and Jenkins only winked at me and laughed. I believe he has bought it to keep for me till I leave school."

"I don't see why you should think that," said Oliver. "I believe uncle bought the pony for himself; he said not long ago how badly he wanted one."

Thomas looked somewhat abashed, but the next minute—appealing to Mrs. Porter,

"Don't you think very likely uncle has bought it for me, mother?" he said.

Mrs. Porter looked fondly at the handsome, eager face.

"I don't see why he should not have bought it for you," she said. "You see," she added, turning to Oliver, "your uncle looks upon Thomas almost in the light of a son."

Mrs. Porter always seemed desirous of keeping the fair prospects of her favourite son in view. Oliver made no reply. After a pause, Thomas said,

"Phil says he knows he has. He says he thinks I am a lucky chap: he only wishes he had got a rich uncle to buy him a pony."

"Well, at any rate, you have some little time to wait for it, my dear," said Mrs. Porter. And no one in that little group seemed to understand how much better it might have been for Thomas, if he had not only had to wait for a pony, but had been obliged to work for one also.

CHAPTER III.

FRIENDLY HELP.

MR. BLAKE did not forget his little friends; but a few days after their accidental meeting, he was summoned to a sick relative, who earnestly desired to see him, and feeling that the visit might detain him for some days at least, and not wishing to disappoint Paul, he deputed his little sister Susie to convey the promised books during his absence. Susie was thirteen years old, but was tall for her age, and her face was sweet and gentle. But perhaps its chief charm lay in the soft, dark eyes, so soft and shy that they seldom rested on you long enough for you to determine what colour they really were. Her mouth was sensitive and mobile, but the firmly-formed nose and chin saved her from any appearance of insipidity, as they had a very decided character of their own. It was soon after the dinner hour at Mr. Porter's that Susie made her arrival, and at the sight of so many comparatively strange faces, she for a moment looked shyer than usual. But Susie could be shy without confusion of manner, so walking quietly up to Paul, she said,

"I think you are the little boy my brother met out in the rain?"

"Yes," said Mrs. Porter, answering for Paul; "and I am afraid he gave your brother a great deal of trouble."

"Oh no, I am sure he did not," said Susie. Then turning to Paul, "My brother has sent you the books he promised you; he wanted to come himself, but he has been obliged to go away from home for a few days, so he told me to bring them instead, and mamma let me come this afternoon."

"It was very kind of you, I am sure, my dear," said Mr. Porter, who from his position on the hearthrug had been looking with envious eyes on the specimen of what a blooming little daughter might be. And certainly, Susie sitting there with a bright colour glowing in her cheeks, and her brown hair falling round her neck in fair, soft curls, looked a very pretty specimen indeed. She glanced up at Mr. Porter with one of her shy, sweet smiles, then opening the packet of books, she turned to Paul, and the two soon fell into friendly conversation, as she pointed out to him those her brother had thought he would especially like to read. As Susie took her departure,—

"That's a sweet little girl," said Mr. Porter with a sigh.

"A very sweet girl," said Mrs. Porter, who in her own mind felt inclined to regard the visit as somewhat of an honour. The Blakes had not long been in the neighbourhood, but there was a prevalent notion that they were people of good standing and connection. Mrs. Blake, who was a widow, and who, with her little daughter Susie, had accompanied her son, was believed to be in possession of a considerable income; and it was generally thought that Mr. Blake would not long remain in his present position, but would be speedily raised from his curacy to an opulent living.

Altogether Susie seemed to have made a favourable impression, for Thomas, seating himself on the table by his mother, said as he toyed with a paper-knife lying near,

"Why don't you ask Susie Blake to tea, mother?"

"Well, I don't know," began Mrs. Porter doubtfully, who was always ready to defer to any proposition coming from Thomas. Had he asked for the proverbial top brick off the chimney, probably she would have given the demand her best consideration. Mr. Porter, however, interposed:

"The idea," he said, "of asking her to meet a parcel of rude, rough boys!"

"We are not rude," said Thomas, "and we wouldn't be rough."

"Your father means, my dear, that there are no girls here to ask her to come to meet," said Mrs. Porter.

"Ask Phil Carter's sister Blanche to come."

The voice was Oliver's, and the very idea of Oliver taking any part in the discussion, made all eyes turn in his direction. Thomas burst into a laugh.

"I never heard Oliver want any girls to come to tea before," he said; "I do believe he is in love."

Oliver laughed slightly, as he rose and stood beside his father on the hearthrug. He was already a little taller than his father, and Mr. Porter, glancing at the straight, manly figure by his side, might be pardoned the look of paternal pride as he said,

"There's time enough for that yet, isn't there, Oliver?"

"Yes, father, I think so," replied Oliver. "I was only

trying to help them a little; but perhaps if we asked Blanche she wouldn't come."

"I don't think she would want much asking," said Sydney, with that rare instinctive insight into character, which though he possessed, he but rarely and almost unconsciously exerted. For few people had a better notion of going through the world with their eyes closed than Sydney; so it was seldom he exercised the latent power within him, and perhaps never where his affections were concerned; for with Sydney, to love, made it impossible to suspect.

Whatever decision might have been arrived at, Mr. Porter suddenly changed the subject.

"It is time to be going to business," he said; "are you coming, Oliver?"

The business referred to was a factory in the straggling manufacturing town about half-a-mile distant. Oliver replied in the affirmative. Thomas suddenly thought of some exploit he had been planning as an afternoon's diversion, and beckoning to Sydney and Theodore to follow him, the little party speedily became dispersed, and Paul was left alone with his books, which promised to open up to him another ray of light in his somewhat monotonous existence.

A few days after Susie's visit, with the exception of Oliver, the boys returned to school, and again Paul missed his companions, and felt dull and lonely. Then a worse turn of illness came upon him, and through the hot, sultry days he lay weak and languid on his couch, or limped wearily about the house; and then during that time of illness and consequent depression, morbid thoughts and fancies, like dark shadows of a dreary

future, for the first time crept over his childish soul.
And it seemed too, as if every one in the house had less
leisure for him than usual, for Mr. Porter was just then
assiduously absorbed in business matters, which at that
time were rather critical, and certain losses had been inevitable; and in the midst of it a feeling of discontent
had crept among the factory hands, and with difficulty
an impending strike had been averted. These things
kept Mr. Porter and Oliver—so far as he was admitted
into confidence—busy and pre-occupied; and Mrs. Porter
sometimes grew anxious and careworn. All these things
had effect indirectly on Paul, and he became complaining, weary, and restless.

At the back of the house was a cool, pleasant apartment, generally used by the family as a breakfast room:
a large French window facing the north, made it a cool
retreat the hottest day in summer. To this room Paul
retired with a book one hot afternoon, when the sound
of voices, and particular the mention of his own name,
aroused his attention. The fact was, Mr. and Mrs. Porter
had just been having a confidential *tête-a-tête* in the
room opposite where Paul was sitting. They had been
discussing an important event, A friend of Mr. Porter's
had written concerning Oliver, telling him of what he
considered would be an advantageous start for him in
life; but Mr. Porter considered the terms too high.

"Much too high," he had just been saying to his wife.
But Mrs. Porter, who to do her justice, had unbounded
ambition for her children, had been urging that every
point should be strained, every other expense curtailed,
so that Oliver's prospects might not be marred. But
Mr. Porter saw the thing in another light; the sum was
unreasonable.

· "And besides," he added, as opening the door he stepped into the hall, "there are the others to think about. Oliver must wait a bit,—he is wasting no time by being at home with me in the business; and as I say, we must think about the others: and there's the little man Paul to provide for."

· "Oh yes," said Mrs. Porter, "we all know Paul will never be able to work for himself; he must always be a trouble and burden to some one."

"Well, well, we must make the best of that," said Mr. Porter.

"Oh, of course," replied Mrs. Porter.

Mr. Porter did not answer, he was going up the hall to the front door. Mrs. Porter herself also walked slowly away, never for a moment dreaming that the object of her complaints had been a listener to her words.

But Paul had heard it all, and like cold iron the words entered into his soul, and his spirit was deeply, sorely wounded within him. For surely they err, who suppose that childhood, because of its fleeting emotions and vague ideas, cannot therefore suffer deep and poignant grief. Truly many a sorrow sweeps across a child's path, which from his very ignorance he is unable rightly to estimate or comprehend; but when a sorrow comes within the range of children's understanding, perhaps the grief then felt is as intense as any more matured troubles that visit later years. For though their feelings be more transient, their faith is more implicit, their confidence more unquestioning, and when that trust and confidence are first rudely torn or shaken, of necessity the shock must be ruder, and the pain more intensely acute. So as Paul sat there with bowed head, a whole storm of sorrow seemed to crush and overwhelm him. All at once he seemed to bitterly realize what life must be to him, and what he would be, not only to some one, but as it seemed to him then to everyone who should have anything to do with him—a helpless burden and trouble.

Then came a sound of steps, and Paul felt he could not on any account just then face his mother, so making, for him, great effort, he effected a hurried escape through the French window. A few paces across the lawn was an arbour, which, standing sideways to the house, would so far shelter him from observation. Towards this arbour Paul wearily crept, and sinking down on the ground, laid his head down on the wooden seat and wept in bitterness of soul. But the arbour stood so that the front was towards the path leading down to the hall door, and along that path Mr. Blake was quietly walking towards the house, and as he did so, plainly saw every movement of the sorrowful child.

Mr. Blake's first thought was to go across to the arbour, but seeing Mrs. Porter at one of the front windows, he walked up to the house instead. He stayed there talking to Mrs. Porter some time, then mentioning that he saw Paul enter the arbour, Mrs. Porter offered to go and fetch him in, but Mr. Blake said he would not have Paul disturbed, but would go and speak to him where he was.

So as Paul still crouched down against the hard wooden bench, he suddenly became sensible that steps were coming towards him, and then a kindly voice said close to him, " Paul, my little friend !"

After a moment, Paul for answer merely lifted his tear-stained face.

"You are not feeling so well, are you, Paul?" said Mr. Blake gently.

But the kind tone only seemed to open up the flood-gates of Paul's sorrow anew, as with a sob he answered,

"Yes, sir; it is not that."

"Well, let me help you to rise," said Mr. Blake; and Paul could not resist the firm, kind touch, as he felt himself gently raised and placed on the arbour seat beside his friend. "There, that is better," said Mr. Blake, as he tenderly adjusted the injured limb. Then noticing Paul's still very sorrowful face, he said, "You are in trouble, Paul; can I help you?"

Paul's first impulse was to pour out at once the cause of his grief, but an instinctive feeling of honour restrained him, so he only told as much as he thought he safely might.

"No, sir," he said, "I don't think you can help me; it is only because I shall never be any better, but always a trouble and a burden."

Mr. Blake looked closely at the child; his quick sense at once told him that the last few words did not fall naturally from the childish tongue, but for reply he only said cheerily,

"I don't know, Paul, whether you are quite right there. Your mother and I have been having a long talk about you indoors, and I think something may yet be done for you. I knew a little child once, who was very much like you, and who got much better again; and I think, though perhaps you will never be able to run about quite so fast as some boys, that much may yet be done, so that you will be by no means either a helpless cripple or burden."

"Mother said so," said Paul, and then stopped short, blushing scarlet at the inadvertently. implied accusation.

Mr. Blake took no notice of the remark.

"Paul," he said, "even if you were really to be a cripple, or very helpless, I don't see why you need be either a burden or a trouble. Do you know the kind of people who are really burdens to others, Paul?"

"No, sir; unless they are cripples, or quite blind, perhaps."

"I mean wicked people, Paul. A bad, disobedient boy must always be a burden and trouble to his parents, or whoever has the charge of him; but many very afflicted persons, by their cheerful and patient spirit, have been real blessings instead of troubles to those around them."

"Yes, sir," said Paul.

"You see, Paul," continued Mr. Blake, "when any-one we love is in pain or ill, and we see them very fretful and complaining, it makes us also full of grief; but when we see them cheerful and trying to bear it all patiently, it makes our own hearts feel so much lighter, and takes away half the bitterness of the trial."

"Yes, sir," said Paul again. Then after a moment's pause, "I will try and bear it all cheerfully," he said, but there was a slight tremor in his voice as he spoke.

"You must ask God's help, my boy, and you will succeed," said Mr. Blake reverently; "and remember, Paul," he added, "no affliction of body need hinder you from being a good and noble-minded man. But you and I will have, I hope, many a talk together yet. I have been asking your mother to let you come to tea

with me one night in every week: I want you to begin
to-morrow night; will you come?"

Paul's brightened face answered for him: "Oh, I
should like it so much!" he said eagerly.

"Very well then, you shall come; your mother says
you can be sent down in your little carriage, and I hope
we shall soon get very good friends. Good-bye, Paul."

"Good-bye, sir," said Paul; but long after Mr. Blake's
departure his words rang in Paul's ears. Paul was intelligent, and with that quick intelligence that so often
springs from physical suffering, and he had understood
the bearing of all Mr. Blake had said to him, and musing
over it all to himself, his heart grew brave with noble
resolves; his mother glancing at him, noticed his brightened countenance, and unconsciously felt her own care
lightened also.

With these visits to Mr. Blake, a new and delightful
era opened in Paul's life. Perhaps most of us, looking
back, can point to a certain period of existence, and
define it as the happiest part of our life. Some will even
thus designate their school days; and certainly that
time so full of the rush, and activity, and enterprise of
life, without its graver cares and considerations—that
time full of promise, without the responsibilities that
attend the fulfilment of desire—is undoubtedly to most
a memorable and happy time. Still, as the old saying
goes, "A school is but a miniature of the world," only it
is the world without its conventionalities, and restraining
laws of society and decorum. They are raw recruits at
school, not the orderly, well-appointed band; and among
the motley throng and undisciplined ranks, sensitive
spirits get many a wound and rub, that go far to dispel

the illusion of school days being the happiest period of life.

Perhaps had Paul been asked, he would have referred to those four years under the tutelage of Mr. Blake, for the connection between them soon drifted into that of tutor and scholar; and under that happy guidance, many a door of knowledge, that, debarred as Paul was then from school life, must have been inevitably closed to him, was now freely opened, and studies, which were so ordered as to seem constant sources of delight, were eagerly followed by the attentive child. And yet through it all, the teaching was almost more of heaven than of earth; for with Mr. Blake as tutor, it was almost impossible it should be otherwise. He was not of those who think a child too young to put on its spiritual armour; and so during those four years, in that childish soul, the seeds of a high and noble life were earnestly and successfully sown.

But in this ever-varying, chequered life, periods, whether happy or sorrowful, are doomed to have a limit and a bound, and so the four years came to an end, and Mr. Blake fulfilled the expectation formed of him, and departed to a living some fifty miles from Clansford; and he also at the same time did what perhaps had not been expected of him—for the young lady lived at some distance, and had only occasionally been at Clansford— he married a wife also; and after his departure, the people of Clansford knew that a good and earnest man had departed from their midst. Susie and her mother still remained; they had made a few firm friends, and Mrs. Blake was getting used to the neighbourhood, and as her son was married, he no longer wanted his mother to superintend his household; and so though Mr. Blake took his departure, it happened that his mother and sister remained still in the old home.

Susie had become quite an established favourite with the Porters, and under the chaperonage of her governess or mother, the tea-drinking proposed by Thomas had several times taken place.

But those four years had brought to Paul physical as well as mental improvemet, for the treatment proposed by Mr. Blake that afternoon he found Paul sorrowing in the arbour, had been tried, and to a great extent tried successfully; and though a very considerable degree of lameness still remained, the evil was in a measure corrected, and as Mr. Porter observed, Paul seemed likely to rub through the world a deal better than he thought at one time he would be able to.

Strictly speaking, it was hardly four years that Paul was under Mr. Blake's guidance, as it was just after the summer holidays Paul began his weekly visits to his house, and it was just before the summer holidays, four years later, that Mr. Blake took his leave of Clansford. Perhaps it was well for Paul that the parting with his friend was immediately followed by the return of his three brothers from school, for then once more the house became cheered and enlivened by the tramp of young, eager feet, and echoed to the sound of the glad happy voices of youth. Four years had of course wrought consequent changes in them all, and Sydney had finally left school that term. He had come home laden with justly-acquired trophies and honours, for Sydney, when he chose, could be an apt and brilliant scholar; still there was an immaturity of idea, a lack of development, that sometimes puzzled his teachers. Sydney mentally was asleep, and alas! for those whose inner nature thus slumbers, for they may have but sudden and rude awakening.

CHAPTER IV.

THE BROWN COB.

URING the holidays it became matter of consideration whether Paul, as he was so far improved in health, should accompany his brothers, Thomas and Theodore, back to school; and it was finally agreed that he should do so, when a circumstance occurred, which for a time put all thoughts of school aside, as it appeared doubtful whether some of that little band would ever go to school or anywhere else again. About eight miles from Clansford, standing back in a spacious park, was a large and stately mansion. A Sir William Harrell then resided there, and his ancestors had resided there before him. It was a custom of Sir William Harrell's, and it had been the custom of his predecessors, once a year to throw open to the public the park and grounds by which the house was surrounded. All sorts of sports, a flower show, the best band the county could produce; all these combined made the day a thorough gala day, and it had become quite a time-honoured institution, and one that was attended by most of the families round.

On this particular summer we are speaking of, a few days before the one appointed for the usual fête,

Mr. Thomas Porter called at his brother's and intimated that two of his nephews could ride to "The Park"— Sir William Harrell's grounds being so called in distinction from all other parks—in his conveyance.

"I shall go very early myself, as I have sent some roots to the show, and want to be there soon enough to see the prizes awarded. Besides," he added, "Robertson asked me to ride with him, and spend the rest of the day with him after we leave the show; but that will make no difference to the boys going; Jenkins will drive them so they get to the Park about the middle of the day. They can walk up to my house in the morning, and Jenkins can drive them on."

The proposal was at once acceded to, and as Oliver would with his father be in London that day on business, Sydney and Thomas were selected for the honour.

Accordingly, on the morning of the fête the two boys started for "The Grove," as their uncle's house was designated, which was about a mile distant. They had gone but a little way when they were overtaken by Philip Carter and his sister Blanche. Philip explained he was going up to Mr. Smith's.

"I think perhaps," he said, "if his son does not happen to be going, I can get a ride with him."

The Smiths were farmers in the neighbourhood, and Philip was making use of a slight acquaintance for his own advantage.

"Mr. Carter is not going, I suppose?" said Thomas.

"No, the governor is not going; and what is more, wouldn't let me go either if he could help it. He says he must take the horse and trap in another direction to-day, *on business* of course. He thinks now that I'm getting a little too fond of pleasure, and it is my belief he has taken the horse for no other reason but because I should not have it to drive to the Park. However, if Smith has got room, he will take me, I know."

"What will you do if you can't get a ride with him?"

"I shall have to think about it," replied Philip philosophically; "foot it, perhaps. We are not all lucky like you, Tom."

Thomas took no notice of the remark.

"Are you going too, Blanche?" he said, turning to Philip's sister.

"No; I only came with Phil for the sake of a walk."

"Jenkins is going to drive you, isn't he?" asked Philip.

"Yes," replied Thomas.

"With the cob or the old mare?"

"The cob; the old mare is lame."

The old mare referred to was somewhat of a favourite with Mr. Thomas Porter. He had bought her on his first settling in Clansford; she was then not quite in her first youth, but her excellent qualities had endeared her to her master, and she had grown into the position of an old friend and servant. But, like other old servants, she had peculiarities of service, and the best faculty horse ever possessed of being lame on all possible occasions. At the time of the fête she had a worse attack than usual, and was so lame that she could not possibly be taken out for any travelling purposes whatever. A high-stepping brown cob had superseded the pony that Thomas had once fondly imagined his uncle had bought for his own especial benefit. So far circumstances had proved Oliver to be right, when he expressed his belief that his uncle had only bought the pony for his own use.

"Then you'll go quite in style!" said Philip.

Thomas laughed, and the four continued their way, chatting merrily as they went along. But when they reached the Grove, an unexpected apparition awaited them in the person of Mrs. Jenkins, who met them at the door with elongated countenance.

"I was to tell you, young gentlemen," she said, "your uncle is very sorry, but you won't be able to go to-day."

Blank silence for a moment fell on her listeners, then Thomas pushed hurriedly forward.

"What's the matter? Where's uncle?" he asked.

"Oh, your uncle has been gone since right early this morning; it's my husband that's ill. I've been up with him the whole blessed night. He's got his old complaint again, which was as near cholera this time as could be."

"Then—he—isn't able to go?" slowly ejaculated Thomas.

"Able to go! He ain't able to stir hisself in the bed. But I mustn't be a standing here, for he can't bear me out of his sight for a minute. There he is now a knocking," she added, as a dull, heavy sound as of some one slowly moving up a chair and then thumping it down again, came from the vicinity of the bedrooms.

"I'm a coming," said Mrs. Jenkins, as she moved down the hall in response to the summons.

A look of disappointment settled on the faces of the little group standing in the doorway.

"Well, that's a settler," said Philip.

"I suppose it is," said Sydney, as moving slowly across the gravel path he threw himself full length on the lawn, and shading his eyes with his hand, lay dreamily blinking at the blue heavens above him.

"I know what I should do," said Blanche.

"Well, what?" said Thomas eagerly.

"I should harness the cob and drive him myself."

"I couldn't do that," said Thomas.

"You couldn't drive, I suppose," said Phil, with a touch of derision in his tone.

"Yes, I could drive," replied Thomas quickly. "Father often lets us drive his horse at home, and I have driven uncle with the mare; but I don't think he would like me to get his pony out without his leave."

"Oh, I thought you did just the same here," said Blanche, "as you would at home,—like we do when we go to see Aunt Jemima; we always do exactly the same there as if we were at home." And indeed there was some truth in her words, as a certain much-enduring maiden aunt, being the aunt Jemima referred to, could have given mournful testimony.

"Well, so I do," said Thomas, half doubtfully.

"I believe," said Philip, "from what I know of your uncle, he would just like your pluck. He promised you his horse to go with; Jenkins is ill and can't drive, and so you drive instead."

"I have a good mind to," said Thomas slowly, in a vacillating voice.

And in truth there was some excuse for his vacillation, for Mr. Porter was not a man who carried with him any power or authority. He was by no means a man of marked individuality. His abilities were small, his aspirations small, his affections and views in general were small, and his anger was of that puny, futile kind, which may be designated small also; and his nephews might be excused if they interpreted this feebleness of character for amiability upon which they might encroach. But Thomas, though he didn't exactly know it, was running the greatest possible risk of rousing his uncle's irate powers to the utmost, for if there was one thing on earth could stir ambition within him, it was the horse he drove. He had a good eye and judgment for this sort of thing, and could not easily be put off with a second-rate bargain: but that the boys would ever think of such a course as taking the horse themselves never entered his head. When Mrs. Jenkins informed him that morning of her husband's illness, he had merely replied, that she must tell the young gentlemen that he was sorry, but of course they could not go. The capabilities for disappointment in a boy's soul, who has been promised a great pleasure, and finds his hopes suddenly overthrown, was a theme beyond the stretch of his imagination. If he thought any more about them at all, he concluded they would walk quietly back again when they found the course events had taken; and any idea of offering any compensation for their disappointment, or attempting to devise any other plan for them so that they could still go to the park, never entered his mind. So perhaps Thomas had a slight excuse for his vacillation, as after a minute's consideration he added,

"Would you go with us, Phil? There will be plenty of room."

"Yes, if you wish it," replied Philip carelessly.

"Well, then, I think we will; I don't believe uncle will much mind it;" and Thomas turned as he spoke in the direction of the stables.

"Don't let me persuade you, you know," said Philip. "What do you say to it, Sydney?"

"I'll do what the rest do," said Sydney laconically, setting up one of his knees, and clasping it round with his two hands.

"Very well then," said Philip as he turned after Thomas. But Thomas had gone only a step or two when—whether his better genius was suddenly at his side, or whether Sydney's indifference seemed to throw the whole burden of responsibility upon himself—certainly a powerful doubt, as to the propriety of what he was doing arose within him, and turning suddenly round, he said,

"I think now we had better not go."

"Just as you like, of course," said Philip; "only if you don't mean to go, I'll be off at once, or Smith will be gone before I get there. You think you'd better not go?"

"Y—es," said Thomas, though with doubtful tone.

"Well then, I'm off," said Philip. "Come, Blanche."

"No, I'm not going any further in the heat," said Blanche sulkily; "I shall go straight home now. I don't see the good of stopping any longer to see one boy go one way and two another. I thought I was going to see quite a grand mount and start off."

"I say, Phil," called Thomas, as that young gentleman began very slowly moving away.

"Well, have you changed your mind?"

"I don't know, but just wait a minute."

Philip waited accordingly, and Miss Blanche, planting her heel firmly in the gravel, began a rapid rotatory movement, that had in it more dexterity than grace.

Stopping suddenly opposite to Thomas, "Why don't you speak the truth," she said, "and say you'd like to go, only you are afraid?"

Thomas blushed scarlet—"But I am not afraid," he said hastily.

"Looks like it," said Blanche, preparing for another rotatory movement.

"Of course I'm not afraid," said Thomas; "there is nothing to be afraid of." Then as if this last question had decided it in his mind, "Come along, Phil," he added; "we will go."

"Have you quite decided this time?"

"Yes, quite," said Thomas; and then the three walked away to the stables, and Blanche threw herself lazily on the grass to wait for their coming back.

The brown cob turned his shapely head and somewhat fiery eye round quickly to the new comers. Perhaps those well acquainted with horse physiognomy, might have surmised from his expression that the cob might not at all times be the most tractable or agreeable of creatures to deal with. His master, Mr. Thomas Porter, averred that there was no vice whatever about him. Still, like many another high-stepping cob, he had certain propensities of his own, and was given at times to disport himself in a manner not always either pleasant or comfortable. By an unwise use of the reins, he would sometimes choose to stand upon two legs instead of four, and the two legs he thus chose to stand upon would place him in such a position, that the driver, fearing he meant to force himself backward in bodily form upon the chaise, would instinctively spring forward and lower the reins, at which juncture the brown cob, with a move-

ment something between a leap and a plunge, would
bound suddenly forward, and continue his journey for a
while at a rather headlong rate. Still, if judiciously
managed, he might continue to travel without any further
unpleasant performances. He had, moreover, a great
dislike to uncouth-looking objects sticking out of hedges ;
and shrill sounds or sudden noises would inspire him
with a considerable degree of irritability and excitement.
However, all these little peculiarities, the three persons
who thus voluntarily took upon themselves the manage-
ment of him, were in happy ignorance of.

"I'm not much up to harnessing," said Thomas.

"Let me alone for that," said Philip ; "I'll harness
anything."

So far so good, and in process of time the brown cob
was duly harnessed to the dog cart, and led round to the
garden by Philip in triumph.

"Will you drive, Phil?" asked Thomas ; "you know
more about horses a good deal than I do."

"No, thank you," replied Philip. You see when you
drive your own horse you can do what you like with
him ; but when you drive another person's, if any
little mischief does come through it, it is not always
pleasant."

Philip did not seem to consider that the argument
applied equally well to Thomas. However, it settled
the point, and the boys at once got in, Philip and
Thomas in front, and Sydney sitting behind.

They had just got down the drive, and Blanche was
waving her handkerchief in triumph, when they were
startled by a sound that was something between a wail
and a cry, and looking round, they saw Mrs. Jenkins

standing on the doorstep with outstretched arms, as she rather shrieked than called upon them to stop.

"It's only old mother Jenkins," said Phil; "she's scared to see us going. Drive on, Tom; don't stop for her."

Thus advised, Thomas did drive on, while Philip, his example followed by Sydney, took off his hat in mock courtesy. As the dog cart passed on into the road despite her endeavours, Mrs. Jenkins rushed hurriedly to where Blanche was standing.

"Where on earth are they a going to?" she asked wildly.

"To the Park, Mrs. Jenkins," replied Blanche coolly. "Your husband couldn't drive them, so they have driven themselves."

"To the Park! They'll be turned over afore they get a mile."

"Not they; my brother is with them, he knows a lot about horses."

"What does he know about this one?" demanded Mrs. Jenkins fiercely; "and that dear lamb, Thomas, a driving. I tell you they're a going to their deaths; but I'll stop 'em yet."

So saying she ran across the lawn, and mounting on a garden chair, which commanded a good view of the road, resumed her vain endeavours. She waved her apron, she shrieked her loudest to them; but by this time the dog cart had got some way down the road, and her cries and exertions were wholly unanswered.

"Don't trouble yourself, Mrs. Jenkins," said Blanche; "they'll be all right."

"Will they? I tell you they're a-going to certain

death—and master away like this; I wouldn't ha' had it happened for all the world. Whatever master will say! Oh dear, oh dear!" she wailed, as she passed Blanche on her way back to the house.

Even Blanche grew a shade paler with undefined apprehension, at the sight of her distress; but Blanche was of too equable a temperament to concern herself very much about the troubles of others, so she turned quietly away towards her home.

Mrs. Jenkins went straight up to her husband, whom she greeted with the news after unceremonious fashion, as she said, "If they haven't been and got the cob, and driv themselves!"

"Who ha' got the cob? What do you mean?" said her husband, slightly raising himself in bed.

"Why young Mr. Thomas and his brother, and young Carter, ha' been and took the cob to drive theirselves with to the Park, cos you was ill and couldn't drive 'em."

Now Mr. Jenkins looked liked a man who had been seriously indisposed, but as the truths of the case became clear to his mind, all look of weariness or pallor passed away from his face, as staring at his wife he almost shouted,

"Why didn't you stop 'em?"

"Stop 'em! I think I did nearly split my throat a bawling to 'em, and they a acting just as if they was crazy, a taking off their hats and a bowing, and would go right on in spite of me. But I believe they're gone to their death, I do."

"Not they; boys have as many lives as a cat; and if they do get a broken limb or two, serve 'em right. But 'tis the cob I'm thinking on ; and I and master ha' been so careful how he's been driv, and trying to break him of those ways of his, and now them boys will just go and ruin him wholly, that's what they'll do."

"I don't care about the cob, if I knew they'd come home safe again."

"That's just like a foolish woman," was her husband's rejoinder. Then there was silence, till Mr. Jenkins, after a pause, in a strangely altered voice, uttered the one word, "Susan." Mrs. Jenkins turned ; by the lowered tone of voice, and the rigidly solemn expression of her husband's face, she knew that a darkly prophetic mood was heavy upon him. "Susan," he said, as she waited for him to go on, "this will be the losing of our place to us."

"I don't see why it should be that," said Mrs. Jenkins, with a downright whimper. "I'm sure I did all I could to stop 'em ; and whoever on earth would ever ha' thought of their doing such a thing ? "

"Well, you'll see we lose our place through it ; " and the sick man uttered a groan so loud and terrible, that Mrs. Jenkins remembering that all night through, though racked with acute bodily pain, he had never once groaned like that, became suddenly apprehensive for the effect it might all have upon him.

"There, pray don't you go to worrying and fretting yourself about it," she said ; "I reckon I never ought to ha' told you a word about it, but I was that done and scared, I was forced to tell somebody. There, do lie still," she added, as her husband with tumultuous heave of the bedclothes, turned suddenly in the bed, and burying his face in the pillow gave another groan heavier and louder than the first. For reply he only uttered another moan, and yet another, till Mrs. Jenkins becoming fairly alarmed for the effect, hurried off to seek something to soothe her husband's excited feelings.

Meanwhile the brown cob had gone beyond the predicted mile. Doubtless he shared the instinctive knowledge, peculiar to every beast that's driven, from the high-bred hunter to the lowly ass, which renders them accurate judges whether it is a competent hand that holds the reins. Still we are bound to give so much credit to the cob; whether he did it through feelings of condescension, or from the absence of vice with which his master accredited him, certainly he trotted along tolerably quietly, and might have continued to do so; but as they passed along a road shaded by low branching trees, Sydney suddenly grasping at a bough just above his head, lost his hat in the endeavour. "Stop, my hat's off!" he cried out. Thomas, in obedience to the call, somewhat sharply pulled up accordingly. Sydney jumped quickly down, but it was a breezy morning, and his hat, like the cob, seemed inclined for a frolic, as the wind getting into it, it rolled swiftly down the road. It took Sydney a minute or two to secure it, and by that time the brown cob was showing unmistakable signs of impatience, and beginning a sort of restless movement with his feet, as though he were going to dance.

"Mind, Tom," said Philip, as the cob rose slightly on his hind legs, "he's going to rear. Come along, Sydney."

Sydney was already panting along at the utmost of his speed, but by the time he took his seat again, the

cob's patience was quite exhausted, and he seemed inclined for a little playful diversion on his own account.
He signified his intention by standing erect on his hind
legs.

"Get out, Phil, and hold him," said Thomas.

"He'd be up again directly I let his head go," said
Philip, who nevertheless sat with every muscle drawn up
like a cat prepared for a spring. "Let him have his
head, Tom," he said quickly, as the cob rose up again.
And in fact the admonition was not unneeded, for
Thomas, whose chief idea of driving was to hold a horse,
was using his knowledge in a manner that threatened to
be dangerous. However, he lowered the reins accordingly, and the cob, responsive to the slackening movement, gave a sudden violent plunge forward, and started
off at a break-neck rate.

"He's running away," said Sydney, peering round
from his seat at the back.

"He will stop at that hill," replied Philip, and so far
he proved correct, though it seemed to all a fortunate
occurrence that a hill came in such timely proximity.
The hill thus designated was a steep one, and by the
time they were half-way up the cob condescended to
walk, and when they gained the summit, ran off again
at his usual pace.

Thomas began to hope their trials were over, and so
possibly they might have been, but on gala days there
are sights and sounds which are not seen or heard on
ordinary occasions. They had nearly reached their
destination when, just at the entrance of the village,
they came suddenly upon a group of tumblers, accompanied by a shrill, tinkling band, which was far more

startling than harmonious. Probably tumblers were a novelty to the cob; anyhow he showed his appreciation of the scene by bounding violently across the road as he passed them. He was scarcely by when the band set up a shrill, discordant strain, and the cob, feeling neither his master's nor Jenkins' powerfully restraining hand, did what Sydney had before feared he was doing, and this time fairly bolted. There was no friendly hill again to stop his career. No one now suggested the idea of his running away, all three were too fully alive to that fact.

"I shall jump out," said Sydney, who in a crisis of events was sure to propose the most unfeasible and impracticable plan of proceeding.

"Sit where you are," said Philip quickly; but his cheek grew suddenly pale with terror, as laying his hands on the reins he found the cob had got his head down in such a fashion, that any power over him was almost hopeless. Up the village street they rushed at headlong rate. A woman standing in a doorway screamed as they passed; and a shop-boy, out of the principal shop, ran with extended arms up the street after them. Then Sydney put in practice his mad proposition, and made a desperate spring from the conveyance. He could never afterwards tell what that leap was like: it seemed to him for a moment as if heaven and earth crashed together, and then he knew nothing more till—well, that was after all the rest had happened.

The two in front never missed him, and if they had done so, would have been powerless to have assisted him, so thoroughly were they at the mercy of the cob. Just round a corner, in a side road leading out of the main

street, was the "Bull Inn," where Mr. Thomas Porter
had occasionally put up, and towards this corner the cob
was unmistakably making his way. Whether he would
safely have rounded the corner must remain matter of
conjecture, but on fête and gala days, not only are you
in danger from the horse you drive, but also from what
you may meet; so it happened, that just as they came
to the corner, three men in a cart driving at unwarrantable speed, came suddenly upon them from the opposite
direction. Both parties made a frantic effort to pull up,
but the result was inevitable: a terrible crash and
collision followed, which unceremoniously ejected the
occupants of the two conveyances. The brown cob
made a few desperate plunges, and then started off with
the wreck of the dog cart behind him. Philip, with a
sort of natural agility, descended safely to the ground;
but Thomas lay on the hard road, becoming every
moment more and more conscious of excruciating pain
in his right arm and shoulder. Of the three men in the
cart, one having fallen on to a stony part of the road,
had considerably bruised his face and head; but the
other two had escaped with but little injury. One of
these went to help his fallen comrade, and the other
started after his horse, which being an old and worn-out
one, and which had been going at its late rapid rate
through being urged on by its half-drunken masters, and
not for its own pleasure, had gone only a few yards and
then stopped of its own accord.

"Are you much hurt, Thomas?" asked Philip.

"I don't know," replied Thomas with a groan.

Philip was meditating helping him to rise, when
glancing down the street, he saw a small crowd gathered

round the spot where Sydney had fallen, and he immediately started off in that direction. In a few minutes he returned with blanched, terror-stricken face, as two men carried by his side Sydney's apparently lifeless form.

As in a dream Thomas saw the procession, and heard a man saying, "I reckon *that* young gent is wholly done for;" then for a moment came strange ringing in his ears, and men, and earth, and sky seemed blending together in one confused mass. Then as the deadly faintness passed he became conscious only of terrible pain, as he felt himself raised and carried in a pair of strong arms, and finally deposited on a bed in the "Bull Inn." Then the garrulous, officious landlady, attempting to remove his coat and waistcoat, Thomas gave such a downright yell of agony that the good lady started back appalled, and as she declared, trembled from head to foot.

Perhaps the next bad thing to getting seriously hurt in an accident yourself, is to be relative or companion to those thus injured, especially when the whole calamity is mainly brought about by folly and indiscretion; so for a time Philip was by no means in an enviable position. Beset with questions on every side, he confessed to the landlady that the two boys were the sons of Mr. Porter of Clansford, and nephews of Mr. Thomas Porter.

"Why, he was in here this morning," said the landlady, "along with Mr. Robertson; and their horse is now a standing in the stables. He's sure to be somewhere in the Park; hadn't you better send and let him know?"

E

Philip seeing no other alternative, assented to the proposition.

"Aye, and send for a doctor too," said the landlady.

Again Philip assented, and the landlady bustled off. In a few minutes she returned: "I've sent for 'em both," she said. Then laying her hand in motherly fashion on Philip's arm, "Are you their brother, my dear?" she asked; but Philip, with all the manly pride of sixteen summers, drew back from what he considered the familiarity of tone and action.

"No, I am no relation," he said, in a tone of impressive dignity.

But Mrs. Wilson, the landlady, was not an impressible woman. "Well, I'm glad to hear it," she said. Then as Sydney gave a low moan, and turned up his eyes in a manner that left only the whites of them visible, she once more drew up to Philip, and fairly clutching hold of his arm, she said, "My soul! I do believe it's well nigh up with him, poor fellow! How I do wish the doctor would come."

In his heart Philip echoed the wish; then a sudden commotion below attracted both him and Mrs. Wilson to the window. It was the brown cob, which having been stopped further up the road, was now brought back covered with foam, and showing still unmistakable signs of insubordination.

A long while it seemed to Philip before any help arrived, and then it came only in the person of Mr. Thomas Porter. Mrs. Wilson hastened to the door to meet him.

"Here's a terrible job has happened, sir!" she said; "but just step in and look for yourself."

Mr. Porter did step in and look for himself accordingly.

"Have you sent for a doctor?" he asked, after a silent investigation.

"Yes, and am expecting him every minute."

Then Mr. Porter turned to Philip, who was standing almost behind the partly-open door.

"Well, sir, this is a pretty business!" said Mr. Porter.

"Yes, sir."

"And pray how came you to take my horse and drive it without my leave?"

"I didn't drive it, sir."

"Who did, then?"

"Thomas drove, sir."

"But you were with them?"

"Yes, I happened to come with them; but Thomas drove."

"And a pretty drive he's made of it: there's my cart smashed, and the horse ruined."

"If he ain't a thinking all about the hoss, I do believe!" said the landlady to herself, in a suppressed, irate whisper. Then going hastily up to where Mr. Porter stood, she said quickly, pointing to Sydney as she spoke, "And that young gentleman there is as good as killed, sir."

"Ha! I believe so," said Mr. Porter; and the tone conveyed so little appreciation of the fact, that Mrs. Wilson fairly bounced out of the room in indignant surprise. At the top of the stairs she met the boy who had been despatched for a doctor.

"Mr. Stirling is out," he said; "and his assistant is out too. They're both gone together miles away, and they don't expect 'em home till late this afternoon."

"Well then," said Mr. Porter, "we must have a fly and take them as they are. They might be got home and have their own doctor, by the time Mr. Stirling could come to them here."

This really seemed the best proposition circumstances allowed, but it was not so easy of practice. However, at length a mattress was so adjusted in the fly, that the two boys could be placed upon it; then there was just room for one person to wedge in close by the door. Mr. Porter appropriated this seat to himself.

"You can ride on the box with the man," he said to Philip; and that young gentleman, who had been apprehensive lest the place in the cab might be assigned to him, obeyed with alacrity.

But Mr. Thomas Porter, in addition to his other qualities, was a nervous man, and he had not proceeded far on his journey before he began to find his position a very trying one. For Sydney at times repeated the upward roll of his eyes which had so startled the landlady, and altogether looked so strange and death-like, that Mr. Porter became full of agitating apprehensions. By way of diversion he began adjusting Thomas' sleeve, which Mrs. Wilson had zealously ripped open; but Thomas assumed such a look of agony at the least attempt to approach his injured arm, and groaned so audibly at every uneven movement of the conveyance, that by the time half the distance was completed, Mr. Porter found the circumstances of the case simply unbearable. Then a happy thought occurred, and he instantly signalled to the driver to stop. Getting out of the cab, Mr. Porter beckoned to Philip to descend. Philip obeyed with a rather alarmed expression, fearing in his own mind that one of the sufferers must be taken decidedly worse.

"Just step in there," said Mr. Porter, holding the handle of the door in his hand.

Philip stepped in accordingly, supposing his advice or help was required ; but the next moment the door was suddenly closed upon him, and Mr. Porter ascending nimbly to the side of the driver, the conveyance again moved on. Then Philip understood that he had been as it were insnared into his present position, and like Mr. Porter he found it to be anything but comfortable or pleasant, and he experienced no small sensations of relief when at last the cab drew up at the boys' home. Mr. Porter got down from his seat on the box, and Philip got out of the cab, and then the two looked at each other. Mrs. Porter had yet to be informed of the calamity, and Philip and Mr. Porter both felt that perhaps the most difficult part of the whole affair still lay before them. Mr. Porter spoke first.

"You just step in," he said to Philip, "and acquaint Mrs. Porter with what has happened, while I and the driver get the boys out."

So saying, he turned to the cab as though immediately to commence the duties before him ; but Philip stood irresolute.

"I am thinking, sir," he said after a minute's pause, "my mother may have heard there's been an accident, and she will be anxious to know if I'm hurt. I think I ought to go home at once and show her I'm all right."

Philip, as he finished speaking, turned and began walking rapidly away. Mr. Porter gazed after his retreating figure in dismayed astonishment. "A nice young gentleman that," he muttered.

But there was evidently no help for him. If Philip would thus desert him, he must take the whole burden upon himself, so with more perturbed feelings than he ever remembered to have experienced all his life, he walked slowly down the garden to the house.

CHAPTER V.

THE CARICATURE.

RS. PORTER really exercised more self-control than might have been expected of her under the circumstances; but many a weak soul wakes up to sudden fortitude and power at the sight of beloved ones stricken down, and in sore need of all the help that can be given.

Then followed days of dire solicitude and watching, for while Thomas' injuries were confined to his right arm and shoulder, Sydney's injuries, being internal, made his case full of much uncertainty, and grave anxiety. But at length youth and hope reasserted their sway, favourable symptoms appeared, and the danger was pronounced nearly over.

One evening Paul was left a little while in charge as nurse. Thomas and Sydney occupied two rooms opening one into the other; but during Sydney's more dangerous illness, the door connecting them had been kept carefully closed. Now, while Thomas was fast becoming convalescent, and Sydney progressing favourably, the door was generally open. As Paul sat by Sydney's bedside, he could hear through the open door if Thomas asked him for anything. Paul sat very still, for Thomas had appeared to be dosing, and Sydney also had been lying with his eyes closed as though asleep. Then Paul, turning his head, became suddenly conscious that Sydney not only was awake, but looking at him with fixed, earnest gaze, his dark eyes luminous with mysterious awe. The gleaming, eager look of his eyes startled Paul.

"Don't you feel so well? Do you want anything, Sydney?" he asked.

Then in low, impressive tones Sydney replied, "I feel very bad, Paul; and, Paul, I don't believe I shall get well any more."

Paul choked down an involuntary sob, and then remembering that he had heard the doctor caution his mother to keep Sydney quiet and cheerful—

"Oh yes," he said, "you will; Dr. Miller told mother to-day the worst was over, and you would soon be yourself again."

Sydney suddenly laid his hand on Paul's: "No, Paul," he said, "I don't feel like getting well. I think I am going to die, and Paul"—and his grasp grew tighter— "I am afraid." For a moment Paul did not answer, and Sydney said, "Dying seems so dreadful, Paul—and then what is it out beyond?"

"Heaven," said Paul, unhesitatingly.

"What is heaven like, Paul?"

"Mr. Blake always spoke of it as home. He often talked to me about it, and he always made it seem to me as if it were a beautiful, glorious home."

Paul spoke the faith of his childish heart, but the words found no echo in the dreamy, speculative soul that had only looked on a vast futurity as a vague possibility, rather than a reality and truth that must inevitably come.

"It doesn't look like that to me, Paul," he said; "it only seems a great blank and darkness. I can fancy judgment and all that, but I don't see anything like home. Paul, I wrote the prize essay at school on death, and I gained the prize; but I didn't think it was like this; I didn't really know anything about it,—and now I am afraid."

"Oh!" said Paul, with tears in his eyes, "how I wish Mr. Blake were here, he would tell you so much better than I can."

Sydney moaned.

"Paul," he said, "I have been taught all about these things; but oh! it seems all dark before me, and I can't find anything to hold on to anywhere."

Just then Mrs. Porter came in; she was advancing towards Sydney's bedside when a low, wailing cry from Thomas startled her, and she hurried to him at once.

"Mother," said Thomas in awe-stricken tones, "is Sydney worse?"

"No, he is much better."

"But he says he is going to die. He and Paul have been talking all about it."

Mrs. Porter turned quickly to Sydney's room.

"You had better go down, Paul," she said hastily; "Sydney cannot bear much talking."

But Sydney's fingers only closed tighter over Paul's hand.

"Let him stop," he said.

Mrs. Porter seeing Sydney's white, haggard face, hastened off for a restorative, and then, as Paul still sat

by Sydney's side, he felt his fingers gradually relax their
hold, as he fell into a peaceful, quiet slumber. When
Sydney awoke, sleep had silently done its restoring
work, and though he could not account for the change,
he felt the springs of life once again strong within him,
and the mysterious shore he had so shuddered to approach was once more receding in the distance.

In fact Sydney had not been so near dying as he
imagined ; but who does not know that the first ebb
and turn of life after severe sickness, like stray gleams
of light in a strange, lonely place, only seem to show us
more plainly the dim outlines and shadows of the
mysterious land to which we have been unconsciously
borne ? Indeed from that time Sydney kept slowly but
surely recovering, and during the time of his convalesence came a long letter from Mr. Blake, a letter
full of friendly sympathy and holy counsellings ; such a
letter, that though Sydney might not realize the fact, it
was another awakening call, for response to which he
would in some manner be accountable.

Thomas recovered speedily, still the accident somewhat retarded his return to school ; but in the meantime,
it having been quite decided that Paul should now commence his school career, he and Theodore started alone,
leaving Thomas till he should be able to join them.

In this enlightened age everyone knows what school
days are like. The ups and downs, the knocks and
rubs, the hasty quarrels, the sudden friendships, and
sometimes the closely-formed ties which often last
through all our after life ; we have all more or less experienced these things ; and Paul's school life, furnishing
nothing particularly different from the ordinary events

incident to that period, it would be hardly worth re-
cording. But one incident it may be as well to relate,
as it formed a prominently connecting link with his
after life. It was the last year that Theodore was at
Dr. Edwards', when there arose in the school one of
those manias that are always occurring in life, when a
certain pursuit or design becomes all the fashion and
rage.

It happened that one of the boys made a caricature
of some passing event, and his example was instantly
followed. Caricature after caricature appeared, and
there were one or two boys among them who obviously
excelled in graphic delineation, till every suggestive
incident became subject for absurd representation.
Then the artists grew bolder, and a certain Mr. Crowfoot,
a grocer in the town, having informed Dr. Edwards that
the bad behaviour of the boys at church had caused
much annoyance to his family, the said boys, by way
of revenge, favoured Mr. Crowfoot with a very appropriate, but anonymous little caricature. But whether
they bungled in their plans, or whether there was a
secret enemy in the camp, or young Crowfoot, the
grocer's nephew, who attended Dr. Edwards' school, got
wind of the affair, certain it is the whole thing was found
out, and the amateur artists were brought into public
notice in a manner that was hardly flattering, and not very
likely to prove favourable to their future artistic career.
But Dr. Edwards dealt leniently with the offenders;
perhaps his own boyish days, and their mischief-making
propensities were still green in his memory; or perhaps
he tacitly sympathized with the indignation every school-
boy feels towards anything of a tale-bearer, anyhow he

dealt leniently, but on one condition only—all caricatures for the future were sternly prohibited, and anyone daring to disobey that prohibition, he warned them would meet with instant and severe punishment. The boys knew Dr. Edwards would keep his word, and it is very probable the caricature mania would have died out a natural death, but an incident arose which proved an irresistible temptation. Perhaps it was not generally known, it was the truth nevertheless,—Dr. Edwards was bald and wore a wig. The boys themselves were mostly aware of the fact, but it was rarely matter for ridicule among them, for the every-day facts of life with which we are constantly familiar, do not prove so mirth-provoking as the chance events that spring up in our lives in quaint, grotesque, incongruous fashion. Besides, beneath that wig was a head that might have ruled a nation rather than a school had opportunity presented itself, so on the whole the boys let the master and his coiffure alone.

But for once in his life, that wig did certainly place Dr. Edwards in rather trying circumstances. It was a Sunday morning, and towards the close of the service there fell a heavy storm of rain, and consequently, when the service was over, people lingered in the porch waiting till the storm should subside. The rain had not been expected, and ladies in dainty dresses, and with perishable-looking sunshades, were waiting and speculating how long it was likely to continue. Of necessity there was much hurrying about for umbrellas, and adjusting of dresses and cloaks, and Dr. Edwards seeing a friend of his, Mrs. Grattan, a lady about sixty years of age, vainly endeavouring to open her umbrella, rushed gallantly forward to her assistance. Dr. Edwards could never quite account for the accident, but in his haste being somewhat precipitate, he suddenly caught his foot in something—possibly entangled it in some lady's trailing skirt—and fell violently to the ground, and in his fall he so caught hold of Mrs. Grattan's dress, that but for the intervening help of a gentleman standing near, the lady would inevitably have fallen also. As it was she was barely saved, and Dr. Edwards' head coming into unfortunate contact with her apparel, his hat was knocked off, and rolled down on to the gravel path beyond. But alas! this was not the whole extent of the calamity; for though before his fall Dr. Edwards appeared to be the possessor of a very tolerable crop of hair, after the scuffle he raised to view a head that certainly was innocent looking, but perfectly bald. To say he fully rose in this condition would not be correct, for before attempting to gain his feet, with inconceivable dexterity he replaced the wig upon his head, then making a hasty exit from the church porch, he went in pursuit of his hat, which was complacently rolling down the gravel path before him; securing which, he walked quietly off through the rain, evidently preferring to brave the elements rather than the suppressed merriment of the spectators in the porch.

Forming a prominent part of those spectators were boys from his own school, for while some had been despatched home, the greater part of them had been ordered to remain till the rain had abated. Among those who thus remained was the chief comic artist of the school, Christopher Brown, or as he was more commonly designated, "Chrissie Brown." Chrissie, shaking back his curly brown hair, which fell in waves over his white forehead, his blue eyes dancing with mirth, stood and fairly held his sides with covert laughter. But the matter did not end there, for on Chrissie's active brain the whole scene was indelibly stamped, and as almost an inevitable result his skilful fingers too readily produced on paper, an apt and striking illustration of the unfortunate scene. Chrissie knew how to give his sketches just that touch of the ridiculous, blended with life-like accuracy, as made them at once such graphic pictures, and yet such absurd representations. So telling was the sketch of the episode in the church porch, that none of the boys privileged to see it could look at it without bursts of appreciative merriment. Chrissie was aware of the risk he was running, and the caricatures were but sparingly distributed, and only to a few thought worthy of confidence, so that to have seen Chrissie Brown's last sketch became a sign of distinction among the boys.

One of the number thus favoured was a youth named Harry Downby, and he not being of a particularly cautious disposition, and having a strong desire to exhibit the fun to a cousin of his living in the town, who was not one of Dr. Edwards' scholars, carried the sketch with him to church the following Sunday, and during the singing contrived to hand it over, enclosed in a hymn book, to the adjoining pew where his cousin was sitting. The paper had such effect on Harry's cousin, that to judge by his distortions of countenance and spasmodic efforts, he might have swallowed the hymn book and been choking in consequence. His father, seeing his indecorous behaviour, though not discerning the cause, leaned suddenly forward and gave his son's head a severe pummelling; and during the disturbance that followed, Mr. Harry Downby, by a dexterous movement, reclaimed his book and put the caricature, as he believed, safely back in his pocket. But alas! on his return from church, in that very pocket there was pocket-handkerchief, penknife, even a bit of enviable looking twine, but no sign of the caricature whatever. Harry Downby certainly felt considerably disturbed at its loss, but solaced himself with the thought that he must have dropt it somewhere in the pew, and that he should safely recover it in the evening. But in the evening no such happy luck awaited him; though he entered the pew first and left it last, and even stayed several minutes under pretence of looking for something, no trace was there of the missing caricature. Then to the parties chiefly concerned, the matter became one of anxiety and grave speculation, and the following morning their worst fears were realized. A day scholar, Alfred Sharpe, a distant relation of Mrs. Grattan, brought the terrible intelligence that the caricature was safely in the possession of the identical Mrs. Grattan herself. He had been at that lady's to tea the previous evening, and Eleanore Grattan, who resided with her grandmother, had told him all about it. She had picked it up in the aisle of the church, and had shown it to her grandmother, and Mrs. Grattan had taken it and securely locked it up in her desk.

"And they mean to use it against us too," said Alfred Sharpe.

"Why didn't you get her to ask her grandmother for it, and then get it away from her?" asked one of the listeners.

"She wouldn't have got it for me. You don't know Eleanore; she's a fearful prig. You should have heard how she went on about the boys who dared to make fun of Dr. Edwards and her *darling* grandmother. She thinks more of that old grandmother than all the rest of the world put together."

Now it was neither loyal nor true of Alfred Sharpe to speak thus, for that same old grandmother, through kindly feelings towards Alfred's parents—who with scant means and a large family, had but a struggling time of it—had very considerably contributed towards his educational expenses; but this part of the matter Mr. Alfred Sharpe did not feel himself called upon publicly to acknowledge.

"Do you think she will bring it and show to Dr. Edwards?" asked an apprehensive voice.

"I believe that's just what she means to do," replied Alfred Sharpe.

"I'm thinking he will know himself if she does," said Chrissie Brown; but though his tone was careless, there was a troubled look in his blue eyes as he spoke.

Just then the school bell rang, and their consultations were for a time at an end. But all during the morning their young heads were unceasingly busy, and they eagerly banded together, as soon as school was over, to discuss what best to do under the circumstances.

"If we could only get it away from her," said one.

"Couldn't we break into the house and get it away by force?" suggested a still bolder spirit.

But the proposition was too unfeasible to meet with even passing consideration, and then some one else proposed that one of their number should watch well his opportunity and steal into the house, carrying with him all the keys they could muster, one of the lot being sure to fit the lock of the desk, and thus abstract surreptitiously the dangerous paper. The proposition was this time gravely considered, and as they talked it over it began to look quite plain and practicable, Then all eyes turned in the direction of Alfred Sharpe: from his very knowledge of Mrs. Grattan's house and its inmates, who could be so fitting as he for the undertaking? But Alfred at once flatly refused.

"I didn't make the sketch," he said, "and I won't have anything to do with it. I dare not," he added, when further urged; "it would be as much as my life is worth to do it."

And in truth Alfred Sharpe did not much exaggerate matters, for he had appreciation enough of Mrs. Grattan's benefits, to know that he would never dare to show his face to his father at home, after conducting himself towards the conferrer of those benefits as a pilferer or a robber. They might call him sneak or coward, threaten or persuade, Alfred stood firm; but he gave a sort of side-long, indirect help that was of considerable value. He agreed to call at Mrs. Grattan's after school that afternoon, and to try and find out if any active measures had at present been taken in the matter, and also when the course would be most likely to be clear for the proposed rifling of her desk. He also further informed them that the said desk was a mahogany one, with brass laid on at the corners, as he had seen Mrs. Grattan use it when he had been there, and she always carried it upstairs to her bedroom, which was the first door on the right-hand side directly you ascended the stairs. So much assistance he proffered, and then sat down with the comforting reflection, that as he took no active part in it, the affair could never in any way be laid at his door; and he really did almost cheat himself into the conviction that he had no part in the matter whatever.

So far the arrangements held good, but it was a melancholy thought, that while they were thus busily laying their plans, Mrs. Grattan might even then be closeted with Dr. Edwards, and spreading out the paper before his horrified gaze. This thought considerably damped their ardour, but they slightly gained courage, when through the afternoon they gathered from Dr. Edwards' serene countenance no sign of impending wrath. Immediately they were all at liberty, Alfred Sharpe was dispatched on his errand. In a very short time he returned with triumphant expression of face: nothing had been done in it as yet. He had learned this by carefully questioning the unsuspecting Eleanore. And what was better still, Mrs. Grattan and her granddaughter had planned quite a long walk that very evening, to visit an old lady who lived quite at the other end of the town.

"You couldn't have a better chance," continued Alfred. "If you let this slip, you won't get another; my opinion is Dr. Edwards will be told all about it to-morrow."

It was at once admitted that the opportunity must not be allowed to slip, but then arose the most knotty part of the question. It was undoubtedly a clever idea for one of the boys to steal into the house unseen and get possession of the paper; but it was like the old fable of the mice putting the bell on the cat's neck—. what boy among them was bold enough for the undertaking? Some of them fairly turned their backs at the bare suggestion. Then at length a happy thought occurred—they would draw lots for the honour: this was universally agreed to. Harry Downby, Theodore Porter, Chrissie Brown, and seven others stood up to take their chances, and the lot fell to Theodore.

Nearly a head taller than the rest, sturdy, stalwart, with open brow and honest eyes, a thorough specimen of an English boy was Theodore; there was nothing about him faintly approximating to the character of thief. Nay, he was most obviously lacking in the very elementary qualities of such a character, and something of this deficiency was apparent to himself as he said slowly,

"I wish it hadn't fallen to me; I shall make the worst possible hand at it."

"No sneaking out of it now," said one of the nine other boys, each of whom had, in turn, heaved a sigh of relief that the hazardous undertaking had not fallen to his own individual share.

"I'm not going to sneak out of it," said Theodore, turning his clear, frank eyes full upon the boy who had just spoken; "but I do say I'm the worst possible one for it: I'm sure to be found out."

"Not you; we will help you through with it."

Theodore, seeing no alternative, put the best face he could upon it. Just then Paul came towards the little group.

"What is it?" he asked.

Now Paul was universally a favourite; his physical weakness at once debarred him from joining in their races and athletic sports, but every one knew Paul might be safely trusted, so by unanimous consent he was let into the secret.　His face grew somewhat troubled as he heard the conclusion.

"I wish it was not you, Theo," he said, half under his breath; but too strict were his notions of honour to attempt to propose any way to extricate Theodore from his trying position.　So he quietly seated himself on the grass, while the boys further matured their plans.

There was no particular difficulty in getting away unobserved, as after certain hours allotted for studies in the evening, the boys adjourned to the playground; and the elder ones being allowed considerable liberty, their absence would not be thought anything of, provided they returned in reasonable time.　The chief difficulty lay in selecting the most fitting time for their adventurous entrance into Mrs. Grattan's residence.　Here again Alfred Sharpe gave side-long assistance.

Half way down the drive leading to the house was an arbour, and anyone standing at the back of it could, as he explained, have a good view of the house and see if anyone came in or out, without being themselves perceived.　The idea was at once acceded to, and Chrissie Brown and two others were chosen to accompany Theodore us far as possible in his undertaking.

CHAPTER VI.

MRS. GRATTAN'S CUPBOARD.

MRS. GRATTAN lived just on the outskirts of the town, about a quarter of a mile from the school. As soon as they were at liberty that evening, the four boys set off walking rapidly in the direction of her house, and arriving there, took up their position safely behind the arbour. As Alfred Sharpe had said, to anyone thus situated, all the front of the house, and the drive leading to it, were plainly visible. And it did really seem as if fortune meant to favour the boys, for they had stood there scarcely five minutes when two people stepped out of Mrs. Grattan's front door, and began walking slowly down the drive. Those two people were no others than Mrs. Grattan herself and her little granddaughter, a girl of about twelve years old. Evidently they were starting on their purposed expedition: Eleanore carried a small satchel on her arm, probably containing certain comforts for the infirm old woman they were going to visit. As they walked down the drive they came quite close to the arbour, and the boys literally held their breath as they passed. Not till Mrs. Grattan and Eleanore had got some way into the road beyond, did one of them dare to move: then considering they were safe, they at once began to carry out their plans.

At the back of Mrs. Grattan's house was a long, narrow garden, enclosed on one side by a high brick wall, and on the others by a thick, well-kept hedge. To this garden, when Mrs. Grattan and Eleanore were considered to have reached a safe distance, Chrissie Brown and another boy repaired, and secreting themselves behind the thick hedge, set up a variety of sounds, varying from a most dismal caterwauling to the moans of a person in dire agony. At first the sounds produced no apparent results; then at length from the kitchen window protruded a head, evidently belonging to Mrs. Grattan's servant, Rebecca. Then, the noises still continuing, the individual to whom the head belonged, walked to the kitchen door and peered curiously down the garden, and finally set off down the path on a journey of inspection. Instantly one of the boys creeping along under the hedge, till he got back within sight of the arbour, signalled to Theodore that the course was clear, and then crept back to his companion under the hedge. Thus encouraged, Theodore, leaving the other boy to keep watch on the front of the house, and to whistle loudly in case of danger, left his position behind the arbour, and going round to the front, walked quickly up the drive. He tried to move in a natural, unconcerned manner. If he was a thief, it would never do to appear like one.

When he reached the front door he found it just ajar; this was a favourable circumstance, so pushing it gently open, he stepped into the hall. Right before him was the staircase, and with as light and nimble a step as he

could command, Theodore ascended. At the top of the
stairs he found a square landing, and right against the
stairs on the right-hand side was the room described as
Mrs. Grattan's. The door was half open, and deter-
mining this must be the right room, Theodore walked
softly in. He glanced carefully round the room, but at
the first survey failed to discover any sign of the
mahogany desk with brass laid on at the corners; but
taking another anxiously scrutinizing gaze, he discerned
on a chest of drawers something that looked like the
article he was in search of, which was so concealed by a
newspaper lying on the top, that only a portion of it was
visible. Theodore went quickly up to the drawers,—
unquestionably that was the desk, but here was another
delaying circumstance: on the newspaper lying on the
desk, with one end placed against the wall for support,
was a glass ornament for flowers of most slender and
fragile make and material. It had evidently been
broken and mended with some kind of cement, and was
thus delicately poised that the cement might effectually
dry. Theodore at once felt that he could not move so
frail a thing, without the broken parts coming to pieces
again through his touch, and peered anxiously round it
to see how best to make the attempt. At last, by
placing one hand at the top and the other at the bottom,
he thought he might possibly move it with success.
Engrossed with this new difficulty, he had got his hands
just so arranged, when he was suddenly startled by a
sound that made his heart stand still with fright: not
the agreed signal whistle, but the sound of voices
evidently at the foot of the stairs. Another moment,
and he distinctly heard footsteps ascending, and then a
young, girlish voice said,

"Lean on me, grandmamma; let me help you up."

Then a voice replied, "Thank you, my dear, I think I can manage."

Surely those last tones belonged to Mrs. Grattan herself, and undoubtedly she would come straight to her own room. For Theodore, standing there almost numb with terror, the circumstances were cruel. To attempt to cross the landing for any other room, would be to discover himself at once to the persons coming up the stairs. He looked round the room in agony; there was the window, and there was the fireplace, and—yes, there was a cupboard, the door of which stood invitingly ajar. Theodore took brief counsel with himself, and stepped hurriedly across the room to the cupboard, and he really had hardly closed the door after him before he heard Eleanore and Mrs. Grattan entering the room.

"Let—me—sit—down, my love," said Mrs. Grattan, evidently speaking with difficulty. "Don't frighten yourself, I think I shall feel better soon; but perhaps you had better run and ask Rebecca to bring me some water, and the medicine I usually take."

Theodore heard Eleanore's light steps descending the stairs, and moved by an irresistible impulse, he slowly pushed the door a tiny creak open, so as to give him a peep into the room beyond. But that one glance showed him his danger; right opposite the cupboard, on a chair at the foot of the bed, sat Mrs. Grattan, her eyes stedfastly fixed on the carpet. Had she been looking as fixedly at the cupboard instead, that hasty impulse of Theodore's would have discovered all. Theodore, with fast-beating heart, pulled the door closely to. After a few minutes—they seemed ages to him—he heard

Eleanore running up the stairs, and the heavier footsteps of Rebecca coming behind her.

"It's the spasms again, ma'am," she said, going up to her mistress, who as she spoke was seized with a spasmodic effort for breath, almost bordering on hysterics. Rebecca hastily dropped something out of a small bottle into a glass, and adding some water, held it to her mistress.

"Take a little, ma'am," she said, "it will make you feel better: I should have been up before, but I was right down at the end of the garden. They boys from the school were some of 'em down there, making believe they was cats, and setting up the hatefullest row. I was just a trying to start 'em, and telling 'em I'd have the policeman to 'em if they didn't go, when I heard Miss Eleanore a calling."

Mrs. Grattan drank some of the medicine, and after a little while professed to feel slightly recovered, and she began breathing quietly and naturally. To Theodore in the cupboard a sudden gleam of hope arose: if she could but recover a little, wouldn't she move from the bedroom; and if so, couldn't he possibly effect his escape—escape being now the only practicable idea. But the next moment cruel was his disappointment, as Mrs. Grattan said slowly,

"I feel a little better now, and I think I will retire to bed at once, Rebecca. I came straight up to my room, for I feel so weak when these attacks go off, that I hardly know how to get upstairs; and I was some distance down the road when I felt the attack coming on, so I had a good way to walk home."

Having said this, Mrs. Grattan, laying her hand on

Rebecca's arm, rose feebly to her feet, and Theodore leaned back against the wall of the cupboard in despair. Just then a clock below struck out eight; Theodore heard it distinctly. At a quarter to nine, all the boys at Dr. Edwards' were expected to assemble for prayers; unless he could effect his escape by that time, discovery was inevitable. To all appearance, he might stop there till midnight. Happily for him, the closet was high and well ventilated, one side was only boarded, forming the back of another cupboard in an adjacent room, and the boards being but roughly and loosely put together, afforded sufficient air to keep off any feelings of suffocation. Still Theodore found his position anything but comfortable, and he was in woful uncertainty as to what degree of freedom of bodily action the limits of the closet allowed. There were a few pegs with garments hanging from them, and shelves on which were placed various sundries; and once in moving his foot he became aware he was in dangerous proximity to what appeared to be a glass bottle standing on the floor. During the process of retiring to bed of which Mrs. Grattan had spoken, Theodore was certain a quarter of an hour or twenty minutes must have elapsed; but even then a forlorn chance appeared.

"I think," said Mrs. Grattan, "if you both go down and leave me quite alone, I may get a little sleep. No, my dear," she continued, as Eleanore asked permission to remain; "go down now, prepare your studies and get yourself some supper. If I want you, or find I cannot sleep, I will ring. No, leave that blind half-way down, Rebecca, and the window a little open; this warm evening a little air will do no harm. Now you may go."

Evidently by the sound of retreating footsteps they were leaving her, and a wild fluttering of hope arose in Theodore's breast. If she would only go to sleep, he might yet steal away unobserved; but he was uncertain how long this process of falling asleep might take for Mrs. Grattan. Two minutes sufficed for himself and his light-hearted colleagues. Considerably more than two minutes elapsed, and Theodore resolved to look for himself; accordingly, as before, he slightly pushed open the cupboard door and glanced anxiously out. That glance showed him Mrs. Grattan, her head resting composedly on the pillow, and her eyes fixed with serene and thoughtful gaze on the open window and sky beyond. Theodore drew back in anguish of soul; that ever anyone intending to go to sleep should lie with their eyes wide open in that fashion! Bitterly cruel it seemed that his last hope should be thus deliberately frustrated. Angry impatience took possession of his soul, and in perturbation of spirit, when a few minutes had elapsed, he resolved to take another furtive glance. This time the sight that met his eyes was if possible more irritating still: Mrs. Grattan—probably as a sleep-inviting process—was complacently reading the pages of a small book she held in her hand. The sight almost threw Theodore into a frenzy of impatience; mad schemes dashed through his brain. At one moment he felt almost tempted to step boldly out of his hiding place, and apologize as best he might. But what apology or explanation could be adequate to the circumstances? how would it sound,—

"Dear madam, believe me, I'm neither a thief nor a burglar; I've only been a little while in your cupboard

If you will allow me, I only want to get out of your house as quickly and as quietly as possible."

Theodore knew at once the shriek and ringing of the bell that would instantly follow such an announcement. Besides, it would be a risk thus suddenly to frighten a person in good health; what the effect might be on anyone just recovering from spasms, Theodore dared not conjecture. Besides, if he was not a thief, his actions surely had all the appearance of one. Meanwhile the time was passing, and the early dusk of the summer evening made the room grow dim and shadowy, and then Theodore, having worked himself almost into a fever, happening to put his ear close to the crack of the door, was certain he heard sounds indicative of sleep proceeding regularly from the vicinity of the bed. At last then there might yet be deliverance! At the thought he moved one foot hurriedly forward, but the hasty movement incurred its penalty. His boot striking suddenly against the glass bottle, produced a sharp, clicking sound; Theodore paused a moment in uncertainty and dread, but the next moment his hopes were finally overthrown, as he distinctly heard the sharp ringing of a bell, too obviously Mrs. Grattan's.

The fact was, Mrs. Grattan had at last really fallen into a dose, but being a light sleeper, at the click of Theodore's shoe against the bottle she had instantly awoke; though she had so far sunk into oblivion that she was unconscious what the sound was that had awoke her, or from whence it had proceeded. Eleanore speedily answered the summons, and then Theodore heard Mrs. Grattan telling her of some light refreshment she thought advisable to take, and the making of which she was entrusting the particulars of to Eleanore.

"Go down now and tell Rebecca to make it, and bring it at once," she said in conclusion; "and you may put down the window and blind first, and give me a light."

Eleanore obeyed, and as Theodore heard her retreating footsteps, he leaned back against the wall of the closet in abject despair. Just then the clock struck again; this time Theodore plainly counted the nine strokes. Then all hope was surely over; but even then, suffer as he had already done, a new train of tormenting thoughts arose within him. How honourable and respectable had been his course at school; only quite lately one of the masters had quoted him to the younger boys as an example of honesty, truth, and uprightness; and now, he felt in his misery, the youngest or wickedest boy in the school could cry shame of him. Nay, for all he knew, the whole wretched affair might yet be made public in a court of justice. His miserable reflections were cut short by Eleanore returning to the room with her grandmamma's supper. Mrs. Grattan swallowed a few spoonfulls, then she said,

"What was that Rebecca was saying about some boys being in the garden?"

"Oh, she has told me all about it," said Eleanore, "they were some of Doctor Edwards' boys. They were not in the garden, but under the hedge outside, and kept making all sorts of annoying noises, so that Rebecca said no one could keep in the house and hear them."

"Ah!" said Mrs. Grattan solemnly, "I am afraid that Doctor Edwards has got one or two unruly spirits under his charge that he will find it difficult to control. But why they should so especially single me out for their spite, is a thing I cannot at all understand."

Poor Theodore, standing cramped up in the cupboard, had only freedom of action and speech been allowed him, would willingly have assured her, that as far as he went at least, he had no desire for spite towards her; his only wish being to escape safely from her dominions. Of this, however, there appeared no chance. Long after Mrs. Grattan had finished her supper, Eleanore still sat chatting to her grandmother; and when she at last quitted the room, it was only to send Rebecca to her mistress.

"Rebecca," said Mrs. Grattan, as that individual appeared in the doorway, "I think if I could get the house quiet I should go to sleep, and a long night's rest would do me good. I want you now to go down, be sure all the doors and windows are securely fastened, and then come up to bed."

Rebecca went down accordingly; Theodore could hear various sounds indicating that she was following out her mistress' commands. A few minutes more, and Eleanore came and wished her grandmamma "a sweet good-night." Then Rebecca followed her, and after the assurance that all was safe downstairs, wished her mistress "good-night" also.

"Rebecca," said Mrs. Grattan, "leave your door a little open, and mine also; if I should want anything in the night, I could make you hear better. Put the light so it does not fall full on my eyes. There, that will do nicely; now good-night."

Rebecca then quitted the room for her own apartment, a small room just across the landing, opposite Mrs. Grattan's, leaving both doors ajar as desired.

Then the house became perfectly quiet, and the only

available plan for Theodore was to wait till Mrs. Grattan was undoubtedly asleep—there must be no mistake about it this time—and then steal carefully from his place of concealment. Once clear of the bedroom and the stairs, he trusted to his ready brain and strong young hands to effect his exit.

Theodore waited patiently, at length he thought he must have waited long enough; surely by that time Mrs. Grattan must have succumbed to the soothing influence of "nature's sweet restorer." He listened attentively, and then pushing the door slightly open, peeped out. There was not light enough in the room for him to discover whether Mrs. Grattan's eyes were shut or open, but the figure in the bed appeared to lie perfectly still. He paused again a few minutes, and then putting his ear to the door, again intently listened, and succeeded in persuading himself that there was a sound of regular breathing, like that of a person in a quiet sleep. Now surely his time of deliverance had come at last, but he was determined that vile glass bottle should not again defeat his successful exit. Feeling carefully on the floor, with something akin to resentment, he laid hold on the innocent cause of his former failure. Towards the back of the cupboard the space seemed quite clear, and Theodore placed it on the floor as far back as he could reach. Of necessity he stooped to effect his purpose, and being very tall, and raising his head suddenly, it came into such violent contact with some article projecting from the top shelf of the cupboard, that as a result it descended over his head and shoulders, unfolding itself a little as it fell. Theodore made a pluck at it which only unfolded it more.　It was a light, woolly material, apparently a shawl.　Theodore hurriedly doubled it together, and placed it beside the glass bottle ; but the effects of its fall did not end there.　That very shawl Mrs. Grattan had herself, about a week previously, placed away with her own hands, and like many another good housewife, being aware that the best thing to prevent moth—far exceeding the use of any advertized moth powder, is a good sprinkling of common pepper—had accordingly sprinkled lavishly of that article in the folds of the shawl as she doubled it together ready to lay by for winter use.

Theodore was not aware of all these circumstances, but he soon became painfully conscious of some new element in the atmosphere of the cupboard, which produced a tickling sensation in his nose, and an irresistible inclination to sneeze.　The sound he knew would be fatal to his plans, but what was he to do!　In vain he held his mouth, his nose, and buried his head in the garment hanging nearest to him.　A loud, prolonged sort of noise, something between a cough, a sneeze, and a groan, was the only result of his endeavours.　Theodore listened in an agony—yes, there was surely a rustling sound, as of some one moving.　Then Mrs. Grattan was awake ; but possibly she would take no notice of the noise.　What a mockery was the thought, for the very next moment there it was again—the tickling sensation worse than ever.　"Tis-shue," uttered Theodore, before he could this time attempt to repress the sound.　There must have been terrible virtue in that pepper, for before he could recover from the fright the noise caused him, again he uttered a sound that to a listener could have been no other than a loud, clear, distinct human sneeze.

"Ahem," said Mrs. Grattan from the bed. She evidently belonged to that class of persons who, in encountering a thief, always first audibly announce their bodily presence as a sort of preliminary to their proceedings.

Theodore felt his fate had arrived, but even then the pepper persisted in doing its fearful work. His eyes were streaming with water, he felt as though he must sneeze or die, and burying his head once more in the friendly garment near him, the sound this time was muffled and less distinct.

Then he heard footsteps moving in the room; were they coming straight to the cupboard? Probably they would have been, had there been lock or button by which the door could have been secured; but the cupboard was an old one, and a piece of string passing through a hole where a lock might have been, was the only means of pulling the door open. Then as he listened, the footsteps ceased; possibly the lady in her fright had escaped from the room. At the thought, Theodore pushed open the door and cautiously protruded his head: the room was much brighter; evidently a candle had been lit from the night-light, and there, before the chest of drawers on which was the mahogany desk, before an open drawer, standing with her back to him, was Mrs Grattan, arrayed in ample *robe-de-nuit*, and long-flowing dressing gown. The sight seemed to fascinate him. Despite his anguish of mind, Theodore stood for a moment silently watching her. Then a thought passed dizzily through his brain; she was with

G

her back to him:—could he possibly pass behind her unobserved? He so far listened to the idea that he carefully drew the rest of himself from the cupboard, and was preparing for the first move when, as though in answer to the bold suggestion, Mrs. Grattan suddenly turned and confronted him; and Theodore felt an unpleasant thrill pass over him, as he noticed she held with determined grasp a pistol in her hand. She advanced steadily within a yard of him and stopped, and Theodore with an endeavour at explanation began,

"Madam, I'm"—

But Mrs. Grattan in solemn tones interrupted him.

"Young man, do you wish me to shoot you?" she asked.

Theodore certainly did not wish any such thing, and was opening his lips to speak to that effect, when Mrs. Grattan continued,—

"Then down upon your knees directly."

But Theodore did not much care for that proceeding either, and again attempting his defence, this time got a word further:

"Madam, I'm not"—

"Down upon your knees," thundered Mrs. Grattan, "or I'll"—and she held the pistol towards him in a threatening manner.

Theodore could see no positive harm in kneeling, so dropped upon his knees accordingly.

"Now," said Mrs. Grattan, "at your peril move a single step and I'll"—and again the pistol was pointed with deliberate aim.

But to tell the truth, Theodore felt more of wrath than fear under the circumstances, and remembering that the prohibition extending only to his actions could not prevent his freedom of speech, was just going again to attempt a word or two in his own behalf, when Rebecca, in tumultuous haste, made her appearance at the door.

She had not only obediently left her door unclosed, but had retired to rest with her ears and senses on the alert; therefore hearing unusual noises in her mistress' room, she had rushed hurriedly to the rescue. Probably the scene before her awakened ideas within her more terrible than just the bare facts themselves, for holding on to the doorway, she uttered a succession of cries, that for loudness and intensity might have equalled an Indian war whoop.

"Oh, oh, ah! oh, oh, ah!" she shrieked.

Then going hastily to her mistress, she threw her arms so violently around that lady's waist, that Mrs. Grattan felt her breath impeded by the movement, much the same as from an attack of spasms.

"Don't, don't, Rebecca," she protested feebly, still keeping the pistol steadily raised, and her eyes fixed on the victim before her.

But Rebecca, whose only idea seemed to be to effect a retrograde movement, only tugged the tighter.

"Come back! come back!" she shouted; and so vigorous was the clasp of her strong arms, that Mrs. Grattan almost staggered and reeled, and of necessity retreated a step or two. So distressing to both body and mind were the importunate efforts of her servant, that she was for a moment taken off her guard; and lowering the hand that held the pistol, she turned to remonstrate with the officious Rebecca. Perhaps Mrs.

Grattan considered a kneeling foe a vanquished foe, or was not aware that she had an expert young wrestler in the supposed robber before her. Anyhow, she was not prepared for the next movement on his part, for Theodore, seeing his opportunity, drawing up every muscle for the effort, sprang suddenly to his feet, and with one bound cleared the room and rushed with precipitate haste down the stairs.

But for Rebecca's restraining grasp, Mrs. Grattan would have instantly followed him ; as it was, Theodore had gained the front door before she was fairly in pursuit. But Theodore found that to let himself out of a strange house, and to undo a door with whose fastenings he was unacquainted, was not so easily effected. He had just succeeded in turning back the key which went very stiffly, when he heard steps coming down the stairs after him. At the sound he redoubled his efforts, but there is an old proverb which tells that speed is not always the result of haste, and the bolts seemed to defy his hasty, eager fingers. At last the top bolt was withdrawn, and he took a furtive glance around. Mrs. Grattan had reached the bottom of the stairs ; Rebecca, the lighted candle in her hand, had half way descended ; and even as he glanced, a young figure clad in long, white robes, with dark hair streaming over her shoulders, appeared at the top of the landing. She gave a quick scream, and then began running down the stairs.

What three women with a light and a pistol might not effect—the last-named article need not have troubled his mind, Mrs. Grattan having laid it down on the drawers before descending the stairs—Theodore dared not stop to conjecture. He gave the door a violent pull, but there

was still an impeding bolt. He stooped down and
had just triumphantly overcome this last obstacle, when
a pair of hands were laid suddenly upon him; then
another, for Rebecca, putting the light down upon the
hall table, came to make common effort with her
mistress. Theodore knew by a few well-directed blows
he could quickly have rid himself of his two opponents,
but he had too much manly sentiment to put forth his
power against two of the feminine order.

"The poker, miss!" said Rebecca to Eleanore, who
stood looking aghast with fright, and uncertain how to
proceed.

At mention of such an unlawful weapon, Theodore
resolved to make good his escape, and giving the sturdy
Rebecca a sudden push which sent her reeling violently
backward, and using a little very gentle force with
Mrs. Grattan, giving himself a dexterous wrench he
made effectual exit, although even as he cleared the
doorway, he felt conscious that his antagonist's hand had
wrested some personal property from his coat pocket.
But not till he got beyond the drive did he stop to consider that point, then clapping a hand on each pocket,
he became aware that he had left his pocket handkerchief in his enemy's power. How far that might affect
his fortunes he stayed not to think, but rushed hurriedly
on. He would not probably have been much comforted, could he have seen Mrs. Grattan at that instant
holding up the handkerchief to the light, and reading
aloud the name in the corner, "Theodore E. Porter."

"We've got a good clue here, Rebecca," she said.

"I'm sure I don't know," sobbed Rebecca. "If only
you'd help me fasten this door, my hands shake so; no-

how can I turn the key, and he may be a-coming back with a dozen more behind him. There, that's done at last," she said after desperate effort, "and I'm sure I'm that done up I could drop anywhere;" and seating herself on the stairs she burst into a fit of hysterical tears and lamentations, while Eleanore hovered round her grandmother like a frightened bird.

"Try and control yourself, Rebecca," said Mrs. Grattan; "I and Miss Eleanore don't behave like that."

"If you'd had the blow in your chest that that young willin give me, perhaps you wouldn't feel no better yourself," replied Rebecca, bursting into a still louder fit of injured sobs, and it really required all Mrs. Grattan's tact to effectually quiet her.

At length she marshalled her and Eleanore up the stairs before her. Still it must be owned that, despite her calm exterior, Mrs. Grattan felt very seriously upset and overcome; and but for her long-acquired habits of self-restraint and composure, might have in a measure followed the example of the more demonstrative Rebecca. There was considerable pallor on her countenance, as gaining her bedroom she sat down on the first available chair. When she felt slightly recovered she rose, and taking the pistol from the drawers where she had laid it before going in pursuit of Theodore, proceeded to put it in its proper place. At the sight of that formidable article, Rebecca suffered a serious relapse.

"I can't help it," she said; "the very sight of that pistol is enough for me; and to think of you a-standing holding it as you was when I come in. I shall always think there would ha' been murder if I hadn't come in just as I did."

"Rebecca!" said Mrs. Grattan, "do you think I should lightly take a fellow-creature's life?"

"But you was a-pointing it at him!" sobbed Rebecca.

Something like a smile passed grimly over Mrs. Grattan's face.

"You don't know, Rebecca," she said, "that the pistol was even loaded; I wanted to frighten that young man, but I certainly should not have shot him." So saying she laid the pistol back in the drawer.

Could Rebecca have examined that pistol just then, and seen its unloaded and rusty condition, she probably would not have entertained any further doubts on the subject herself.

The truth was, Mrs. Grattan, as a young woman, had been fully capable of firing a pistol, and had somewhat prided herself on her acquirement; but of late years she had wholly discontinued the art, though she still kept the pistols as kinds of relics. Nay, she kept them in a drawer in her bedroom, possibly in much the same way that some people will keep an old, rusty sword, that could be of no available use, at the head of their bed. In the late case of alarm, it had occurred to her mind to try their effect as means of intimidation.

It was some time before Rebecca could feel sufficiently composed to retire again to her bed, but Eleanore still lingered by her grandmother's side.

"May I stop all night with you, grandmamma?" she asked. Mrs. Grattan gave her consent, and then Eleanore, with eyes in which still lurked a latent gleam of terror, said gravely, "Grandmamma, did you really think of shooting him?"

There was in fact little of a courageous kind, or out of

the common range, that Eleanore would not have given
her grandmother credit for.

"I thought, Eleanore, you knew me better," Mrs.
Grattan replied; "you at least, child, must not mis-
understand me.   Look here," she said, going to the
drawer and reproducing the pistol, "it was not possible
to have shot anyone with that : I only used it thinking
to intimidate him into confession.   Had Rebecca helped
me," continued Mrs. Grattan gravely, "I think now we
might have captured him."

CHAPTER VII.

BEGGING FOR MERCY.

MEANWHILE Theodore sped rapidly on in the direction of the school. As he expected, the doors were already fastened. He crept cautiously round to that side of the house where his room was situated; all was perfectly quiet. There was among the boys a certain article designated a rope ladder, which had done service on rare and desperate occasions; but no friendly ladder was in sight. Theodore only concluded one thing, the silence portended ill; failure and discovery had most likely produced depression and silence.

He was partly right in his conjectures. The boy he had left in charge behind the arbour, for a few moments watched zealously, then concluding that Mrs. Grattan and Eleanore being absent, there could be no further need for disquietude, began wondering how the two were progressing at the garden hedge, and went several paces to reconnoitre. At length, returning to his assigned post, he was literally terror-stricken at the sound of voices, and at perceiving Mrs. Grattan and Eleanore slowly walking back up the drive. In such close proximity he dared not give the agreed whistle; he felt rooted to the spot, and could only stand and mutely watch their entrance to the house. Then he ran wildly round the arbour to the road, and advanced some paces up the drive, and in his agitation actually attempted to whistle, but so feeble was the attempt, that the sound could not possibly have reached Theodore's ears. Then in his perplexity he rushed round to the back, making as he went various tokens of distress to the two behind the hedge; they became aware of his signals just as Eleanore appeared at the back door calling Rebecca.

The three then held hurried counsel a few minutes, and all was communicated, and they at once realized the perils of their situation. In vain they watched the house, no sign was there of Theodore, till at last, seeing it useless to remain longer, they went disconsolately back. It was miserable work telling their utter failure, and the terrible turn affairs had taken, to their expectant companions.

Just before prayers, a band of those concerned in the matter were gathered in the lobby adjoining the back hall that led to the schoolroom, anxiously discussing what was best to be done.

"It will all come out at prayers," said Harry Downby; "Theodore will be sure to be asked for then."

A tall, thin boy, named John Wicks, with a cunning expression of countenance, and evidently a year or two older than the others, pushed his way forwards.

"I tell you what," he said, "we'll say we don't know where he is; we can say so much with truth anyhow."

"It would be no use saying that," said Chrissie, with a doleful voice; "it must all be found out now."

"No, it needn't," persisted John Wicks. "Suppose

we say he went to bed with a bad headache; if they find he's not there, then we know nothing more about it. But Dr. Edwards is out for the evening, it will only be West to read prayers to-night, and West is half a muff; if we say that, he'll never think anything more about it, and we shall get Master Theo in all right."

"I won't have a lie told about it," said Chrissie.

"You just leave it to me," said Wicks confidently.

"I tell you," said Chrissie, with suddenly crimsoning face and flashing eyes, and stamping his foot imperatively as he spoke, "I won't have any lying; I'll let it all be found out first. I won't have any sneaking lies told."

"If West asks, that's the tale I shall tell," said Wicks coolly.

"If you do, I shall get up and contradict what you say; there shall be no lies told over Theodore."

The speaker was Paul Porter; John Wicks turned on him a contemptuous leer.

"A nice muddle the truth will bring you into," he said.

At that moment Mr. West, who was one of the principal masters, and generally regarded as next in authority to Dr. Edwards, passed quite close to where the boys were standing. How near he had been to them, how much he had heard, no one could determine, and they followed him with apprehensive hearts to the schoolroom. The place where Theodore sat at prayers was close to the master's right hand, therefore his absence was at once observed.

"Where is Theodore Porter?" asked Mr. West. An ominous silence followed the question. "Does anyone know where he is ?" Mr. West gave a scrutinizing glance round as he spoke.

If Mr. West was a muff, he had a very considerable degree of discrimination, and it did not require a great deal of discernment to see that something unusual was amiss. Paul Porter almost hid his troubled face behind the companion sitting next to him. Chrissie's blue eyes were full of perturbation, and Harry Downby kept alternately looking intently first at one of his feet, then at the other, as though his toes were all at once become objects of peculiar interest to him. More or less, all the guilty party by their looks betrayed themselves, with the exception of John Wicks, who with folded arms sat complacently regarding the opposite wall.

Mr. West looked carefully from one to another, but receiving no answer, evidently thought it wisest not to press the matter further just then, and opening the books, he began to read.

Theodore, Paul, Harry Downby, and Chrissie Brown, all occupied one room : to this room Mr. West came after all the other boys had gone to bed. He was hardly surprised to see that neither of the boys had begun to undress, but were all gathered together in earnest consultation. At his entrance, Harry Downby made a hurried effort to hide something under his bed.

"What is that you are putting under your bed, Downby?" asked Mr. West.

"It's nothing particular, sir."

"Just show me what it is."

"I—I—I'd rather not, please, sir."

Mr. West moved at once to the bed, and stooping down, pulled out the identical rope ladder.

"I suppose," he said, "this was to assist Theodore in getting into the house; if so, it will not be needed, as I intend to see him myself and let him in when he returns. I can see," he added, "that you are in some way connected with this escapade of Theodore's, or are endeavouring to screen him. I do not say this to pry into your secrets, or to force you to confession; but you are aware that if a really guilty transaction comes under my notice, I am bound to inform Doctor Edwards of it. I should not otherwise discharge my duty towards you. Only I shall be grieved to have to bring trouble upon so good and honourable a boy as Theodore Porter."

"That's just it," said Chrissie, suddenly veering round; "and as I'm at the bottom of it all, I should like to tell you all about it, Mr. West. I don't suppose you can help us; still, as I was the cause of it, I think I ought to tell you."

He glanced interrogatively at Harry and Paul, and receiving from them no dissenting voice, suddenly springing to his feet and standing before Mr. West, he gave him a truthful account of the whole matter. Mr. West's face became grave as he listened.

"I did not expect anything so bad as this," he said; "what the end will be of so rash a proceeding I cannot conjecture. But it will do no good for you to sit up talking any longer: all of you undress for bed at once." Then, as the boys began to obey him—"Whose is this rope ladder?" he asked.

"I think it mostly belongs to me," said Harry Downby in a doubtful voice, as though uncertain whether the ownership of it would not appear culpable.

"Then," said Mr. West, "I restore it to you, and I

trust to the honour of you all not to attempt to-night to use it. Remember, I have undertaken to see Theodore in."

"Wicks says West is a muff; I say he is a brick," said Harry Downby, as Mr. West retired from the room.

Then followed for the boys a time of anxious suspense. In vain they strained their eyes and ears at the open window, no sign could they catch of Theodore's return; at last ensued a time of depressing silence, and during that interval Theodore returned. He had stood but a minute under the bedroom window, when he heard steps approaching, and turning, he suddenly confronted Mr. West. Mr. West laid his hand quietly on Theodore's arm.

"Chrissie Brown has told me all about this unfortunate affair," he said, "and I have been on the watch for your return. Doctor Edwards is out this evening; had he been at home, he would probably have let you in himself."

An unpleasant thrill passed through Theodore's mind at the idea, and he walked silently into the house and into the bedroom with Mr. West. Chrissie greeted his appearance with a subdued shout.

"Oh! how did you get here?" he asked. "Mr. West knows all about it, so you may tell us for all him— mayn't he, sir?"

"If he wishes, he may," replied Mr. West; and Theodore, seating himself on the bed, gave a truthful and vivid description of all that had occurred.

Perhaps a comical affair never sounds so truly comic, as when told in a thoroughly matter-of-fact or mournful manner; so by the time Theodore's story fairly came to an end, Chrissie, with that instinctive discernment of the ridiculous peculiar to his nature, after vainly endeavouring by sundry contortions of face to assume due gravity of expression, at last entirely overcome, buried his head in the pillow, completely convulsed with laughter. Then looking up and meeting Theodore's aggrieved countenance—

"I can't help it, Theo, I can't," he said; "only to think of you in the cupboard, and Mother Grattan and her pistols; I can't help it," and again he shook with untimely mirth.

Even Mr. West for some reason turned aside his head, but at length looking round, he said,

"I am afraid you will not laugh over this long, for it threatens to be a very serious affair. I do not see that I can give you either help or advice. I see no reason to tell Doctor Edwards, as of necessity it must undoubtedly reach his ears: for if Mrs. Grattan gets a distinct clue from the handkerchief, she will of course at once know where to apply." Then, noticing Theodore's haggard face—"You are faint and tired," he said kindly; "could you eat anything?"

"No, sir, I could not eat a mouthful," said Theodore mournfully, a queer sensation rising in his throat.

"Then take my advice and go to bed at once," said Mr. West.

To go to bed was one thing, to sleep was another; and for the first time in that room, in each bed there was restless tossing to and fro, and it was long past midnight before sleep closed their eyelids. Even then one of their number refused to be thus comforted: Paul

Porter still lay awake, with wide-open eyes staring at the window. Then a something arose in his mind that was at first but a vague idea or project, then it fashioned and developed itself as projects will in the night season, till it grew something tangible and practicable, and then it became as a duty which must of necessity be performed. Thinking over all the details of the question, just as the grey dawn began to struggle in at the window, Paul fell into a restless slumber.

When he opened his eyes, after the first memory of their common trouble, the project of the former night arose before him. But it seemed as if even during that light slumber the thing had changed its garb, and what at night seemed feasible and proper, now appeared vague and impracticable; but with the memory that a brother's honour, as it seemed to Paul—life—was at stake, he determined that practicable or not, no plan to which attached a chance of hope should be rejected. So with profound countenance he rose and gravely dressed himself, then beckoning Theodore aside, he communicated to him his project. Theodore heard him in silence and astonishment; the proposal Paul made was to go himself to Mrs. Grattan after school that morning, and by explaining all, put themselves at her mercy.

"That would be just the thing," said Chrissie, who came up in time to hear the end of the suggestion. "If I hadn't done the picture I would go myself, but that would never do. I couldn't have the face, and I do believe I should laugh."

But Theodore had by this time given the matter deliberate consideration.

"You shall not go, Paul," he said firmly; "you are innocent about this, and I won't have you put your foot into it now."

But though Theodore was honestly resolute in his denial, public opinion was so much in favour of Paul's plan, that during the morning he finally gave his consent. The only dissenting voice was John Wicks'.

"I should think," he said, "you've had enough already of going uninvited to Mrs. Grattan's house."

But his remark was unheeded, and so after school, having obtained leave of absence, Paul set off on his errand. He went steadily along; his lameness still so much impeded his movements, that he could not get over the ground so quickly as any other boy would have done. As he went, he so far matured his plans as to carefully prepare exactly what he would say to Mrs. Grattan, how he would begin, and so forth; but as he reached the drive leading up to the house, one of those variable moods peculiar to a sensitive temperament, and which sometimes make actions appear inconsistent and changeable, passed suddenly over his mind. Again, as in the early morning, the thing he was doing appeared chimerical and inexpedient, and under the force of the passing impression Paul might have made a momentary pause, but the all-conquering concern and anxiety for a beloved brother stimulated him onwards; and again renewing his courage, he made his way to the front door and rang the bell. Directly after he had rung, a new train of thought occurred to his mind; Mrs. Grattan might not be at home; nay, she might even then be putting the matter in the hands of the police; or worse still, one of that order might already be in the house examining the spot where the affair took place, and going over the chief circumstances of the case. But the bell was rung and he must take what followed. Rebecca answered the summons.

"Please, is Mrs. Grattan at home?" asked Paul.

"Yes, she is," replied Rebecca shortly.

"Then can I speak to her? I want very much to see her."

Before answering, Rebecca looked him down from head to foot; to tell the truth, boys were her distinct aversion, but something in the wistful face and pleading manner of the specimen before her, rather went in his favour.

"I don't know as you can see her," she said; "my mistress is anything but well this morning. Still, if you like to send in your message, I can hear if she'll see you."

"Will you tell her that one of the boys from Doctor Edwards' school wants particularly to speak to her?"

An abrupt change passed over Rebecca's face.

"If you're one of that owdacious lot, the sooner you're gone the better. I ain't a-going to trouble my missis nothing about you." So saying she shut the door suddenly in Paul's dismayed face.

In excuse of Rebecca's behaviour, it must be urged that the conduct of the boys down the garden the evening before, which she chose to look upon as direct personal insult to herself, was still fresh in her mind. But she never for a moment connected Paul with the more momentous circumstances that occurred later. In truth, her mind was so imbued with the magnitude of the whole affair, and with the idea that she and her mistress had nearly succeeded in capturing a really villainous burglar, that such a thought as associating Paul with the event, or the idea that the robber was no other than a very big school-boy, never entered her head.

But courtesy and hospitality were fixed laws in Mrs. Grattan's house, and Rebecca, as she stood with the door handle in her hand, felt half uncertain whether she was doing quite the right thing; so opening the door a little way, she looked out.

"Oh, you ain't gone," she said.

"No, I must see your mistress, I really must," urged Paul.

Rebecca would most probably have yielded at this point, but just then Mrs. Grattan appeared on the stairs.

"Who is there, Rebecca," she asked.

Rebecca threw wide open the door, so that Paul stood full in view.

"It's some one from Doctor Edwards'," she said, with a tone and expression betokening that such was no very great recommendation. Mrs. Grattan came forward.

"Do you want to see me?" she asked.

"Yes, ma'am, I have something I want particularly to say to you," replied Paul earnestly.

"Then step in here," said Mrs. Grattan, opening a door on her right hand, and Paul, glad to have so far prospered, stepped in accordingly; and Mrs. Grattan following him into the room, shut the door, and asking Paul to be seated, sat down herself almost opposite him. Then after a minute's silence,

"I think you said you had something particular to say to me," she said.

Paul looked up; he was familiar with Mrs. Grattan's face, he had seen her nearly every Sunday at church since he had been at school, but he had never noticed before how singularly impressive and dignified was her whole appearance and bearing; and at the same moment every word of the carefully-prepared introduction, which was to have been as a prelude to the rest, vanished entirely from his mind. To have saved his life he could not remember how to begin; he looked alternately at the carpet and at the window, and finally, feeling Mrs. Grattan's gaze fixed full upon him, he made a precipitate beginning.

"I am come to speak about—I mean—" he said, "I am afraid you were very much frightened by some one being in your house last night."

"Some one was in my house, certainly, and in my cupboard."

"But it wasn't a robber; it was some one who never for a moment thought of hurting you. He would not even have frightened you if he could have helped it; he would have got quietly out of the house without disturbing you at all, if he had been able."

"And who, pray, was this person?"

"It was my brother," said Paul, with a suddenly crimsoning face.

Mrs. Grattan looked neither surprised nor puzzled by these statements; her quick, intelligent mind had that morning been putting this and that together with a sagacity that might have done honour to one of the detective force, so she said quietly,

"Your brother Theodore?"

"Yes," said Paul; "and oh, believe me, he did not

intend any harm; he only hid in the cupboard when he heard you coming upstairs."

"And what was he in my house after?"

This was the knotty point, but Paul before coming had concluded that nothing but a full confession could avail; still it did seem difficult to disclose this part of the matter, and his memory still continuing painfully treacherous, no happily-framed sentences would come to his aid.

"Haven't you, ma'am," he said at last, "a caricature of you and Doctor Edwards?"

"Yes, I have such a thing. What of that?"

"That is what Theodore wanted to find."

"Did he succeed in getting it?"

"No, you came home before he had time to find it."

Events were beginning to look clearer to Mrs. Grattan, still there were some points that mystified her, so she said,

"I think if you want to make me fully understand about this, you will have to tell me the whole story quite plainly."

Paul had expected nothing less than to have to make an unreserved confession, so in the best way he could he complied with Mrs. Grattan's request, and told her the whole story, only according to his strict code of honour, he made careful mention of Alfred Sharpe's name, so as if possible not to implicate him. Mrs. Grattan quietly heard him through, then she said,

"And what is the purport of your visit this morning?"

"Oh, ma'am, if you would only forgive them and let it pass over. It will come so especially hard upon Theodore if it is all found out. He has worked so hard all the last year, and is sure to take honours at the examination; and now if Doctor Edwards hears of this he will be openly disgraced, and I believe expelled from the school. I am come on purpose to ask you to have mercy on him."

Mrs. Grattan showed no outward sign of being moved by the pathos of the appeal, and her next question really sounded a very unimportant one.

"What is your name?" she asked.

"My name is Paul."

"Then, Mr. Paul Porter, you have not lived so many years as I have; had you done so, you might know that it is not always right or wise to let people who have done wrong go off without any penalty at all. If a thief breaks into your house, you are neither right nor justified in allowing him to escape without any punishment whatever."

Paul felt he could say nothing in contradiction of all this, and his countenance considerably fell as he listened. If these were Mrs. Grattan's views, then he had done the cause he sought to espouse unspeakable harm by thus putting the names of the guilty parties, and all the details of the affair at her merciless disposal. Then a new thought occurring, he said,

"But you see, ma'am, Theodore would not have come into your house like that if the lot had not fallen to him. After that he was almost obliged to do it."

But Mrs. Grattan's intellect was too acute to be deceived by any such specious sophistry, so she said quietly,

"I don't think that tells anything in your brother's favour: his guilt lay in agreeing to the undertaking.

Every one of those boys who stood up to draw lots were equally guilty; whoever the lot fell to, that one had pledged himself to undertake the affair. Your brother only appears more guilty than the rest, because the lot happened to fall to him."

Again Paul felt he could not deny the statement, as with downcast eyes he sat looking sorrowfully at the carpet. Could he have seen Mrs. Grattan's face at that moment, the predominant expression of which was pitiful kindness and compassion, he might not have felt quite so dejected in mind.

"Then, ma'am, you won't pardon them?" he said without looking up.

"I think," said Mrs. Grattan slowly, "I must talk to Doctor Edwards about it."

Paul glanced up quickly.

"It will be all over with them then at once."

"Perhaps if you knew Doctor Edwards as well as I do, you would know that in speaking to him I should be speaking to one of your truest friends."

Paul made no reply, and a minute afterwards Mrs. Grattan rising, Paul in courtesy rose also. Going to him, Mrs. Grattan laid one hand on his shoulder.

"But I have got a little more to say to you, Paul," she said. "You are a brave boy to come thus boldly to plead your brother's cause; and I like bravery wherever I see it. You have also given me your confidence, and I hope no one will ever say that they gave me their confidence and I afterwards abused it. Besides, in what you have told me I believe you have given me a thoroughly truthful account (Paul smiled brightly); therefore I will promise you this much—neither your brother, nor any of the other guilty parties, shall be brought to exposure or punishment for this. You may tell them from me they have my pardon."

"Then you won't tell Doctor Edwards?"

"I didn't say I would *tell* Doctor Edwards; I said I would *talk* to him about it. Won't you trust me, Paul? You must have had some sort of confidence in me to have come here this morning. Are you going to trust me less after our interview than you did before it?"

Paul looked up into Mrs. Grattan's face, and as he did so the thought passed through his mind, that as a young woman she must have been very handsome; traces of beauty still remained, and there was much power and sweetness in her soft, dark eyes.

"Yes, I trust you entirely," he said almost reverentially.

"That is right; then you and I part good friends, Paul."

Mrs. Grattan let him out of the house herself; on the threshold of the front door Paul suddenly paused:

"I don't think I have really thanked you," he said; "I am sure we are all most grateful to you."

"Your friends are welcome, if for the future it makes them more careful and consistent."

Mrs. Grattan stood looking after Paul; she had not noticed in the house how lame he was, but as she noted that fact and stood watching him, intense motherly kindness and sympathy once more softened and beautified every feature of her face. Mrs. Grattan had not seen fit to tell Paul that she had already despatched that morning a messenger to Doctor Edwards, telling him that she had suffered considerable annoyance, and asking him if he had not in his school a boy named Theodore Porter, and if so, if he would call and see her as early as convenient. But for the unexpected visit of a friend from a distance, Doctor Edwards would have complied with her request after morning school, and most probably would have encountered Paul on his expedition.

Right at the drive gate, Paul came face to face with Eleanore Grattan: she took a good look at his face, and then hurried on, wondering who he might be. In the hall she encountered Mrs. Grattan.

"Come here, Eleanore," said her grandmother, "I have something to tell you. I have found out who our thief was; it was one of Doctor Edwards' boys. Did you meet a young lad in the drive? Well, he has been here telling me about it, and has so made good his tale, that I have granted the intruder my pardon. I tell you this, as I wish no more said on the subject. I can trust you to tell you thus much, but I do not expect you to mention who it was to Rebecca, as I do not wish to have the affair any further talked about."

But Eleanore seemed capable of only taking in fully one idea.

"You have pardoned him!" she said, looking fairly aghast. "Oh, grandmamma, you ought to have had him punished!"

"I am satisfied with what I have done, Eleanore."

But Eleanore was evidently of a different opinion.

"Grandmamma," she said, after looking angrily out of the window for a few minutes, "I hate that boy."

"What boy, my dear?"

"The boy who got in last night and frightened you so. I do—I hate him."

This quick, vindictive spirit was one of Eleanore's worst traits, and threatened to mar what might otherwise have been a lovely disposition.

"Eleanore," said Mrs. Grattan, "I shall have to forbid you to use that word 'hate.'"

"But I do hate him, grandmamma."

"I must insist upon your not repeating that, Eleanore," said Mrs. Grattan severely.

Eleanore knew her grandmother would be obeyed, and dared not repeat it in substance; but after a minute she indirectly urged the point.

"But we ought to hate evil, grandmamma?"

"Yes, dear, we cannot hate all evil too strongly, but that does not include hating the evil doer; and I think, dear, if we could see the misery and punishment that even in this life wicked people bring upon themselves, we should feel them so much to be pitied, that we should hardly find room in our hearts for hatred."

Eleanore did not fully appreciate the sentiment, but she did believe her grandmother to be a very wonderful woman; still in this case she felt very inclined to be self-willed and obstinate. In her hurry of mind, or else because Mrs. Grattan did not speak very explicitly, she had understood her grandmother to say that the boy who had been caught in the house the previous night, had been himself that morning and obtained pardon, and therefore concluded Paul was that identical young gentleman. She made no further remark to Mrs. Grattan, but formed in her own mind a hasty determination, that if her grandmother accorded the young gentleman her pardon, she herself would not do so.

"I should know him again," she thought, "and if ever I should meet him, and should get the chance of speaking to him (such a chance appeared vague and unlikely), I will tell him of it to his face."

But the opportunity came sooner than Eleanore expected: all this happened just before the expiration of the term. The very day the boys were taking their departure from the school, Eleanore was at the railway station waiting on the platform for a train. Suddenly her attention became drawn to two boys standing a little further down the platform, and as she looked she felt assured one of them was the very boy she wanted to speak to. She took another glance—she was almost sure; then another good look, and she was quite certain. Should she put her hasty resolve into practice? Possibly she would hardly have hesitated but for the presence of that other boy, who, tall and manly in appearance, looked rather formidable; and we all know, when we have an unpleasant office to perform towards anyone, we are generally glad to dispense with a third person. It was not a pleasant idea to have that tall boy listening to all she said. Then as though in answer to her thoughts, the tall boy moved quite to the other side of the platform; at once Eleanore saw her opportunity, and acted on it accordingly. Feeling sure he was the right boy—Paul's was a face that from its distinct personality was more recognizable than some—she stepped up to where he was standing. When quite close to him she paused; she had not had time to consider how she would begin the threatened denunciation of his conduct.

"Are you—" she began, and then stopped.

Paul looked half wonderingly at her, yet he fancied

her face was familiar to him, so in courtesy lifted his cap and waited for her to speak further.

But Eleanore, though at first seeming not quite clear what to say, was too direct and positive in her manner and address to be given to hesitancy or stammering. So in answer to his look of inquiry, she said at once,

"Are you the boy who came to see my grandmamma, Mrs. Grattan?"

Paul's face slightly flushed.

"Yes, I am," he said.

"And my grandmamma forgave you all, didn't she?"

"Yes; Mrs. Grattan was very kind."

The words were said earnestly and quietly, as a person would speak who remembered gratefully a past favour; but there was no sign of the confusion or shame that ought to attend a person who has been mercifully pardoned for some unwarrantable transgression. The quiet tone and look were exasperating to Eleanore: he didn't even look ashamed of himself, and only said Mrs. Grattan had been very kind. It seemed to Eleanore he ought to have stood covered with shame and confusion, and acknowledged humbly how unmerited had been his pardon. But then, it only showed how barefaced he was, and how confirmed in his wickedness.

"Kind!" she said; "I think she *was* kind. She could have had you severely punished for getting into her house and frightening her so: you might have frightened her to death. I think you are a bad, wicked boy, and ought to be made thoroughly ashamed of yourself."

Paul, if he did not look penitent, at least now looked satisfactorily confused and bewildered.

"I don't quite understand—I think—" he began, when he was suddenly stopped by the tall boy, who having unperceived by Eleanore recrossed the platform, had overheard her remarks. Confronting her he said,

"You have made a mistake; it was I who got into Mrs. Grattan's house. My brother Paul here, had nothing at all to do with it; he only went to Mrs. Grattan's the next morning to—to explain a little. If you have anything more to say, you must say it to me."

Theodore's face flushed as he spoke; certainly he exhibited more the signs of guilt than Paul had done, but Eleanore did not seem to have any more to say. Looking up at this new adversary, she felt her ardour suddenly checked—checked by that restraining influence which even physical power and might can occasionally exert. Besides, she had made every effort for her first sally on the enemy, and had expended her courage upon Paul; still possibly she would have rallied her forces for another attack, but at that moment a shrill voice was heard calling, "Miss Eleanore! Miss Eleanore!" Looking in the direction of the voice, Eleanore saw Rebecca standing vociferating in the doorway of the waiting room, and without another word she turned and walked away.

"What were you a-doing, Miss Eleanore?" asked Rebecca.

Eleanore deigned no reply.

"You were a-talking to them two boys!"

"I shall talk to whom I choose, Rebecca."

Rebecca said no more; she understood that "Miss" was in her "high ways," which indicated a state of mind with which Rebecca had found it vain to cope. There was some truth in her oft-repeated assertions, that at times there was no one on earth could manage Miss Eleanore but her grandmother. Well was it for Eleanore that such restraining influence was at work in her young life.

Just then the station bell rang; the train Theodore and Paul were going by was in sight, and the two boys walked up the platform. Paul was not looking his best, he had been studying hard, and the study and confinement had told upon his health. He walked lamer too than usual, and Eleanore, as she stood at the waiting-room door, and noticed how pale and thin he looked, felt seized with a thrill of compunction that she should have made such a fiery attack upon a boy who was not only innocent, but obviously an invalid. To do her credit, Eleanore was no stranger to generous impulses. As she looked at Paul she wished she could speak to him, just tell him she was vexed for what she had carelessly done. Would she?—yes; the quick young heart was willing enough. Could she, with that other boy by his side? Yes, she would brave him too; so stepping across to Paul as he stood against the carriage door, she said,

"I am sorry I made that mistake and spoke so unkindly to you."

Paul, looking round at her, was startled at the change the mobile face had undergone. The haughty, imperious look had all disappeared, and the dark blue eyes were full of genuine kindness and gentleness.

"I am sure it does not signify. Don't think anything more about it," he said quickly.

"But I am very sorry I said it; I felt I must just tell you so. Good morning."

"Good morning," said Paul; and then stood looking wistfully after her as she walked back to the waiting room.

"We must get in," said Theodore, giving Paul a hoist into the carriage.

As Paul seated himself he still looked lingeringly towards the waiting room, but the young lady had quite disappeared.

"I suppose she didn't think me worth apologizing to," said Theodore.

When the train had moved quite away from the platform, Eleanore once more stepped to the waiting-room door and stood looking earnestly after it. Rebecca, from her place by the table, in charge of sundry small articles of luggage, had been a spectator of the last little scene on the platform, which she had regarded with much inward dissatisfaction.

"If I were you, Miss Eleanore," she said, "I would come and sit down quietly till our train comes up; your grandmamma wouldn't like to see you going in and out, and walking about. Why don't you come and sit down still, like a young lady?"

Almost to Rebecca's surprise, Eleanore walked quietly across the waiting room and sat down as desired.

Eleanore was going on a long visit, and Rebecca was travelling with her to see she reached her destination safely. A few minutes, and the train they were going by came up to the platform. In the same quiet mood Eleanore entered the carriage, and remained silent and thoughtful during the first part of her journey. Eleanore had protested against this visit, but now, sitting back in the railway carriage, she was thinking how opportunely it had happened. Mrs. Grattan was that autumn going to leave the neighbourhood where she had for some years been residing. The house in which she had been living, belonged to a family who for some time had been residing abroad; they were coming back to England that year, and claimed their house to live in themselves. Mrs. Grattan had selected another house; Eleanore, who hardly liked the idea of leaving, said the name of the place where the new house was, began with "C" and ended with "ford," and she knew before they went it would be a stupid place. Of course all this involved journeys to the new abode, and Mrs. Grattan concluding that for the time being, and during the still busier time of packing and actual removal, Eleanore would be best out of the way, accepted an invitation of some standing for her to go to a friend of hers on a long visit.

Against this arrangement Eleanore had raised a futile rebellion. If she did not care to leave the old home, still the idea of packing, and its consequent bustle and excitement, had considerable attractions for her; but Mrs. Grattan, as was her custom, ruled in the matter, and Eleanore had to go accordingly.

Now, as she ruminated over it all in the train, the idea of seeing Paul again at church or elsewhere, was exceedingly unpleasant to her; and she remembered with a thrill of consolation, that when she again rejoined her grandmother it would be in a new home, and, as she fondly believed, far enough removed from both Doctor Edwards and Doctor Edwards' boys. Having arrived at this consoling point, her spirits considerably rose, and she fancied the little scene in which she had that morning so voluntarily forced herself to act, would speedily be passed over and forgotten. To do her justice, in her first letter home she gave a correct account of it all to her grandmother; it was a truthful, ingenuous letter, with just a feeling of conscious wrong-doing running through it. Mrs. Grattan smiled as she folded it together after reading it, and when she wrote back she spoke carefully and guardedly to her young charge. Mrs. Grattan knew that the events of life often teach better than lengthened precepts; and if only Eleanore's eyes were open to the foolish circumstances in which her rash, hasty spirit had placed her, Mrs. Grattan felt content to let those circumstances and their silent teaching alone.

So the autumn came and passed away, and Mrs. Grattan removed to her new home, and still Mrs. Chignall, the friend with whom Eleanore was staying, wrote to say she could not yet spare her young guest. Her own little daughter Kitty Chignall and Eleanore were becoming such fast friends; they rode together, walked together, shared each other's studies and pursuits, and were so happy in each other's company, that it seemed cruel to separate them till they were obliged to do so.

So winter set in and Christmas time came, and still Eleanore did not return. Then Mrs. Grattan decided the matter, Eleanore must be home in time for Christmas day; and so Christmas week Eleanore once more rejoined her grandmother.

"You are willing to come home, dear?" said Mrs. Grattan.

"Oh yes, yes, grandmamma. I love Kitty like a sister, but no one can ever take your place, grand-mamma dear; you are mother, sister, everything."

Mrs. Grattan kissed her grandchild tenderly; Eleanore's wealth of love would have atoned for more serious faults than she in reality possessed.

CHAPTER VIII.

STARTING IN LIFE.

CHRISTMAS day that year came on a Sunday, and Clansford church was even fuller than usual; brothers, sisters, sons, daughters, seemed all gathered home for that Christmas Sunday.

Mr. and Mrs. Porter walked to church with their five sons; Oliver was now three and twenty, and tall and manly-looking beyond that age. Mr. Porter, as he walked along, was indulging in feelings of paternal pride, and thinking fondly to himself that on the whole his boys were certainly turning out well. Oliver had left home almost a year; another good chance in life had opened to him, not again to be refused. Mr. Porter had this time seen the advantageous side of the thing, and the matter was speedily settled.

Oliver had left Clansford in the early spring, but he with the others had come for a Christmas at home. Sydney, when he had quite recovered from the accident he met with the day he was going to the Park, had been placed in a large house of business in London, and had continued there ever since; and Theodore, almost directly after leaving school, had been apprenticed to an engineering firm. The only one who did not do quite as could have been desired was Thomas. All efforts to start Thomas in life had been futile and unavailing. At first he had been placed in the same house of business with Sydney, and in three months' time, back he was, thoroughly disgusted with the whole affair. Business hours strictly kept, orders promptly and diligently executed, were not at all to Thomas' taste. Trade was horrible, dirty, degrading; he could not and would not stop at it.

Mr. Porter looked at him with wide-open, indignant eyes. Perhaps Mr. Porter was not in one sense a very ambitious man; he had not striven that his children should be great men, superior in attainments to their fellows; but to the best of his abilities he had brought them up to be honest, straightforward, and business-like; and he looked on Thomas' indolent manner with indignation and aversion.

"What do you mean to do?" he asked.

"I am sure I don't know, father."

The words were accompanied with an indifferent yawn.

"Look here, my boy, you'll have to know, and know very soon too."

This time Thomas did not answer; there was a quick look in his father's eyes, and Thomas knew it was not a fit time to gainsay or contradict him.

Mr. Porter set about the matter in earnest; the longer Thomas idled about at home doing nothing, the worse it would be for him to turn out. Another opening was secured to him, and again he threw it all up and came back in disgust. Then Mr. Porter waxed severe, and Thomas grew sullen.

"I will go back if you wish me," he said; "but I shall never get on at a thing I hate."

"Then what is it you do want to do?" and a fresh idea striking him, Mr. Porter looked fidgety. Had Thomas set his mind on a profession? He would rather have seen all his sons fairly established in business, but the boy must do what he had a mind for. In a dubious tone he asked, "You don't want to be a lawyer, or doctor, or anything else professional, do you?"

Thomas looked blankly at his father for a moment, then his blue eyes danced with merriment, and for reply he threw his head back and laughed aloud.

"No, no, father; nothing of a profession for me," he said. "I should get bored to death with the study."

Mr. Porter's face somewhat lightened.

"Then what do you want? What would you like?" he asked.

"I shouldn't mind a nice house, father, and a thousand or two a year, and plenty of servants to do everything. I think perhaps I could manage that."

Mr. Porter looked at him in amazement. Then he took stern counsel in his own mind, and came to the conclusion that Thomas should have one more chance—choose his own line of life, and then once again put out, he should be forbidden to return.

But between Mr. Porter and his stern resolves, his wife raised up a barrier of vain excuses. Thomas was very young, she urged, and didn't know his own mind; then he had always seemed a little different to the others, and had always been told he would be a gentleman some day; and besides, if his uncle made him his heir as he had promised, why he would have no particular need of business—just a little something to keep him employed or to amuse him, would be all the business he would require. Mr. Porter saw the fallacy of all this, still he was almost unconsciously influenced by it, and it so far produced effect upon Thomas, that it strengthened his praiseworthy determination to do nothing worth doing, or rather nothing the doing of which involved trouble or unpleasant exertion of any kind.

So the months passed by, and then a happy idea occurred: would Thomas be a farmer? The thing seemed to offer just that sort of easy occupation Mrs. Porter thought so well adapted for him; and Thomas, whose chief ideas of farming were, that the corn grew of itself, and that stock were raised much on the same principle; that what work there was to do, the men did it all, and the master only now and then looked at them; and that a farmer's life consisted in shooting, hunting, and riding about at his pleasure, eagerly seconded the proposal.

A Mr. Gray, a farmer in the neighbourhood, trained agricultural students, and to his house Thomas was sent. Mr. Gray's terms per annum were high, but Mr. Porter would have paid even more than the required sum to have seen his desultory son satisfactorily settled in life.

Thomas started off again, this time with a light heart; but when he found that farming like any other business required much care and attention; that to properly cultivate land and successfully rear stock, implied much prudent forethought and diligent toil; that unless a farmer was rich enough to keep a bailiff, the men expected to take their daily orders from the master himself, and that men left to themselves would bring a farm to ruin; that if farming did not mean sitting up late, it certainly involved rising early; when Thomas saw all this, the delusions of farm life fell from his eyes, and he hated the whole thing worse than he had done trade. It was stupid, plodding, toiling work, without any of the enlivening circumstances of town life, and he soon summed it up as something altogether unbearable. He communicated his feelings to Mr. Gray, and Mr. Gray wrote to Mr. Porter. For reply Mr. Porter wrote back to Thomas, that he insisted upon his staying and doing his best. Then after a little while Mr. Gray wrote again; he did not wish to trouble Mr. Porter, but he should never be able to make anything of his son; he had nothing of the farmer about him, and it would be simply robbing his father's pocket for him to remain any longer.

Then Mr. Porter grew very wroth, more wroth than he had ever been with one of his children before, and again Mrs. Porter pleaded for her favourite son. It might have been well for Thomas had he had no home to which to return, and it was some little time before Mr. Porter would consent that he should do so; and when Thomas actually came home, Mr. Porter, to use his own expression, made it as hot as he could for him.

Then Oliver left home, and Thomas himself made a proposition—might he not take Oliver's place? Mr. Porter shook his head gravely, but at length unwillingly complied. And certainly the arrangement brought to Mr. Porter more than his share of discomfiture and vexation, as he soon found the difference between an industrious, diligent son, and one whose only idea of work seemed to be how much it was possible to leave undone.

But that bright Sunday morning, Mr. Porter, being in a genial mood and inclined to look on the best side of things, thought to himself that on the whole his boys were turning out tolerably well. As for Thomas, as his mother said, he was still young, and the best must be hoped for him.

Opposite the Porters' pew sat Susie Blake. Susie had not much altered from what she was as a child; her face had still the same soft outlines, and the dark eyes were as shy and sweet as ever. Mr. Porter, as he glanced across at her that Sunday morning, felt in a vague sort of way the old desire revive, and that to have owned just such a daughter would have consummated all earthly happiness. Just in front of the Porter's was the Carters' pew; Philip had grown up to be tall, and somewhat foppish in appearance, though the keen, restless, dark eyes rather belied the assumed nonchalance of manner. Blanche had developed into what some people thought a very attractive-looking girl. Like Philip, she was tall and straight; her features were straight also. Her nose was straight, her mouth was straight—much too straight for the softer curves of beauty, and her dark brown hair fell somewhat low over her forehead; her eyes were of that dark, impenetrable shade which so defies the physiognomist. There were times when all her features seemed to contract, and her face then wore a cold, hard look, but this was by no means her habitual expression. Then Blanche had a smile peculiarly her own. Some people's faces when they smile seem to ripple all over with gladness, sure index of the happy sunshiny heart within; but Blanche's smile was not of this order. It had nothing very genuine about it, but it was so frequent as to be almost habitual. If she only spoke to you, or replied to some most common-place remark, there came the inevitable smile. Still that smile did Blanche good service, it made people call her merry, lively, and attractive. Mrs. Carter, a fat person, with a greedy, dissatisfied-looking face; and Mr. Carter, a small man with very quick, dark eyes, completed their party.

But there was one stranger in Clansford church, who certainly had never appeared there before. In one of the seats nearest the pulpit sat a lady, rather on the shady side of life, but whose figure still retained much power and dignity, and by her side sat a young girl with dark blue eyes, and dark hair falling in long curls over her shoulders, It was Eleanore's first introduction to Clansford church, but she had been too well trained to stare about her during service; but as she and Mrs. Grattan rose to go out, Eleanore took a good look round, and as she did so her eyes encountered a sight that made her draw back and clutch suddenly at Mrs. Grattan's sleeve.

"Look, grandmamma!" she said.

Mrs. Grattan, following the direction of Eleanore's eyes, saw Paul looking earnestly at them. Mrs. Grattan instantly recognized him. As she walked down the aisle, Paul was standing just at the entrance of his pew; Mrs. Grattan paused and shook hands with him, and Eleanore, feeling more ashamed than she ever remembered to have done in all her life before, stopped and shook hands with him also.

"How came you to know that lady?" asked Mrs.

Porter, as they walked away from the church. "That's Mrs. Grattan, who has lately come to live at Hill House; I didn't know you knew her."

"I knew her at school," said Paul slowly.

"Well, I never heard you say anything about her. Did you know her too, Theodore?"

"Yes, a little," said Theodore; but his tone was so equivocal that Mrs. Porter looked round at him sharply.

"I suppose you don't both want to seem ashamed of it," she said. "Thomas," she began, but looking round she saw only her two youngest sons were accompanying her.

A few paces behind came Mr. Porter, Oliver, and Susie Blake. An onlooker might have supposed that perhaps after all the nearest approximation to Mr. Porter's pet desire was to be granted in the shape of a daughter-in-law: possibly Mr. Porter thought so too. But if it was a love affair, it was one of those quiet, natural attachments that excite but little speculation or remark. Even Clansford did not gossip about them. But perhaps things that appear fixed and settled, and happening just as they should happen, seldom do excite much public feeling. Had Susie walked through Clansford with a stranger, all the rambling, dirty town would have been rife with rumour and speculation; but as it was, Clansford had so long ago settled it that Mr. Oliver and Miss Susie were making a match of it, that they rarely troubled their heads further about the business. Anyhow, it was by no means the first time those two had quietly walked home from church together.

Not far behind them came Thomas with his friends, the Carters. They were walking rather slowly, when there came a hasty step behind them, and Mr. Thomas Porter from the Grove joined them. Mrs. Carter looked quickly round.

"Dear me, Mr. Porter!" she said; "I declare you get quite young. You walk so light and quick, I thought it was some young lad coming up."

"Ah, I wish I could be a young man again; I wouldn't be a miserable old bachelor if I could have my time over again."

He looked down at Blanche as he spoke, and Blanche smiled and glanced up at him with her unfathomable dark eyes.

As they walked along they came to a road forming a short cut down to the Grove.

"No, I'm not going that way to-day," said Mr. Porter, as he noticed a slight pause as though to bid him good-bye.

"Uncle always has his Christmas dinner with us," said Thomas.

"Ah, it is an old bachelor's fate to have to get his dinner out on that day," said Mr. Porter.

"I think it is nice going out to dinner Christmas day," said Thomas, "when one is at home all the year."

"Ah, some young people always want what they don't have," said Mr. Porter, who at times seemed to imagine he had particular right to snub his nephew.

Thomas made no answer, and Philip Carter nudged him dexterously in the ribs, then they both seemed suddenly attracted by some object on the opposite side of the road, so intently were their heads turned in that direction.

"We must say good-bye now, I suppose," said Mrs.

Carter, as they came to another turn in the road leading to their own house; and the party thus dividing, Thomas and his uncle walked on alone.

If Paul and Theodore thought they had successfully parried their mother's remarks, they were disappointed, for at dinner time Mrs. Porter revived the subject, and as the result of the close cross-examination which followed, they confessed to the truth about the matter; but the story only being told in reply to sharp questioning, and in a disjointed manner, they hardly conveyed to their listeners a clear statement of facts, but Mrs. Porter understood enough to come to the conclusion that it was something to be ashamed of.

"Well," she said, "I wish you hadn't behaved in that way; Mrs. Grattan coming to live here, you will get quite talked about."

"You never told me a word about it," said Thomas half reproachfully.

"Well, it was a bit of a secret," said Theodore.

"Only shows what pranks some boys will be up to," said Mr. Thomas Porter, with a look round on his nephews which was intended to be very severe. A remembrance of a former prank, in which some of the present company had taken prominent part, probably floated before his mind at that moment. Thomas looked slightly disconcerted, but his father interposed.

"This is Christmas day," he said; "we won't have any fault-finding to-day. Had Mrs. Grattan thought so badly of the boys, she would not have spoken to Paul this morning. Anyhow, we will let the matter rest to-day."

And the matter seemed likely to rest, for Mrs. Grattan,

contrary to Mrs. Porter's opinion that she would get the boys unpleasantly talked about, seemed only desirous of pursuing a friendship with Paul, an intimacy which soon extended to the other members of the family. In one of her early interviews with Mrs. Grattan, Mrs. Porter ventured to hint that she was afraid Mrs. Grattan's acquaintance with her boys began under rather unpleasant circumstances, and Mrs. Grattan replied,

"We will let by-gones be by-gones. Whatever the circumstances were, they have ended, so far as Paul and I are concerned, in making us very good friends."

Mrs. Porter rightly concluded that if Mrs. Grattan took this view of the matter, nothing further need be said on the subject.

After the holidays Paul returned to school, and continued there an earnest, diligent scholar; and when the time arrived for him finally to leave, he came home with a desire in his heart which, from its very intensity, he felt it almost impossible to utter.

Thomas still continued a hanger-on at home; truly, Mr. Porter had placed certain limits to his indolence, and there were duties he dared not shirk, still he managed to get much more liberty and many more idle hours than Oliver in the same position would have deemed possible. This unsatisfactory conduct on the part of Thomas, only made Mr. Porter feel more anxious than he otherwise would have done about Paul's future. Had it not been for the trouble his careless, indolent son gave him, as Paul was the youngest, and never very robust or strong, he would probably have been well content that the boy should wait awhile before he decided upon future plans for him; but as it was, he felt anxious to know in what direction Paul's inclinations might lie, and determined to lose no time in settling the matter. If the boy had anything in view, perhaps he would speak of it, but Paul expressing no direct wishes, Mr. Porter took the matter in hand himself. But in answer to the question, if he had thought at all about what business or occupation in life he would like to follow, Paul's face flushed a vivid crimson, and instead of replying, he only turned his hot face towards the window as though the view beyond could help him with an answer. It was some minutes before he spoke, then he said,

"No, father, I don't know any business I should like."

A sudden qualm seized Mr. Porter's heart.

"What do you mean?" he said quickly. "One son idling about home is enough; I cannot have another. If you don't know your mind, I must try and find something for you. There is nothing you wish yourself?"

"Yes, father; I know what I wish, but I am afraid you won't like it."

Mr. Porter's brow slightly cleared; here was something definite at any rate.

"Well, what is it? Out with it, my lad," he said.

"I am afraid you won't approve, father; but I want to be like Mr. Blake. I wish to be a clergyman."

Had Mr. Porter on the spot sternly negatived the idea, Paul would not have been at all surprised; but when his father, after softly whistling to himself, merely said, "Oh, that's it, is it? Well, we must think about it," and then without another word walked quietly away, Paul was very much surprised indeed.

The truth was, Mr. Porter was not particularly startled

by the declaration. Thinking about Paul as he had done of late, he had felt a sort of instinctive idea, that the boy would want something out of the common line of ordinary business life. By a sort of presentiment he felt half prepared for something of the kind, and though he could have wished differently, still he was not altogether surprised by Paul's avowal. It was not a line of life much within his range, none of his family had ever taken up the clerical profession, and he was aware he had no interests to push the boy on with. He felt that Paul might pass his life in some obscure curacy, unless he could bring extraordinary talents into the field. Still it was a definite aim and desire, and something about Paul he admitted seemed adapted to it; and a distinct aim, though difficult of attainment, was better than the idle spirit of choosing nothing professed by Thomas. So when he saw Paul again, he only said,

"I have been thinking it over, my boy. When Oliver comes home for a few days this autumn, we will see what can be done."

And Paul's heart bounded in him with delight as he listened.

Yes, Oliver was coming home for a few days in September, and some one else also was coming back to Clansford just then. Mrs. Blake, the previous autumn, had been taken seriously ill, and at the advice of her medical man had spent the winter in the south of France; of course Susie had accompanied her. Mrs. Blake got quite strong again by the next spring, but they had spent the summer travelling about, and were coming back that autumn.

It was a September day when Mrs. Blake and Susie

once more arrived at the Clansford station. It was one of those bright, sweet, pure days that so often come in September, and which seem like loving, lingering memories of the summer so rapidly passing away. Susie herself looked bright and happy as the day. When they came within sight of Clansford Church, nestling among its green trees,.

"Look, mamma!" she said; "there's the church. Don't you like to see the dear old spot again?"

"Yes, love; it seems very nice to be at home again," said Mrs. Blake.

Susie sat back in the carriage quietly musing; that church had certain happy memories for her. Soon they came within sight of their own home, with its green lawn and trees, and again Susie's face lit up with pleasure.

"There's our home at last, mamma! It all looks so quiet and lovely, doesn't it?"

"Yes, dear. After all, what place is there like home?"

But the house, like the church, had certain memories of its own, and as Susie sat looking at it, a soft light stole into her eyes. She was thinking of one evening not quite a year ago, when she and some one had been walking in that garden in front of the lawn, and the some one had been so near saying something, the saying of which Susie felt might have altered all her position in life. At that moment, Mrs. Blake had thrown open the drawing-room window. "Susie, my love," she said, "come in now; I am sure you will be taking cold." The words seemed to break the spell. "Good-night," said Susie, as she turned in obedience towards the house, but Oliver snatched her hand—"Good-night, if you must go," he said; "but you and I understand one another, Susie?" He held her hand for an answer,—"Yes," said Susie, very faintly; "good-night," and she broke away from him and ran into the house.

It was of that evening Susie sat thinking; she had not seen Oliver since. Soon afterwards Mrs. Blake had been taken ill, and their going abroad had been hastily arranged. So the sight of the garden seemed to bring the scene back to her afresh; but her ruminations were cut short as the carriage drew up at the front door.

Only a day or two after her return home Susie received a visit from a friend of theirs, a Mrs. Meadows, who resided near Clansford. She was about to give a large pic-nic, and invited Susie to be present at it. Susie consented to go.

The day before the pic-nic, as she was driving herself through Clansfrod, she met Thomas Porter coming up the street, and stopped to speak to him. Thomas came forward quickly.

"I heard you were coming home," he said. "How well you are looking too! Is Mrs. Blake quite well again?"

"Oh, yes, thank you; quite well and strong. We enjoyed ourselves so much while we were away: I must tell you more about it another time. You are all well, I hope?"

"Yes, thank you."

Still Susie lingered.

"Are any of you going to Mrs. Meadows' pic-nic to-morrow, Thomas?"

"Yes, all of us; I mean, I am going, and Paul, and Miss Wilturn."

K

" Who is Miss Wilturn ? "

"Oh! you're not in the secret, I see," said Thomas laughing; "and I mustn't tell tales, you know, out of school. Oh, and Oliver is coming home to-night; he'll be there to-morrow."

Thomas looked mischievous; Susie's face slightly flushed, she seemed all at once to think she must be moving on.

"Good-bye, Thomas," she said; "I suppose I shall see you there to-morrow?"

But as Susie drove away she wondered what he meant. Who could Miss Wilturn be, and what were the tales Thomas mustn't tell? Were she his own sweetheart? he scarcely would have spoken in that careless way about her. Then she wondered she had not stopped and asked him again; and then the latter part of the news Thomas had told her, for the time drove all thought of Miss Wilturn out of her head.

Some people thought it was rather late in the season for a pic-nic, but Mrs. Meadows said it was her little daughter's birthday, and she had promised her the treat, and the evening would be moonlight; and as nearly everyone invited accepted the invitation, she accordingly carried out her plans.

Happily the day was warm and favourable. The spot selected for the pic-nic was called " The Grove ; " it was close to where Mr. Thomas Porter lived, and from it his house derived its name. It was a pretty, rural spot, part of it extending over a grassy hill, and there were green winding paths running through it. It was the hill side of the Grove where the pic-nic was to be held.

Susie arrived rather late; a green lane led from the

road up to the Grove, and the sound of voices guided
her to the right spot. Susie found most of the people
had arrived before her, and several were busy laying the
cloth, and getting out cups and saucers, and piles of
cake and bread and butter, and various other eatables.
Susie took a hasty glance round, and then her eye fell
on two figures standing quietly a little distance off; they
were Oliver, and her quick sense at once told her, the
Miss Wilturn Thomas had spoken of. She was a little
creature, with a bright, animated face; even at the
moment Susie noticed what a bright, changeful face it
was, and there was a sort of spirituality and life about
her every look and movement. For a moment Susie
lost sight of the pic-nic, of Mrs. Meadows in a rather
loud voice issuing her order, of the people, of the place;
she saw only those two standing together there. Twice
some one spoke almost in her ear without her heeding
the voice, then turning she saw Mr. Thomas Porter
standing near her.

"Really, Miss Susie, I am delighted to see you back
again," he said.

"Oh, thank you; but Mr. Porter," she asked hurriedly,
though trying to speak naturally, "who is that young
lady standing there with Oliver Porter?"

"You are looking quite charming, Miss Susie!" he
began; but she interrupted him.

"Who is it, Mr. Porter?"

"Who—what—oh, that young lady? Oh, then you
haven't been introduced to the lady-love, eh! Shall I
take you over to her?"

"No, thank you," gasped Susie, as stepping quickly
past him she turned away behind a cluster of sheltering

trees. For a few minutes she lost sight of everything, save a numb feeling of crushing misery. She would go back: she would go home. So she thought for a few minutes, then she remembered she had been already seen. No, she would stay and bear it out. A fresh tide of strength came with the resolution, and she walked firmly back again to where the others were standing. This time Oliver saw her, and crossed over to her at once.

"I thought you would come the other way," he said; "I didn't look for you on this side. How are you, Susie?"

Susie answered that she was quite well, but her manner fairly startled him; there was a quick, restless look in her face he had never seen there before. She soon found an excuse for getting away from him, and he stood and watched her busy with the busiest, arranging the tea, livelier and merrier than any of them. A perplexed look stole over the young man's face as he watched her; but all through the evening she continued the same. He thought she studiously avoided him, but she was the first in all the games, and introduced one or two that had not been tried before. Once she found herself standing close to Oliver and Miss Wilturn. Oliver touched her arm.

"This is Miss Wilturn, Susie," he said; "I don't think you have spoken to her yet. You will know each other well soon, I hope," he added, as Susie turned and shook hands with her.

He was evidently about to say more, but the next moment Susie turned and moved away.

All the while she was wondering how long she could

keep it all up, and then the grass beginning to get damp, and Susie, suddenly remembering that Mrs. Blake had charged her to return early if the grass became dewy, felt she had a good excuse and need stay no longer. Bidding Mrs. Meadows good-night, and telling her the reason for leaving early, she walked quietly away; but just on the outskirts of the Grove, at the top of the green lane, she met Paul.

"Where are you going, Susie?" he asked.

"I'm going home, Paul. It is getting damp, and I promised mamma I would leave early."

"Then I will walk with you; it is getting dusk."

"No, I like to go alone, thank you. I went about so much by myself when I was out with mamma, I got quite used to it, and I should never think of being afraid here." She waved him back with her hand as she spoke, and ran lightly down the lane to the road.

Susie went on quickly at first, then when she fancied herself safe from pursuit she slackened her pace. The road there formed a bridge over a babbling brook, and leaning on the wall of the bridge she stood and looked over wearily at the gurgling water beneath. Very faintly she could hear the sound of the people's voices still in the Grove. They would not come away yet; they had threatened to have one dance by moonlight before they separated. She was safe from interruption from any of them; and as Susie stood there, a few hot tears fell fast on the old mossy wall of the bridge. She thought she saw it all plainly at last; they had been friends, great friends, never anything more. Quietly she told herself this, as a lesson she must strive to learn, yet barely comprehended in that first stupor of pain how hard that lesson might be, when a glowing vision born of a happy past, should have faded away like a deceitful dream. She was turning slowly away when the sound of steps startled her. Some one was walking quickly after her, and the next moment, turning, she found herself face to face with Oliver.

"Paul told me you had left, Susie; he said you were going home."

"Yes, so I am," said Susie hurriedly. "Don't stop me, please."

"I don't want to stop you; I am coming with you, Susie."

He made an effort to take her hand and place it on his arm, but she drew it hastily away. The two walked on a little way in silence. Over the hill the moon was rising brightly.

"How red the moon is rising, look!" said Susie, with a desperate effort to act and speak quite naturally.

Oliver looked accordingly.

"Yes, I see it is; but I didn't come to talk to you about the moon, Susie, though that is what lovers generally do talk about, isn't it?" he said, with a little forced laugh.

Was he coming to force the relation of his love affairs upon her? Susie asked herself. If so, she must be equal to him.

"I don't know," she said, "but you have had some recent experiences of that sort, haven't you?"

She spoke the words carelessly, but there was a harsh ring somewhere in her voice as she spoke.

"I don't know that I have," said Oliver slowly; "I have never had but one love. Don't you know who that is, Susie?"

"Your uncle Thomas told me this afternoon; I didn't know it before."

Oliver looked down on her with a perplexed face.

"What do you mean? What did uncle tell you?"

"Only about Miss Wilturn. She is your lady-love, Oliver."

Oliver suddenly stood still, and taking both her hands looked fixedly into her face.

"I don't know what uncle could mean," he said; "either he or you must have made a great mistake. Miss Wilturn is no lady-love of mine; Sydney is the happy man. He met her in London, and they have been engaged but a very little while. He brought her on a visit to us a few days ago. He was obliged to go to town to-day, and as Paul was too young, and Thomas so careless, he left her under my especial care, as he thought she would feel strange among so many strangers. But she is no lady-love of mine: I have never had but one love. I thought you knew me better, Susie. Had anyone told you I was married, then you would have believed them."

Susie felt his keen blue eyes fixed upon her.

"Why shouldn't I?" she said quickly. "Let my hands go, please."

"One minute more, Susie," he said, looking down closer into her downcast face. "You are my one love! I have never loved anyone but you. Look at me, Susie."

Susie raised her eyes to his face; tears were on the dark eyelashes, but the eyes had a wondrous tell-tale light that spoke to Oliver more eloquently than words. Taking her in his arms, he pressed his first lover's kiss on her lips; and from henceforth, through joy or pain, through life, through time, those two hearts were one, perhaps all the more surely one for that first shadow of misunderstanding between them.

Mrs. Blake received her daughter's confidence with mingled emotions. In a worldly sense possibly Susie might have done better, but still on this point Mrs. Blake felt satisfied, and she believed that in Oliver she would have a faithful husband and protector. The pain lay in the prospect of losing Susie, and the tears which sprang to Mrs. Blake's eyes at the thought, showed how good and sweet a daughter Susie had been.

But no conflicting feelings disturbed the joy of Mr. Porter's heart, as folding Susie in his arms, he tenderly kissed her; and in taking this newly-found daughter to his heart, the old hungry desire, the fruitless yearning, was at last laid to rest.

One benefit at least seemed at once to spring from the engagement; the two families being drawn closer together, and Mr. Blake hearing of Paul's latest aspiration, proffered his help. A clergyman in the next parish to where he was living, further added to his income—the living being but small—by taking young men to read with him as a preliminary preparation for the ministry. He had at the time a vacancy, and Mr. Blake using his influence, the vacant place was offered to Paul, who gladly accepted the offer. Never surely did anyone enter upon a course of life with more intensity of desire and earnestness of purpose than did Paul. During that preparatory time, and the sterner period of study that followed, Paul worked with zealous, untiring industry. Not so much to be clever above his fellows; not so much for a famous name; but that in every way he might be fitted for, and highly adorn, the post of duty, the high calling in life to which he believed himself chosen.

During the time that thus passed, events were happening at Clansford. In the first place, Susie and Oliver were married. It was not a long engagement; they were married the spring following that September pic-nic. The wedding was intended to be quiet, and so perhaps it was so far as the guests and family arrangements were concerned; but somehow Susie was a favourite in Clansford, and then the fact got abroad that their old friend, Mr. Blake, was coming to assist in the marriage ceremony, and so it happened that on that bright May morning, people seemed by one accord to be gathering together to Clansford church to see the wedding. To all appearances everything went off very pleasantly, but after all, in weddings there is a great diversity of feelings and experiences. There are weddings when the eldest son or daughter makes a prosperous match, when everyone seems to participate in the general joy, and when even the pang of parting is borne down and silenced by the thought of the happy future, and bright prospects of the newly-married couple. There are weddings when the bride and bridegroom have reached more mature years, whom people seem tacitly to agree to let alone; they are old enough to know their own minds, and as long as they are pleased it matters nothing to anybody else. But there are weddings when the dearest or last bird leaves the home nest, when every peal of the ringing bells echoes like a knell in the loving hearts, that cannot but mourn the departure of the beloved one; when all the sunshine of the wedding day is blotted out and clouded over by the bitter pain of separation.

Such were Mrs. Blake's feelings; she felt that the little daughter who had nestled against her heart so long, whose hand had clasped hers so tightly on their journey through life, was now virtually consigned and given over to the care and keeping of another.

Susie had with tears entreated her mother to take up her permanent abode with her and Oliver in their new home, but Mrs. Blake had quietly and steadily refused. Every wife, she said, especially every young wife, should have no third person interfering with, or even influencing her household arrangements.

"You will be your own mistress, my love, and you can be that best when you rule in your own house alone, and rely only on your own judgment. I will come to you often, and stay with you as long as you desire, but we have separate ties and duties in life, and you and your husband must be all in all to one another."

Mrs. Blake held good to her resolution; still on that wedding morning she was beginning to realize, and knew when all was over she should realize even deeper still, how desolate her home would be without the gentle presence that had cheered and brightened it so long. And she could not resist, when the ceremony was over and the wedding party returned from church, seeing Oliver standing alone, going up to him, as with tears in her eyes, she said,

"Oliver, I have given you to-day my best and dearest in life, promise me you will be always to her a good and faithful husband, and that you will always love and protect her."

There was an unwonted mistiness in Oliver's clear blue eyes, as in a low voice he said,

"You forget how much I love her."

"No, I do not; and you may think me foolish and anxious, but promise me."

He took one of her hands gently in both of his own as he said,—

"Yes, I faithfully promise you. I have loved Susie ever since I first knew her, and I will love and protect her my whole life through. I promise you."

He kept his promise faithfully.

Mrs. Blake was probably about to express herself satisfied, when a noise outside attracted them, and they moved to the window to see the cause. On the grass lawn in front of the house, two persons were figuring prominently; they were Thomas and Mrs. Jenkins from the Grove, who being an old and respected servant, and having considerable skill in certain culinary proceedings, had been invited to give her aid for the occasion. She had responded gladly to the invitation, and in honour of the event had arrayed herself in a new dress of somewhat conspicuous colour, and a towering head-gear profusely adorned with ribbons and flowers, and altogether was on her best manners and behaviour. Thomas, seeing her standing in the doorway, had beckoned her on to the lawn, then jauntily placing one arm round her waist, he began waltzing with her round the lawn, to the no small amusement of the postillions and grooms who collected in a knot to view the proceeding. Round and round Thomas dragged his unwilling partner, who kept up a running strain of expostulation:—

"Mr. Thomas, my dear, pray don't; and all the ladies and gentlemen will see—what will they think? Mr. Thomas, pray let me go—and master too; what will he say? Let me go, Mr. Thomas—my dear."

Then Thomas, when he thought he had had enough of it, giving her his arm, politely escorted her back to the house. Mrs. Blake a few minutes before had been nearly crying, but at the scene before her she laughed in spite of herself.

"What a light-hearted fellow that brother of yours is!" she said.

"Yes," said Oliver, who in his own mind hoped Thomas would not be too light-hearted before the day was over.

Then followed the wedding breakfast and the customary toasts, and Mr. Porter twice rose essaying to speak, and twice sat down after a futile endeavour. Poor man, he had intended saying something about the wish that had long lain dormant in his heart, being that day fulfilled; and that he had always felt that could he have had a daughter of his own, he should have wished for just such a one as Susie. But whether through the train of remembrance this latter thought gave rise to, or whether through the excitement incidental to wedding days, certainly he failed to produce these sentiments in words; and rising the third time, he only gave utterance to the customary expressions of good feelings and good wishes.

After him rose Mr. Porter from the Grove. Forcible oratory with him meant the introduction of long and seldom-used words, and not having the heart experiences which had impeded his brother's speech, he gave what was certainly a lengthy, and as he considered it, elaborate address. Perhaps the most genuine part of it was the deep regret, that in conclusion he expressed, that he had let all his youth and best part of his life go by, without having tasted for himself the happiness of married life. Silence for a moment followed his speech, till Thomas, looking across the table at him, said,

"If I were you, uncle, and felt so about it, I would try a taste of married life now. It is never too late to mend, you know; and if I were in your place, I would make a start in life now."

"Would you really?" replied Mr. Porter, with suddenly brightening eyes.

"To be sure I would," said Thomas; never for a moment dreaming that his carelessly-uttered advice would in reality be acted upon.

The final parting passed off quietly. Whatever were Mrs. Blake's feelings, she did not cloud her daughter's departure with useless lamentations; so with the accompanying, "God bless you, my darling," she smiled bravely back into Susie's wistfully questioning eyes. And for the sake of her guests, Mrs. Blake continued a placid exterior.

But there is often in festive days a time when the general merry-making seems to flag, and every one looks at his neighbour, as if it was his especial duty to produce the next effort at diversion. So it happened that on that wedding day, just as the bright May evening was closing in, everyone seemed inclined to be quiet, and to be conjecturing what it was most expedient to do next. Outside, a clear full moon touched the lawn and budding trees with silvery beauty. Mr. Thomas Porter, standing in the doorway, was quietly admiring the placid scene before him, when all at once he heard what seemed the confused noise of many people talking at once. The sound proceeded from the direction of the road, and as Mr. Porter listened, the voices came nearer; evidently a crowd of people were coming up the road. Just then Sydney crossing the hall, his uncle beckoned to him to listen, and Sydney running across the lawn and looking down the road, came back with the intelligence that the road, as far down as he could see, appeared one mass of people coming along in a disorderly fashion. Then Sydney signalled his father to the door, and soon most of the company assembled on the spot. By that time it was very evident that a noisy crowd of some sort was advancing. Then the dark mass surged up in front of the house, and one or two of the foremost climbed up on the gate and hedge, and looked over on to the lawn.

"It is a mob," said Mr. Thomas Porter apprehensively.

Mrs. Blake had been having a private *tête-à-tête* with her son, and came forward only in time to catch Mr. Porter's words.

"What do you mean?" she asked hurriedly; and as they drew back for her she looked eagerly out. After one glance she turned back with a white, scared face: "Oh, what is it?" she gasped.

Again Mr. Thomas Porter expressed his opinion: "A riot, I believe, ma'am. Ha! Thomas, what are you nudging me, and jogging my elbow for?" he added, turning sharply in the direction of his nephew.

Perhaps Thomas was about to explain, but Mrs. Blake had a secret horror of riots and mobs, and her one dislike to the manufacturing district of Clansford had been her terror of a fray in case of a lock-out or strike; therefore, at the words "A riot, ma'am," she started back with a sudden scream; and as though her shriek was the signal, from the crowd outside arose a long, loud, deafening cheer, which to the startled nerves of Mrs. Blake, sounded like a loud shout of defiance.

Excited feelings kept under powerful restraint, are apt to find tumultuous outlet on the first occasion that presents itself, and so at this point of affairs Mrs. Blake lost all her wonted self-control, and as another and yet another roar of cheers swelled from the crowd outside— giving frantic directions to bar the doors and windows— she lapsed into a violently hysterical condition, and one or two of the others catching the infection of her fears, for a few minutes the hall became the scene of general confusion and agitation. In the midst of it all, Thomas stepped up to his father:

"Don't you know, father?" he asked.

"Know what?"

"Who the people are."

"No."

"They are our own factory men; they are only come to give Oliver a cheer or two."

"A cheer or two indeed! and after having given them as good a supper as they could wish, down the street at the 'Vine Inn;' but I'll start them."

"Don't go like that, father," said Thomas, placing himself in front of him; "I—I—knew they were coming."

"Did you tell them to come?"

"Well—I knew they were coming."

"Stand out of my way," said Mr. Porter, attempting to push Thomas on one side; but just then Theodore, who had overheard the conversation, interposed:

"I will go out to them," he said, looking valiant and

powerful enough for a much more formidable undertaking.

"You had better neither of you go," said Thomas.
"The men have most likely been drinking, and if you go
thundering out to them, they'll be troublesome. I'll go
and start them all quietly in five minutes."

Mr. Porter had a sort of hazy idea that Thomas was
the right one for the undertaking, and standing back, let
him go past him.

Thomas was correct when he owned to his father that
he knew the men were coming; still it was owing more
to his carelessness than to his direct planning. The
previous day some of the men had been regretting that
they were not able to see Oliver and bid him good-bye.

"I should like to have seen him and given him one
good cheer," said one of the younger hands.

"You can do that as it is," said Thomas; "you can
come up to Mrs. Blake's and give him a round," forget-
ting in his carelessness that Oliver would not be there to
respond to it.

"May we?" queried the young man who had just
expressed his desire for the cheering.

"Yes; I'll give you leave," said Thomas heedlessly,
and thought no more of the matter till the crowd in
front of Mrs. Blake's house showed him they had taken
him at his word. For though the older men shook their
heads and refused to join the expedition, knowing, as
they said, that "the old master liked things done quietly
and orderly," the notion took among the younger
portion of the men; and so after the supper at the
"Vine Inn," a little band of the most heedless of them
sallied forth to render their salutation to their young

master. But as they went along, they were joined by
hands from the other factories and women and children,
till they became the motley throng that eventually
gathered before Mrs. Blake's house, and startled its
inmates with their clamorous shouting and noise.

Thomas was also right in saying he was the best one
to go to disperse them, for in a sort of free-and-easy
fashion, he had a kind of friendly understanding with,
and influence over the men. He never attempted to
command or rule them, nay, he would often screen their
delinquencies from his father's notice; and so while they
feared and respected Oliver, Thomas was a sort of
favourite with them, as the one who had always a careless
joke or merry word for them. So that night Thomas
was true to his word; and though his pocket became
somewhat lightened by the process, for he distributed to
them every penny in his possession, still he dispersed
them speedily and quietly.

"They are all gone," he said triumphantly, as he
re-entered the house.

"And would never have come but for your nonsense,"
said Mr. Porter angrily. "There is Mrs. Blake in
hysterics, and half the others ready to follow her example."

"It was all uncle's fault," said Thomas; "he frightened
her telling her it was a mob or a riot."

But whether Thomas or his uncle was the most to
blame, the consequences were as Mr. Porter had said;
and though after a time Mrs. Blake recovered her composure, still there lingered among her guests a feeling of
depression and restraint, and as a natural result everyone
left a little earlier than they might otherwise have done.

L

"Well," said Mrs. Porter, as she leaned back in the carriage on her way home, "I think on the whole we have had a very pleasant day."

"We should have had but for Thomas' foolery," said Mr. Porter, looking sternly across at his son.

Thomas only joined his thumbs to his forefingers, and placing them before his eyes looked through them quizzically at his father.

"If you don't leave off your foolish addle-headed ways, you'll never be good for anything at all," said Mr. Porter angrily.

Thomas made no reply, but leaning back and folding his arms, closed his eyes complacently.

"I do think," said Mrs. Porter, "that Mrs. Blake made a stupid fuss; she ought to have controlled herself better."

"Ah, but," said Mr. Thomas Porter, who had joined them in the carriage, "you see, on these occasions ladies cannot always control their tender emotions and feelings."

"And there are feelings at these times peculiar to a mother," said Mrs. Porter, whose maternal emotions—by the way she sought for her handkerchief—seemed suddenly on the alert.

"Ah, to be sure," replied Mr. Thomas Porter, and forthwith lapsed into a rapt state of silent rumination, and soon became lost in the tender beauty of his meditations.

They all proceeded in silence till Thomas, who had appeared to be asleep, suddenly springing forward and laying a hand on each of his uncle's knees, shouted loudly in his ear.

Mr. Thomas Porter started violently.

"When will you learn to keep your vivacious spirits in bounds?" he said, as he testily reseated himself in the carriage.

"Well," said Thomas, "there's father sits frowning in one corner, mother crying in another, and you looking lost in the contemplation of the folly of all earthly things. Instead of being jolly as we should be, we look for all the world as if we were going home from a funeral rather than a wedding." Then seeing his father's face relaxing into a smile, "That's right, dear old dad, look a little pleasant again, and don't think any more about it. The men didn't mean any harm, and I'm sure I didn't."

"Still it was very foolish," said Mr. Porter; "but there, I don't know I want to say any more about it."

Thomas knew by that the offence was looked over, for his father never kept recurring to a thing; having once expressed his opinion he was content to let the matter rest.

"That's a good dad," said Thomas. "Now let's sing, 'We won't go home till the morning;' you can take bass, uncle," and Thomas started the strain accordingly.

"Thomas, Thomas," said Mrs. Porter entreatingly; "the man will hear you outside."

"Well, and he'll like to hear me," said Thomas, starting afresh.

"Leave off, Thomas," remonstrated Mrs. Porter; "we are now coming to the street. What do you suppose people will think of us?"

"There, I'll leave off then," said Thomas, once more settling himself in mock decorous fashion, and he continued quiet till the carriage drove up to their home.

CHAPTER IX.

EVIL WAYS.

LIFE after a wedding is like a pool of water into which a stone has been thrown. There must be certain vibrations before the surface can become placid and quiet again; but after a few days, things seemed to take their usual course. Paul went back to his studies, Sydney and Theodore returned to business, and Thomas, under pretence of working, lounged about at the factory, literally doing nothing, or getting as near to that experience as possible. There were times also, though happily few and far between, when of a morning Thomas could hardly attend to the work before him because of the confused, aching head, consequent upon the reckless dissipation of the preceding night.

One scene Paul never forgot. Some time had elapsed since Susie's wedding. It was Paul's last year of study and preparation for that great life work to which he looked forward with such zealous earnestness. He was at home for a vacation; Theodore was also spending a few days at home. Susie too, who with her little three-year-old son Frank, had been making a visit to her mother, had come to pass a day or two with Mrs. Porter before returning home; Eleanore Grattan and Kitty Chignall had been spending the day there with her. It had been a hot, sultry day, followed by one of those calm, quiet evenings, when not a breath seems to stir the oppressive stillness. In the garden in front of the house, under the shade of the ash tree, whose graceful branches swept low towards the soft, green grass, the inmates of the house had gathered together with the exception of Mr. Porter, his wife, and Thomas. Mrs. Porter owned to a headache, and was lying down in the little, cool breakfast room at the back of the house, and her husband was keeping her company. Thomas had gone out with Philip Carter for a day's pleasure; he had ridden his horse to the station in the morning, and they were expecting him back shortly.

A happy group they looked sitting there that balmy summer evening. Kitty Chignall had just been describing the beauties of some picture she had lately seen exhibited, and Paul looking round at them all—at Susie, who sat watching Frank with such maternal pride in her gentle face; Kitty Chignall, with her merry blue eyes and pretty golden-coloured hair; and Eleanore with her stately young head bent over the work she held in her hand, with bright blue ribbons at her throat and in her glossy dark hair, and with it all that pretty, girlish dignity peculiar to herself—all these made in Paul's estimation a very fair picture indeed.

"I was thinking," he said, "we should make a nice picture, our group here under the ash tree. What do you think?"

"I think it is just like your vanity, sir," said Kitty, throwing a full-blown rose at him.

"Oh, I except myself of course; but supposing I were an artist, I should make you all my next picture."

"Who would you put in the foreground; I mean who would you make the leading figure?" asked Kitty.

"You, of course," replied Paul drily.

Just then little Frank peered curiously round into Paul's face, as though trying to make out the tenor of the conversation.

"There's a candidate for the honour," said Susie laughing; "you would have to take Frank, I think."

"Perhaps I should;" but Paul was looking straight at Eleanore as he spoke.

"I really wish one of us were artist enough to try," said Susie. "Couldn't you, Theodore?"

"No; I could do anything of designs, but I am afraid I could not manage portrait-taking. If we had Chrissie Brown here, he would do it; he is getting on capitally as an artist. But I know I couldn't do justice to the picture."

"We ought to have some one capable of doing that, I'm sure," said Susie.

Just then Mr. Porter came up.

"Theodore," he said, "I am going as far as Jones' (Jones was foreman at the factory); will you walk so far with me? I have a thing or two I want to talk to you about."

Theodore instantly rose to accompany his father, and the two set off down the road in the direction of the street.

"Minus an artist, I suppose our scheme fails," said Paul.

"Yes," said Eleanore; "but don't you think word-painting is sometimes as effectual as any direct picture? I have read scenes and sketches so forcibly pourtrayed, that the whole thing has risen up before me almost as plainly as though I had actually seen it all."

"Yes," said Paul; "and how much easier some books must be to illustrate than others. Where things are graphically delineated, skilfully set forth, the whole scene, as you say, rises before you, and the artist has only to transfer to paper the picture already plainly visible to his mental eye. Has Theodore shown you those drawings he has of Chrissie Brown's? He has a series of them taken from Tennyson's 'Brook,' and according to my judgment they are particularly unique and ingenious."

"I should like to see them," said Susie.

"Theodore has got them in his room; I will go and get them," said Paul.

Paul went to Theodore's room accordingly, but the drawings were not easy to find, and some minutes elapsed before he discovered where Theodore had put them. He was about to return with them in his hand, when glancing out of the window he saw a horseman ride up to the gate, a horseman whose safe arrival at home was evidently far more owing to the sagacity of the animal he rode, than to any skill or power of his own, as it was only too visible he was in no condition to exercise any control over it. As Paul looked, Thomas made futile efforts to dismount.

But Paul was not the only witness of the scene; the group under the ash tree had also seen his approach, and at the same time comprehended the whole situation.

"Oh! he will fall, I am sure, and the horse will tram-

ple on him," said Susie, making a terrified clutch at
Eleanore's dress.

Eleanore lightly shook off Susie's grasp, and springing
to her feet, ran quickly down the garden to the gate.
As Paul looked, he saw her tall, lithe, young form
suddenly take its stand by the horse's head. She took
the bridle in her hand, the horse felt the touch and stood
still, and then Thomas, laying one hand on her shoulder,
and leaning heavily upon her, descended safely to the
ground. Paul did not wait to see all through, he was
hurrying down to give his assistance, but someone else
was there before him. Theodore returning along the
road, opposite the way Thomas had come, saw the whole
scene, and sprang quickly forward. Thomas was just
attempting to speak connectedly to Eleanore when
Theodore almost roughly seized his arm, and with an
angry, indignant face led him quickly towards the house.
Half way Paul met them, but he still hurried on. With
the bridle hanging loosely in her hand, so that the horse
getting his head down was beginning quietly to munch
the turf, Eleanore was standing perfectly still. She
never turned her head as Paul advanced, and when he
said anxiously, "Oh, I hope you are not hurt," save by
a slight tremor of the hand that held the bridle, she gave
no sign of hearing him. Again Paul spoke solicitously
in her ear, and this time she turned and looked at him
with a strangely white face, every muscle of which
seemed quivering with suppressed agitation.

"No, no," she said hurriedly, "I am not hurt, I assure
you, not in the least;" and before Paul could answer
her, she passed quickly by him towards the house. She
found Susie and Kitty in the hall. "Come with me,"

she said, catching hold of Kitty's hand as she spoke; and almost before Kitty knew what she was doing, she found herself following Eleanore upstairs.

"What are you going to do? Where are you going?" she asked.

"I am going home at once; don't you see we mustn't stay any longer? How do you think his mother will bear to have comparative strangers looking on? Don't you see this is no place for us? We will go at once."

Kitty was too used to obey Eleanore's imperious moods to gainsay her, and so the two put on their hats, and with a few words of farewell and explanation to Susie, walked quietly away. But once beyond the garden and precincts of the house, Eleanore moved on at a rapid pace, till Kitty had hard work to keep up with her. When they reached home, leaving Kitty to tell what tale she chose to Mrs. Grattan, Eleanore went straight to her own room. After a little while she came back, and except by a slight paleness, showed no sign of agitation. But when Kitty went out of the room, she moved at once to her old seat at her grandmother's feet.

"Kitty has told you, grandmamma, hasn't she?"

"Yes, dear."

"I did right to come away, didn't I?"

"You did just what my sensitive, impulsive Eleanore would be sure to do."

"But I did right, grandmamma?"

"Yes, dear, I think you did. I know there are some people who can complacently look on these scenes, without seeming acutely alive to their shame and degradation; but you are not one of that kind, Eleanore, and

I think you did right to come away at once. But I am sorry, very sorry," continued Mrs. Grattan musingly; "just about to enter on his life's duties, too; I am very sorry."

"Who are you sorry for, grandmamma?"

"Paul I was thinking of; I am sorry for Paul."

"Yes, I am sorry too."   A bright flush suddenly rose to Eleanore's face; then as in her childish days, she laid her head down on her grandmother's knees, and gradually into her dark blue eyes stole a look of quiet and peace. Perhaps of no one else on earth did Eleanore deign to ask counsel, but Mrs. Grattan had lost none of the influence that from her earliest youth she had exercised over her grandchild; and well was it for Eleanore that such an influence was at work with its controlling power in her life.

This was the most serious outbreak Thomas had been guilty of, but it caused Mr. Porter to see plainly, what in fact he ought to have seen years before, that Philip Carter was no fitting person to be Thomas' chosen and boon companion, and in his own mind he resolved the close intimacy should cease. He spoke to his son to this effect a few days later.

"I don't wish you to be so intimate," he said; "of course you can be friendly, we always have been friends, but there is no reason you should always be after him and constantly with him as you are. He leads you into temptation, and you are too weak to resist. I wish you to break with him. Do you understand me?" he asked, after waiting in vain for an answer.

"Yes, father; but I cannot do it."

"Why not?"

But Thomas found it difficult to look his father in the face and tell him the reason that was in his mind. At last he spoke.

"I—I cannot break with the Carters, father; I and Blanche are engaged to be married."

"Engaged to be married!"

"Yes, why shouldn't we?" Thomas felt bolder now the actual declaration was over. "Oliver is married, and Sydney has been engaged ever so long, and why shouldn't I?"

"You are not fit to be compared to Oliver. He worked long and steadily till he had a comfortable home to which to take his wife; and Sydney, according to all I hear, is going on too, industriously and well. But what right have you—a ne'er-do-well, without a groat to call your own—to be setting up to take a wife! Who do you think is going to maintain her? I tell you plainly at once, you won't bring Blanche Carter here."

Thomas as a child had been sweet and easy of temper, but what temper he did manifest was always of a sudden, fiery kind, and dissolute habits never tend to equanimity of mind or feelings; so with an angry flash in his eyes, he started to his feet as he said,

"I don't want to bring her here, or anywhere else, to be a trouble or annoyance to anyone!"

"What are you going to do then?"

"Wait. Blanche is in no hurry, neither am I, so we mean to wait."

"Wait for what?"

"I don't know—till things improve a little, and I get a better position."

"Then I am afraid you will have to wait some time.

I am sorry it has happened. I don't like it; I don't like it at all."

There was more sorrow than anger in Mr. Porter's face as he turned away. He did not say any more at that time, but the next day he reverted to the subject again.

"Is it quite settled," he said, "that affair you spoke of yesterday?"

"It has been settled some time, just as far as Blanche and I are concerned; I don't think anyone else knows much about it."

"And it must be, Thomas?"

"Yes, it must be." But Thomas was in one of his promising, conciliatory moods, when he would be full of candour and amendment, and when no virtue but seemed possible for him to attain to. "Yes," he said, "it must be, father; I love Blanche too well to give her up. But I mean to do quite differently; I am going to turn over wholly a new leaf—stick to business, and all the rest of it. You shall see."

"I will believe it when I do," said Mr. Porter drily.

"You shall see it, father."

Mr. Porter looked fixedly at him. "There is one thing, Thomas, I hope I shall never see again what I saw the other evening."

"I promise you, father, you never shall. It was hardly my fault then."

"No, that's the sorry part of it."

"It shall not happen again. I mean to be quite steady and diligent from this time forth."

"I am sure I hope you do," said Mr. Porter with a sigh.

"I do, father; and in that case, you would have nothing to say against it?"

"No, I will not promise that; and you may as well fully understand me. I should never at any time have chosen this union for you, and as things are I disapprove of it very strongly, and I should be glad to hear it put a stop to. But you say the thing has been kept quiet; let it continue so."

Thomas had no objection to this. The engagement was fully binding in his own estimation, but it was little more or less than a sort of quiet compact between himself and Blanche. Mr. Porter said no more on the matter. The one favourable point was, that Thomas' affections, such as they were, seemed deeply concerned in the affair, and Mr. Porter was not blind to the truth, that a steady, sincere affection may sometimes go far to rectify an idle, desultory life. So, feeling powerless in the matter, he thought it best to let it rest, and see what would come of it.

CHAPTER X.

TREACHERY.

VERY frequently, when people are inclined to do evil, circumstances seem to help on their inclination; but in the case of Thomas, things appeared to work favourably for his good resolutions. Soon after that conversation with his father, came a letter from Sydney. Mr. Harrows, in whose house of business Sydney had been placed, owned the principal shop in the little country town of Elmsbridge, about four miles from Clansford. The business had been in the occupation of the Harrows for a long time. Mr. Harrows had managed it for himself in his younger days, and during that time he and Mr. Porter, then both young men, had become friends, and it was mainly owing to that former intimacy that Sydney so readily obtained a situation with him in London.

Since Mr. Harrows' removal from Elmsbridge, a trusty foreman had been placed over the business; that foreman had recently died, and Sydney wrote to say that Mr. Harrows had offered the post to him. It would seem a sort of preliminary step to independence, and would materially increase his present salary, and he thought he ought to accept it. Mr. Porter wrote back urging him at once to do so; and so it happened that very shortly after, Sydney was fully installed at his new duties.

The following spring was a very busy time, and Sydney found it necessary to take in a fresh hand. Thomas earnestly solicited to take the place requiring to be filled. He was just as anxious for the life he had once renounced, as he had then been eager to relinquish it. And in truth Thomas did cordially hate the factory; all those years at it had only engendered in him an unconquerable aversion. Sydney wrote to Mr. Harrows, and Mr. Harrows left it to Sydney's discretion, so finally Thomas was appointed to the situation. Mr. Porter gave him a stern word of parting.

"Now," he said, "you've got this one chance; but don't you go playing ducks and drakes with Sydney as you have done with me; and remember, if you by your idle ways hinder instead of help him, don't come back to me; for if you fail this time, I will never try to give you a start in life again. Now I have spoken plainly to you, and you understand, it is your last chance."

A last chance is generally thought to be a forlorn chance, but with feelings anything but forlorn Thomas entered on his new duties, and with as much good faith in himself and assurance of success as though he had been the most virtuous person living. Perhaps Sydney was not quite the right sort to have the oversight of him; he was too unsuspicious, too apt to leave it to Thomas' conscience whether his duties were thoroughly performed. Still on the whole Thomas certainly did better than could have been expected of him, and Mr. Porter began

to entertain a kind of hazy hopefulness for his unsatisfactory son. One benefit he considered was derived
from the arrangement,—going to Elmsbridge took
Thomas in some degree from the society of the Carters.
Against Philip Carter, Mr. Porter gave Sydney a warning word.

"Oh, of course, I shall not allow him to come interfering," was Sydney's answer, and then with characteristic
indifference he dismissed Philip Carter from his mind.

Of necessity too, Thomas and Blanche met less often,
and a careful observer of that young lady's proceedings,
might have doubted whether the prize were ultimately
for Thomas' winning at all. For if Thomas was seldom
at the Carters' house, a certain gentleman rather more
advanced in years, who aped the jocular ways of youth
till it was almost pitiful to behold him, certainly by his
very frequent visits made up for the absence of his
nephew; and there were people in Clansford who were
saying, that old Mr. Porter from the Grove, old enough
to be her father—some said grandfather—was going
courting Miss Blanche Carter.

But of all this Thomas lived in happy ignorance.
Once or twice he met his uncle at the Carters; but love,
which in some natures begets fierce jealousies, with
Thomas only produced unquestioning confidence: it was
to him much easier to trust Blanche than to doubt her.
Neither did any of his family hear the rumour; had they
done so, they would hardly have believed it.

Perhaps no young woman, through any individual
desires of her own alone, would ever seek one of these
ill-assorted unions, still less likely would she be to do
so if surrounded by high and noble influences; but

when the tenor of family feeling abets the project, it is a different thing; and to what depths will not weak humanity sink when our whole surroundings influence and assist the fall? So with Blanche. Mrs. Carter certainly was in favour of the prospect for her daughter, and Mr. Carter said nothing against it; but there was a stronger power still at work. Philip, in an indirect sort of way, had always exercised a certain influence over Blanche. He had always been leader and governor in all their childish sports, and as they had grown up, had in a measure still continued his sway. So in a sort of underhand manner the thing went quietly on. Not long before the affair eventually came to Thomas' ears—for of course as a natural occurrence his eyes were at last opened—one evening, Philip, as he was entering the house, encountered Thomas going out. Thomas hardly stayed to speak, he was, as he said, in a hurry. Going in, Philip found Blanche alone.

"Have you just been starting him?" he asked.

"No," said Blanche in a short, angry tone.

In fact, so far from starting Thomas, she had never felt so much inclined to start some one else instead. Thomas had that very evening been detailing to her his future plans—chimerical perhaps and vague—but Blanche could not be insensible to the love that prompted them all. Philip looked quietly at his sister.

"Look here, Blanche; when do you mean to tell that foolish fellow the truth?"

Instinctively Blanche recoiled from the coarseness of the question, and her face flushed hotly as she said,

"If I never tell him at all, it will be nobody's business but mine."

M

Philip began to see Blanche was not in a compliable mood. With all her selfish indolence, which often made her easily persuaded rather than give herself the trouble to raise an opposition, Blanche could at times be hard and self-willed. Philip watched her a moment, and when he spoke again he began in a conciliatory tone.

"Of course it won't be pleasant for you to tell him, but you had better not let things go on any longer like this; and after all, he is a silly fool, who will never get anyone a decent living. If he does seem to mind it a little bit, he will forget all about it the next day. If you choose to take him, you will only bring an extra burden on us all; but on the other hand, you can have riches, and everything woman's heart could desire. You have been hard up sometimes, I know, but then that would be all over, and you would raise your whole family. And what is more, Blanche, I tell you in confidence, I am terribly hard up myself just now."

"I don't know why you should be, any more than anyone else," said Blanche sulkily.

"Nonsense, Blanche! as long as you have a new dress or bonnet or two, you have no calls for your money. Women don't understand the many expenses men always have to meet."

"If you will get into debt, I can't help it."

Philip leaned closer to her. "You can do something that will make matters worse, and you can do something that will make matters better. Which will you do, Blanche?"

"That is my concern," said Blanche, still with sullen resentment in her tone. She knew well to what Philip alluded, but even she shrank from the baseness of the proposition. Still all this had its weight upon her mind, and strengthened her for the end.

The end to it all was brought about by Thomas going down one evening to the Grove with a message to his uncle. At the door he met Mrs. Jenkins, who informed him her master was not at home.

"I want to see him rather badly," said Thomas; "where is he gone?"

"I'm sure I don't know, unless as usual he's gone courting."

Thomas stared at her with wide-open eyes.

"Gone courting! That is the best joke I've heard lately. Whatever do you mean?"

"Why, Mr. Thomas, my dear, don't you know?"

"Know what? Where is he gone?"

Mrs. Jenkins seemed as if she were about to enter the house, and kept her head turned away from him. As she owned afterwards, she didn't know how on earth to answer him.

"What do you mean?" again asked Thomas.

"Oh, Mr. Thomas, my dear, I thought you knew; though certainly at one time, if anyone had asked me, I should have said it was you who was the young lady's lover. Why, haven't you heard how my master goes a-courting Miss Blanche Carter?"

Thomas leaned back against the door-post, and at first his face flushed crimson, then grew terribly pale, so pale and strange-looking that Mrs. Jenkins, in motherly solicitude, feared he was going to faint.

"Come in and sit down a bit," she said gently. "I suppose I oughtn't to ha' told you, but you would know."

A ghostly attempt at a smile crept over Thomas' face. "Mrs. Jenkins, you are joking," he said.

"As true as I stand here, I'm not joking; they're engaged if ever anyone was. Miss Blanche was here the other day, looking round and giving orders like; and 'twas 'Mrs. Jenkins' this, and 'Mrs. Jenkins' the other. I knew what it all meant; thinks I, it won't be 'Mrs. Jenkins' long, for I can see none of the old ways will suit my lady, and so of course the old people won't either. Some years back, when there was that to do at the Park, and you took the horse, my husband thought we should get turned off through it—but I didn't. Master hasn't got spirit enough to turn off a flea, but come to get a young mistress about, and we shall soon find out where we are. We shall go now in earnest."

All this the good woman said more by way of diverting Thomas, than from any thought of soliciting his sympathy. Just then her husband came up.

"Do you know where master is gone?" she asked.

"To a meeting about the Clansford schools, so he said."

Thomas heard so much, and scarcely stopping to speak to old Jenkins, hurried away.

Tears were in Mrs. Jenkins' eyes as she stood watching him: with all his faults, Thomas was a favourite with the old people.

As he walked along, Thomas resolved one point in his own mind—from Blanche's own lips only would he learn the truth, and without further debate he walked at once to the Carters' house. He found Blanche at home and alone. His quick, agitated manner at once told her the time for the *dénoucment* had come.

"Blanche," he said, "I have heard something this evening so strange I cannot believe it,—so strange, I can believe it from you only."

Blanche bent her head closer over her work. Had Thomas been calmer, the downcast face, and the hands that suddenly trembling stitched with nervous haste, might have seemed to him sure evidences of guilt. Blanche instinctively felt the anticipated time had at length arrived. After a moment she somewhat recovered her equilibrium, as she asked quietly, though without looking up,

"Have you? What is it you have heard?"

Thomas went closer to her, and he tried to speak in an incredulous, careless tone.

"Blanche," he said, "I have heard you are engaged to my uncle at the Grove."

Blanche knew the time for her to speak was now fully come, but with Thomas' eager eyes full upon her it was not easy work, but somehow she managed to speak, and to speak to the point.

"You have heard the truth," she said quietly.

"Blanche!"

For a moment it was all Thomas could utter, then through the midst of his pain and bewilderment of soul came a new idea—they were making fun of him, practically joking him, and Blanche had conspired with them to do it; or she was trying him, proving him. It could not be true; he would not believe it.

"Blanche, you don't mean it," he said; "you are saying all this just to trouble me—to prove me; still, you would hardly do so if you knew how much I care for you. I may not have been all I ought to have been,

but, Blanche, for your sake I will be steady, quiet, industrious, everything you could wish.   Oh, Blanche, you
cannot mean it !   He is getting an old, old man, and you
are a young woman full of youth and happiness, and
you would be throwing all your best young days away.
Come to your young lover, Blanche, who will do anything on earth to make you happy.   Say it isn't true;
say you do not mean it, Blanche ! "

Laying down her work, Blanche had risen and stood
silently before him.   As Thomas finished speaking, he
took her hands each in one of his, and looking into her
face, tried to call a reassuring smile to his lips, a smile
that only made his features look still more wrung and
distorted with trouble and pain.   For a moment Blanche
hesitated ; how easy a way he had made for her to get
out of it all—only to say she was joking and didn't
mean it.   She had played and trifled with that man's
love as a child with a new toy.   She had never cared for
him, she had told herself when listening to the proposals
of her older suitor ; but now as he stood there before her
holding her hands, looking into her face with such
earnest, troubled eyes—as in a moment she realized that
she had deceived herself.   At once she awoke to the
truth ; this was the man she loved and cared for—and
her love would be everything to him, the building up of
his life.   For a moment a high and noble aim, the aim
of helping, restoring a human life looking imploringly to
her for aid, sprang up within her soul.   All that was
womanly, all that was good, all the love her nature was
capable of, for a moment swelled and stirred within her.
Then almost like an actual whisper came the words,
" He is a silly fool, who will never get anyone a decent

living. If he does seem to mind a little, he will forget
all about it the next day. If you choose to take him,
you will only bring an extra burden on us all; but on
the other hand, you can have riches and everything
woman's heart could desire, and would raise your whole
family."

The evil suggestions did their work; like a fleeting
gleam of light the better feelings died out of her soul.
Still she could not look him in the face and say it.
Glancing out of the window, she said,

"Yes, I do mean it, Thomas."

The voice did not seem like Blanche's. Thomas felt
like a man in a dream, and the tones sounded far away,
as though some one else, not Blanche, had spoken the
words. Grasping her hands tighter, he once more
pleaded,

"You cannot mean it, Blanche."

"Yes, I do."

She spoke naturally now, and the truth took possession
of Thomas' soul. Suddenly he dropped her hands and
paced hurriedly to the door, then back again, and to
and fro in bewilderment of pain. Blanche, watching him,
felt startled at the agony his face revealed. If a few
minutes before all her best feelings had been stirred,
surely all his worst, most vehement passions were now
brought into existence. It was no longer the careless,
jovial spirit she had known, but a man wrestling with
fierce, cruel pain, and the sight cowed and startled her.
Up and down the room he walked; yet even in that storm
of passion he could not speak ungently to the woman he
had loved. Once again he paused before her, once again
he took her hand in his. The touch of that hand, that

despite all was still so dear to him, seemed to break down the harsher, sterner thoughts within him; tears sprang to his eyes, and his voice trembled as he said,

"Have you nothing more to say to me, Blanche?"

"No, nothing more;" and she drew her hand away as she spoke, and once more looked away from him.

"Then good-bye, Blanche. May Heaven forgive your treachery; you have ruined me."

Another moment and he was gone, and Blanche sank down by the open window, and laid her head down wearily on the window sill. A few minutes after, Mrs. Carter came in.

"Wasn't that young Thomas Porter who went out?" she asked.

"Yes, mother."

"And you've been telling him at last, I suppose?"

"He had heard it when he came in. He came to hear if it was true."

"Well?"

"I told him it was true."

"And what did he say?"

"He didn't say much, mother."

So far Blanche, with bent head and guilty, suppressed tones, had answered her mother's questions, but she felt the examination must go no further. As she rose and suddenly confronted her mother, Mrs. Carter was startled at the whiteness of her face. She forgot to question further about Thomas.

"You are ill, Blanche," she said hurriedly.

"No, I'm not ill."

"Well, you look so. But it is no use upsetting yourself now it is all over. If I were in your place now, and had had to do it, I should be all in a red heat; so hot as it is, too, this evening." And Mrs. Carter threw herself into an easy chair which, to do her justice, she amply filled, and began fanning herself vigorously. "If I were in your place," she continued, "I should look all in a flame, and there are you looking as cool as a cucumber. You can't be much like me, I'm sure."

A very ghost of a smile crept to Blanche's lips, and her hand trembled as she gathered her work together preparatory to leaving the room. Upstairs in her own room, for the first time there went out from her heart a long, hungry, bitter yearning; but in her misery she knew it was a yearning that came all too late.

It was well for Thomas that, walking on with hurried steps, he did not come into contact with his uncle, or the smouldering fire within him might have burst out suddenly into a furious blaze. He had thought of stopping the night at Clansford, but now his one idea was to get back to Elmsbridge, as far as possible from painful associations. But as he came to his father's house he paused: he would go in and tell his father himself. Going down the garden path, he pushed open the door and entered. At the bottom of the hall, the breakfast-room door stood open; Thomas knew his father often sat there alone of an evening, so walked at once to the door. Looking in, he saw Mr. Porter sitting quietly reading his newspaper. He looked up, and something in Thomas' face fixed his gaze. Thomas advanced close to where he was sitting, and laying one hand on the table, plunged at once into the subject.

"Father, didn't you say once, you should be glad to hear the engagement between me and Blanche put a stop to?"

"Why—yes, I did say so."

"Then you have your wish, father."

"What do you mean?"

"I mean it is all over between us, and over for ever. She is engaged to my uncle Thomas at the Grove."

Not another word added Thomas; turning hastily round he quitted the room, and Mr. Porter sat staring after him in blank amazement.

In the hall Thomas encountered Paul, who was just appointed to his first curacy, and was at home for a few days before starting to his new duties. He had just been visiting one of the factory hands who was ill. His face wore the quietly happy expression of desire fulfilled. That very peaceful serenity of countenance was maddening to Thomas' unquiet soul.

"Where are you going?" asked Paul, as Thomas pushed hurriedly past him.

"Going to destruction," said Thomas, as he walked quickly away, and passed hastily down the garden path and out into the road beyond.

Paul stood a minute looking after him in silent wonderment; then going into the breakfast room, he found Mr. Porter just recovering from the surprise into which Thomas' announcement had thrown him.

"What is the matter with Thomas? Where has he gone in such a hurry?" asked Paul.

"Gone! is he gone, then?" said Mr. Porter, rising suddenly from his chair.

"Yes, gone down the road."

"Then I must go after him; I must speak to him," and Mr. Porter went out at once in quest of his son. But when he got to the end of the garden he saw no trace of Thomas, but he saw someone else coming along with brisk step and jaunty air, and that someone was his brother from the Grove. Mr. Porter, looking him down from head to foot, felt a new light break upon his mind. In the bygone days Mr. Thomas Porter had been apt to exhibit a lingering affection for the garments that adorned his outer man. Coats worn till they were rusty, hats whose beaver was rough and staring, dingy collars, soiled gloves, all showed he had retained them in his service as long as possible. But as Mr. Porter looked at him that evening, he could not fail to discern the appearance of newness and freshness in his attire, and that his whole toilet was sprucely and carefully arranged.

"Have you seen Thomas?" asked Mr. Porter, as his brother came up to the gate.

"No, I have been at the school; I was just coming in to tell you how the meeting got on. You were not there to-night."

"No, I was busy and couldn't get away; but come in," opening the gate as he spoke, "I want to speak to you."

Mr. Thomas entered, and as the two walked down the garden path, Mr. Porter, out of the corner of his eye, took another silent survey of his brother's general appearance. Opening the hall door, he gently pushed him in. Mr. Thomas was about to enter the usual sitting room, but Mr. Porter opening the door leading to the room on the other side of the hall, beckoned to his brother to enter. Mr. Thomas entered accordingly, and seated himself in a chair by the window; Mr. Porter sat down opposite him.

"You say you didn't see anything of Thomas?" he said.

"No, nothing of him whatever."

"He was in here just now, and has been telling me a most improbable tale about you."

Mr. Thomas' face for the moment was a curious object of study. An expression half conscious, half guilty crept over it, but his small, bright blue eyes scintillated with covert delight, as of a man who is hugging to himself some secret joy. He raised his walking cane in his right hand, and bringing it down into his left he clasped it tightly in his palm, as though by way of confirmation of what Thomas had said.

"I dare say he has," was his only answer.

"Why," said Mr. Porter, feeling half aghast at his brother's manner, which seemed to confirm the tidings, "he told me you were going courting—engaged to Blanche Carter!"

"Well, and what then?"

"What then! Why at your time of life, after having lived single all these years, it would seem absurd for you to be courting any one; but a young woman like Blanche—it's too absurd, Thomas; I don't believe it."

"Whether you believe it or no, it is true. I and Miss Carter have been engaged now for some long time."

Mr. Porter coughed slightly, stared at his brother and coughed again.

"And whether you know it or not," he said, "my son Thomas has also been engaged to Miss Carter for some long time."

"Nothing of the kind at all. Miss Blanche has herself

told me, and her mother has confirmed it, that there never was any real engagement between her and Thomas. Mrs. Carter told me at once that her daughter would never think of binding herself to such an idle fellow as he is."

"And what do you think she is binding herself to you for?"

"Why, of course, I am her choice."

"Her choice indeed!" and Mr. Porter brought down his hand so heavily upon the small work-table standing near him, as to threaten to shatter it. "I'll tell you what she's binding herself to you for—because she thinks you will one day make a fine lady of her: that is what she is doing it for. She cares no more for you than she does for this table, but she's marrying you for just what she can get."

"Who says so? Who dares to say such a thing?"

"I do. Everyone who hears it will say it: everyone will see the reason at once why she marries you!"

This was scarcely flattering, but Mr. Thomas was inclined to turn philosophical in his views. Perhaps he felt, "Never noble man but made ignoble talk;" anyhow he said composedly,

"I am quite aware that in marrying the best and prettiest girl in all Clansford, I shall bring down upon myself the ill-natured remarks of many who will only envy me my good fortune."

Mr. Porter for a moment did not reply. If this thing was really thus, another train of thought had risen in his mind in consequence, and the grosser part of his human nature was urging him to propound a certain question, and the grosser part of him prevailed.

"Of course you remember," he said, "you have always promised to do for Thomas—to provide and do for him as though he were your son."

"I have never made any but verbal promises; never given any written agreement of any sort."

Mr. Porter did not strike the table again, but he lifted one of his feet and brought it down again on the floor in an emphatic manner.

"Verbal or not verbal, what do you mean to do?"

"Well, that depends; marriage, you see, sometimes makes great alterations."

"Do you intend doing anything or not?"

"Well—of course—that must depend on how you all behave yourselves."

Now it was the lowest part of Mr. Porter's nature that had prompted the inquiry, but he was no craven, and at the words, "that must depend on how you all behave yourselves," he felt only conscious of contemptuous wrath. Rising hastily he opened the door, and going into the hall, threw the front door wide open also, then returning and taking the unsuspecting Mr. Thomas by the arm, he unceremoniously conducted him into the hall, and giving him a little push out of the front door, shut and bolted it in his face. Then returning to the room he had just quitted, he threw up the window sash, and putting out his head he said quickly, "There, that's how I mean to behave, and you may go and behave yourself as you like." Then shutting down the sash with an angry bang, he stood back from the window and watched his brother walking up the garden path with what he intended to be a dignified demeanour, but looking in reality decidedly cowed and crestfallen.

There is a general belief that some men are the better for being knocked down, though perhaps the belief is safer in theory than in practice; still, certainly that unceremonious ejection from his brother's house, did have on Mr. Thomas Porter's mind a different effect from what might have been expected. In the first instance it greatly upset and confused his mental powers. It had been his intention, after a quiet chat with his brother, to go on a visit to his lady-love, but he had gone some way towards his own home before he discovered he was walking in a direction contrary to what he had intended. After a few minutes' hesitation he determined not to retrace his steps, and fortune, which seemed to be baffling and thwarting him, was really behaving very kindly towards him; for he could not have chosen a more inauspicious time to visit Blanche than upon that identical evening.

As he walked along, and especially after reaching the quiet of his own home, he felt that things were not altogether turning out quite as he could have desired. He had no wish for an open rupture with his brother, and in anticipating the explanation which he knew must sooner or later take place, he had fancied by a carefully chosen sentence or two, to have placed his brother decidedly in his power, and have gained moreover that sort of servile homage, which is choice food for puerile spirits only. But he had not calculated upon the burst of honest indignation with which his brother received his propositions; and though the last thing at night he told himself he had been grossly insulted, still the next morning, having slept over the affair, he quite came to the conclusion that peace with his brother must be restored somehow. The thought of an offended brother, and consequently his offended household, was not pleasant or comfortable, and he felt that even the shield of his beloved's affection would not wholly cover him from so formidable an array. So after breakfast he started off at once for Mr. Porter's house, anxious to see him before he set off for the factory.

Arriving at the house, things did not seem very encouraging. Mrs. Porter put her head out of the dining room to see who their early caller might be, and catching a glimpse of the visitor, instantly drew in her head and shut the door. A servant told him her master was in the breakfast room, and thither Mr. Thomas at once repaired.

Now Mr. Porter had himself been undergoing a process of mind not altogether unfavourable to reconciliation. All that was manly in him still rose up against what he considered the cowardly proposition of his brother; but all that was sordid and worldly-minded within him suggested, that whereas he could get nothing by quarrelling with his brother, he could do himself no harm, and might do himself much good, by behaving and being on friendly terms with him. So when Mr. Thomas entered the room, and going up, proffered his hand, Mr. Porter certainly condescended to take it with a very tolerable grace. To say Mr. Thomas Porter smiled would be hardly correct; to say he grinned at his brother would be much nearer the truth.

"I think," he said, "there was a misunderstanding between us last night. I didn't mean to offend you in any way, and I have come this morning to say so."

All this time he watched narrowly his brother's countenance, and seeing no sign of the tide of anger suddenly returning, gaining a little courage, he continued,—

"What I said last night was quite right. I dare say the news was unexpected to you, but things must depend on how you deal with me. Of course if you turn me out of your house like a scoundrel, why there must be an end of all communication between us; but if you are willing to be friendly, so am I; and though I cannot make any definite promises, I will see what I can do for Thomas."

Now how is it that a person righteously offended, though in the absence of the offender he may have thoroughly made up his mind to pass the matter over and to pardon him, still feels, when once again in the presence of that offender, all the irate feelings he thought subdued rising again in sudden revolt? Mr. Porter certainly felt this subtle influence arising from his brother's presence, also, perhaps, from the sort of cringing manner that accompanied his peace-making, and robbed it of all genuine appearance. Certain it is, he had to desperately swallow down a conflicting emotion or two before he could bring himself to answer,

"Yes, I am willing to be friendly with you just as we always have been, but of course you don't expect me either to approve or applaud this engagement of yours. The lady is nothing to me; still I must say I am not sorry Thomas has thus done with her, though in another sense, I cannot but feel that my son has been badly and scurvily treated."

Mr. Porter looked fixedly at his brother as much as to say, "There, wear that cap as far as it fits you."

Perhaps Mr. Thomas thought of the sudden opening

N

of doors of the preceding evening, and the manner in which he all at once found himself outside them ; anyhow, he made no answer to his brother's significant pause, and Mr. Porter continued :

"What you please to do about Thomas, I leave to your conscience entirely;" and the old independent spirit reasserting itself, he added, "I wish no child of mine to be beholden to any man for his money. So there, if you like to be friendly, there's my hand, and we'll have done with it. I'm off to the factory now; would you like to go so far with me?"

Mr. Thomas declined the invitation which, to say the truth, was not over-cordially given, and feeling the atmosphere of the house to be scarcely genial, made good his departure without encountering any other of its inmates. And in fact the friendship thus forcibly re-established between the two brothers, was a friendship simply nominal. Mr. Thomas found himself treated by his brother's family with almost studied coldness. Thomas positively avoided him, and one evening, making a somewhat unexpected visit, he heard that young gentleman, previous to effecting a sudden escape through the window, decline meeting his uncle in no very complimentary terms. Now all this jarred on Mr. Thomas' nerves; he was a man of peace, and liked to be gently approved and encouraged in the affairs of life in which he was involved. Had he been a few miles distant, he would not have cared the toss of a penny about the dissensions or vexation his conduct might cause in his brother's family ; but living so near to them, to feel them secretly antagonistic, ruffled the placid surface of his soul in an uncomfortable fashion, and for

all this there was only one remedy. He would feel
quieter and more at rest when the wedding was over,
and so the time for the marriage must be fixed as soon
as convenient. This was in July, and accordingly the
wedding was arranged for the latter part of October.

CHAPTER XI.

PAUL'S FIRST CURACY.

EANWHILE Paul had departed to his new duties, and entered on them with all possible earnestness of purpose and ardent zeal. But that purpose seemed doomed to be overthrown, and that ardour damped even at the commencement of his career. The curacy he had accepted was in one of those low, marshy districts, just so near to the sea as to catch its breezes only as they crossed the intervening marshes, teeming with sickness, fever, and death. A great part of the parish was marsh land, and the whole neighbourhood proverbially unhealthy. Natives, or those who had lived there some considerable time, might experience no evil effects; but strangers settling there, unless of very robust constitution, were almost sure at first to fall victims to the baneful influences. Paul, not being by any means robust, could have but little chance of escape. The danger was not a visible, apparent danger, to be openly faced or avoided, but the foe was none the less deadly because its approaches were subtle and insidious. The fever in Paul's veins was just that low, intermittent kind, that most surely undermines the health of its victim. Paul only wondered in a kind of vague way what could ail him, till at last there came a day when the faint heart and dizzy brain could go no longer. Mrs. Bonner, the mistress of the farm-house where Paul was lodging, went herself for the doctor.

Mr. Burton was just starting on his rounds as she came up, and represented to him what she considered Paul's dangerous illness.

"I think you had better come round and see him as soon as you can, sir. I don't like the look of him," she said.

"What is it—ague?"

"No, not that exactly, sir."

"Low fever, then?"

"Yes, that's more what he seems like."

"Humph! He's tall and delicate looking, isn't he? not the sort of man for these parts. The best thing you can do is to go back and tell him to pack up his trunks and be off."

"He looks more like taking to his bed than going a journey, sir."

"Oh! so bad, is he? well, I'll be round soon and see him."

Mr. Burton went round accordingly and prescribed for Paul to the best of his ability, and for a time the remedies seemed effectual; but the improvement was only artificial, and the temporary rally was followed by a relapse that threatened to be really serious. So serious did Mr. Burton think it, that having obtained from Paul the address of his friends, he sat down to do what the sick man was unable to do for himself,—to write and acquaint them with the nature of their son's illness.

Mrs. Bonner bustled to and fro in a state of suppressed excitement. The doctor was writing to Paul's friends, that of itself foreboded evil; and at the bottom of her heart surged up a spring of motherly compassion and sympathy for the young man who, coming to her house an entire stranger, had by his gentle, kindly manners, caused himself to be regarded as a true and earnest friend.

"I hope you don't think very badly of him," she said, going up to Mr. Burton's side.

"I am only writing to his friends to come and see him, and get him away from this place as soon as ever he can be moved," replied Mr. Burton drily.

"Then you don't think he will be able to stop. I am sorry enough to hear it; but you don't think we can keep him?"

Mr. Burton had just finished his letter; he rose and took a few paces in one direction, then a few paces in another, as though he were stepping the exact measurement something would require.

"Yes," he said, "you can keep him here, and that's about how much room he'll take."

Mrs. Bonner understood his meaning. "You really think that, sir?" she said.

"Yes, I do," said Mr. Burton, as he went out, letter in hand.

And so it came to pass that, at the very time that Mr. Thomas Porter of the Grove was being quietly married in London——for whatever splendid anticipations the bride entertained as the after result of her married life, she had common sense enough to see that the wedding had better be celebrated away from Clansford, and as quietly as possible—at the same time Mr. Porter and his wife were hastening to Paul's bedside, in answer to the summons from Mr. Burton.

From that sick bed Paul rose with the one inevitable result before him, of resigning his duties and giving up the work to which he had so zealously put his hand. Till the last he protested against such a course, but his mother and the doctor were too strong for him, and against their officious arrangements he had no power to contend, so there remained nothing for him but to give a reluctant consent, and relinquish his post with the best grace he could. And it seemed that a long trial of patience was before him. In answer to his enquiries of how long it would be before he would be wholly well and strong again, his own doctor at Clansford, who had known him from a boy, merely told him that he had had a sharp pull through, that he must think himself lucky to have escaped as he had, and that several months of care and quiet would be necessary before he must think of again resuming duty. So the hands so eager to work were forced to lie passively still.

To say that Paul bore this trial well or patiently would not be correct; not that outwardly he murmured or repined, but his was not a nature to show by outward demonstration the tenor or strength of his feelings within. Still in the depths of his soul a sort of mutinous warfare was perpetually going on. There was a persistence of purpose in Paul, that made it painful and difficult for him to resign a thing once thoroughly commenced. Besides, during that short time among that simple people, he had formed and set on foot many little plans for their help and benefit, and now he was asking dismally, Who would carry on the work? Why was he, in the midst of true-hearted exertion, by an unseen hand suddenly and effectually removed from his labours? And so, during nights still haunted with feverish unrest, or through days of wearisome convalesence, Paul was constantly seeking, in a spirit of morbid unbelief, the solution of this problem in his life which puzzled him. And seeking for it among the weird phantoms and distorted fancies of a weary mind and troubled imagination, no wonder that the answers received were such as to lead to depression and bitterness of soul.

Like many a one in trouble, Paul was looking down instead of up; looking inward at his own narrow experiences and blind reason; looking too with petulant impatience, not with that true humility which looketh and is sure to learn. So what with the gloomy thoughts thus engendered, and the physical prostration accompanying them, and which doubtless powerfully influenced the tenor of his mind, Paul gave way to unwarrantable ideas and suspicions of himself. He had been stopped right at the outset of his work. Why? because of his inability. Surely he had run and not been sent; he had made some grievous mistake; he who sought to teach others, needed teaching himself. Perhaps in this last supposition Paul was not far wrong, but the teaching came from an unexpected quarter.

That Christmas they were a small party at Clansford; Sydney was in London, Thomas had gone to spend the holiday time with Oliver, and so only Theodore and Paul were at home. It troubled the honest, practical mind of Theodore to see Paul so seemingly prostrate in mind and body. Between those two there was still a close bond of union: there was still in Theodore's heart the old chivalrous feeling, which had led him in earlier days manfully to espouse the cause of his younger brother; and Paul's affection had by no means diminished towards the brother, for whom once he had so importunately sought for pardon from a stranger. But close as was the union between them, Paul could not even to Theodore reveal the experiences of his soul; only vaguely he hinted at the gloom that inwardly oppressed him.

One afternoon he and Theodore were alone together; Paul was lying on a sofa by the fire, listlessly perusing the pages of a book he held in his hand, and Theodore sitting opposite him, leaning his elbow on the table, his hand shading his eyes, was looking stealthily at Paul from under his fingers. Paul's inanimate manner puzzled him. After a few minutes Paul closed his book, and lay looking wearily into the fire. The book was a record of a life full of noble and successful effort, a career which seemed attended by success from its very outset. Such histories, as a rule, tend to stimulate our courage and ardour, but have exactly the reverse effect in times of sensible failure and depression.

"You don't care much about that book," said Theodore; "I thought now it would please you."

"It would have pleased me a few months back; but things seem so different now."

"Why, Paul!" said Theodore, suddenly removing his hand from his face, and looking straight at his brother, "you seem as if you thought you were never going to do any more good in this world at all."

Paul looked up quickly; he had indirectly comforted

his soul with much such sentiment, but the statement from another's lips sounded almost startling.

"Why not that exactly," he said, the listless expression stealing back over his face; "still it was not very encouraging what Dr. Miller said this morning, 'You must not think of work again for some time to come,' he said; 'and even when you are well enough, you must take things quietly and not throw all your strength and might into what you do. Some men can go day and night and all seasons, but you are not one of that sort.' So after all I suppose I am to be only half a worker, and the work requires all a man's utmost energy and strength; but Dr. Miller is right, I think I have proved that. Only those few months, and thrown by useless. I don't quite understand it; I think I must have made a great mistake."

Again Theodore placed his hand before his face, and looked through his fingers at Paul. He guessed enough of the working of Paul's mind, to tell that those last few words gave the key note to the depression under which Paul suffered; but Theodore was too clear-sighted not to see matters in a proper and definite manner.

"Yes," he said slowly, "I think you did make a great mistake." Then in answer to Paul's look of wistful, almost agonized inquiry, "A little common sense might have spared it all : you ought never to have gone to that place. You will be all right again if you have patience, and as busy again as ever,—but you see, you were never the man for the marshes."

Paul looked up earnestly. Theodore seemed quite unconscious of having made any great or extra wise statement, and in truth he had not done so; but the

statement was one that in its straightforward truth and
simplicity Paul found it hard to answer, though twice
he essayed to speak and could not find anything suitable
to say. Was this then the result of all his speculative
enquiry? Was this the sane, unbiassed view another
person took of his situation? If so, if Theodore was
right, then the exaggerated ideas of the matter arose
from his own morbid imagination alone. He had been
unfitted for the post: yes, but physically, not morally so.
Providence had dealt very plainly and simply, though
decisively with him, in removing him from a sphere for
which he lacked the very first element of success—
physical adaptation, and where left alone he would
have consigned himself to a sort of voluntary martyrdom,
sacrificing health, strength, and all the mortal powers
God had given him, that he might continue at what he
obstinately chose to consider his allotted work. He had
chosen to direct and model his own life, and because a
Higher Hand had intervened to wisely direct his course
contrary to his own ill-judged plans, he had been at first
rebelliously angry, and then unwarrantably cast down
and depressed. With suddenly awakened soul Paul
saw all this, and in that first hasty retrospect discovered
also, that the arch accuser of souls was still busy about
his defamatory work; and the recent experience of
gloomy distress stood out plainly before him as a subtle,
yet tangible temptation; a temptation to which he
humbly owned he had fallen an easy victim and prey.
But those few commonplace words of Theodore's seemed
to break the spell that bound him, and Paul began to
see light through the oppressive darkness that had surrounded him.

So long he lay quiet with averted face and closed
eyes, that Theodore, thinking him asleep, stole gently
from the room ; and when after a considerable absence
he returned, he found Paul sleeping indeed, with a look
of such peace and quiet as Theodore had not seen
upon his face since his illness.   And the peaceful
countenance was but expressive of the peace within.
The warfare was over ; Paul was no longer the mutinous
subject rebelling against the stern mandate of his Prince,
but a confiding, trusting child once more, safe in his
Father's arms, and the mighty clasp of Omnipotent love
and care.   He was learning, perhaps, the most difficult
of all earthly lessons, how to wait, and to be willing to
do any appointed work ; whether it should be by powerful faith to remove mighty mountains, or only to give
the cup of cold water to one of the very least of the little
ones.

And truly there are sermons, beside those preached
from pulpit or platform—lives, that by their earnest
purity and loving consistency are living sermons ; and
not till the lowly preacher is called up higher, do we
know and realize how sweet an evangelist has been
among us.   And if Paul could have known it, there was
one at least of that little home circle sorely in need of
this sort of daily evangelizing ; some one who was only
too often seeking by forced exuberance of spirit to hide
the gnawing pain within.   Thomas had promised his
father he would do better, and had fully intended to
keep his word ; but he never for a moment foresaw the
trial directly ahead, and so it was no wonder that
his ship of good resolutions foundered at once upon
the hard rock of treacherous temptation.   The first

instinct of his nature had been to flee away from the
scene of his vexation, but there was a sort of latent
manliness about him that forbad the step. Had Blanche
been a sweet young wife, and his love been laid to rest
with her under the green sod, Thomas would probably
have started at once for the uttermost end of the earth
for consolation; but what change could blot out the
feeling that he had been treacherously deceived and
betrayed? People would only smile and think him
additionally simple. Besides, there were other really
potent reasons. To become even a wandering adven-
turer requires capital, and of that commodity Thomas
was always short. Mr. Porter made no secret of the
fact that he had had losses, heavy ones too; and Thomas
knew too well that old scores had been settled over and
over again for him, till the conclusion was come to that
Thomas, and Thomas alone, must settle those little
pecuniary difficulties for the future.

And then there were old associates at Clansford, and
Philip Carter had somehow contrived to inveigle himself
back again into his old position of friend and counsellor,
though it was an understood thing that silence reigned
absolutely on one point. So Thomas went about, outwardly seeming, except during moods of restless excitement, much as before; and there was no one to whom
to confide the overcharged heart within. There was
Sydney truly, but Sydney with his dreamy, speculative
temperament, would probably have written an ode
on the subject, and have there ended his sympathy.
His father would have had but little patience with him,
and have told him in few words that he considered he had
cause to be thankful for his deliverance from a designing,

deceitful woman. And his mother already sighed over
him, was for ever hinting at the injustice done him, and
pitied him with that sort of pity which proverbially kills
the cat, till Thomas always assumed an extra degree of
gaiety in her presence, but felt in his heart that the
burden might one day become too much for him to bear
alone.

Meanwhile the bride and bridegroom seemed in no
hurry to return, and the honeymoon was prolonged to
four months, and then came a letter from Mr. Thomas
Porter to his brother, informing him that they were
coming home at once. The letter was a short one,
hardly such as a delighted bridegroom might be expected to write; but the writer excused himself on the
plea that he had been very ill, and still felt too weak
for much exertion. Then the letter became nearly
pitiful in almost childish longings after England and
home, and ended with an earnest request that his brother
would come and see him as soon as possible after his
return.

The exact day they would arrive in Clansford was
not specified, but somehow on the morning of the day
fixed for the return, the greater part of Clansford were
aware of the fact. The news found its way to the
factory, and after their dismissal that afternoon, became
subject of discussion among a group loitering together
before returning to their homes. Just past the factory
the road was straight and narrow, but a little further on
anyone going in the direction of Clansford would come
to a sudden curve in the road, leading directly to
Clansford street; opposite this corner was a narrow
lane, and an open space forming an entrance to the

lane was a favourite spot, where several of the factory
hands had a habit of stopping and grouping together
for a while after their day's business was over. So on
that particular afternoon they were discussing the return
of the married couple.

"I'm thinking," said one of the younger lads, "that
the young master won't much care about giving 'em a
welcome."

"I'd welcome 'em; they should have music—a regular
good, rough band," replied another.

A man named Bill Watts, one of the older hands,
looked at the last speaker reproachfully.

"Don't you know," he said with due assumption of
importance, "that every man in England is free to marry
what wife he thinks best?"

Considering that Bill Watts for the third time in
his existence had just entered upon matrimonial bliss,
he had some right surely to an opinion on the subject;
moreover, Bill Watts was a sort of acknowledged
authority among the men, and so no one raised a voice
in opposition; but a minute after, one of the men stepping into the road, after a good look to thoroughly
assure himself, came hastily back.

"They're a coming now," he said, "their carriage and
man. What say you to a word o' welcome—just cheer
the old gentleman up a bit?"

Sundry nods and winks given in mute reply, testified
to approval of the proposition, and so just as the carriage
swept up to the corner, the inmates were startled by a
series of shrieks, and yells, and shouts that were almost
deafening. In vain the driver signalled to them to stop,
his voice was drowned in the uproar.

"There," said a tall youth, "they can't say we didn't welcome 'em home."

"And you've scared the horses. Look! they're going like mad," said Bill Watts.

Bill was right, the driver was evidently exercising all his powers to control the frightened animals, and some of the men ran down the road to watch their progress. In a few minutes one of them returned.

"They're stopped," he said breathlessly, "but they was after bolting clean off; but a man in the street stopped 'em. The master himself come up a minute after, and was speaking to the man that stopped 'em, and so I'm a thinking if master *should* walk round this way, just to see what scared the horses—you understand, boys!"

The hint seemed perfectly understood, judging by the fact, that when a few minutes later Mr. Porter, as had been predicted, did walk round that way, he found only two or three men slowly walking towards Clansford, and these were so impenetrably stupid or ignorant on the matter, that Mr. Porter found no grounds for concluding them to be of the guilty party. Besides, Mr. Porter had his own private ideas on the subject, and as the result of his cogitations, when that evening Thomas happened to come in, he at once passed the honour of the transaction to his account. At the accusation Thomas' face flushed scarlet, as he indignantly denied all knowledge of the affair whatever.

"You are quite sure?" persisted Mr. Porter.

Thomas rose quickly to his feet as he replied hotly, "You need not doubt my word, father; the old—I mean my uncle is quite safe with me. I should not at any rate set the factory hands on to hoot him."

Mr. Porter said no more, and soon after left the room, and Paul and Thomas remained alone together. Thomas was standing with his arm resting on the mantel-piece, his whole face clouded with sullen resentment and pain.

"I suppose there is nothing so mean or bad, but that father would conclude I was at the bottom of it," he said moodily. "They say a bad name hangs a dog, and I'm bad, and going to the bad, I expect. I'm sure I don't see what's to stop it."

Paul did not answer, but tears sprang to his eyes as he looked at the face before him, every feature of which had grown suddenly hardened by sharp mental pain.

"Don't look at me like that, Paul," said Thomas, as he met his brother's fixed, earnest gaze, "and don't preach to me; I know you ought to, but I couldn't stand it; and don't pity me—mother pities me, and well nigh drives me mad."

"I won't preach to you, Thomas, or pity you either; but you must let me do one thing—believe in you."

"You'll have good grounds for belief," said Thomas bitterly, and then he looked wistfully at Paul.

In one sense the two had little in common, none of that sympathy of experience which is so inviting to confidence; but then sometimes the very absence of all similar occurrences in the history of the person to whom they confide, leads some natures to proffer more freely their confidences, as though it were some small consolation to blend something of the initiative with their recital; so after a minute's pause Thomas added,—

"But then, Paul, you know nothing at all about all this. You were never bad, or tempted to be wicked, I believe—there, don't look shocked—of course I suppose

O

you have your little sins, but I don't see or know of
them; but you see, Paul," and his mouth relaxed
grievously at this juncture, "I did mean to do thoroughly
well, I told father so, but then who could stand it—to
be tricked, and cheated, and deceived! And after all,
I wouldn't have cared if *she* had not done it. I
haven't much good in me—father thinks I haven't any
I believe; but I've got some sort of feeling, and, and,"—
with a sudden stamp of his foot,—"I loved her, loved her
truly, rightly, and honestly; and I know I ought not to,
she is another man's wife now; but there, I shall go mad
if I don't tell some one; I love her, I can't help it, even
now." Thomas half hid his face from his brother as he
spoke. "I tell you what, Paul," he added, looking up,
"I fairly cannot stand this any longer; I shall cut it
and go abroad. I think I know of a good opening, and
I shall take it."

This was all news to Paul.

"Where did you hear of it? Who has been telling
you of it?" he asked thoughtfully.

Thomas fidgeted from one foot to the other.

"The murder will out, I suppose," he said hastily;
"I am going with Philip Carter."

Paul looked up in blank surprise.

"Thomas, you must never do it," he said gravely.

"Yes, I must; I cannot stop here. What's against
it?"

"Nothing, as I can see, against your going away somewhere; I believe it would be the best thing you could
do; but you must not go with Philip Carter. I wonder,
after what has happened, you can wish it."

"Nonsense! what has happened doesn't hinder us

being friends, and why should it hinder us going out together?"

"But why be friends with him at all?"

Shifty natures always dislike plain reasoning, and Thomas looked uncomfortable.

"We always have been friends, and it wouldn't be easy to be anything different now; besides, it is not fair to blame Philip for what he couldn't help: but remember, Paul, this is in strict confidence; for pity's sake don't breathe a word of it to either father or mother."

Paul looked thoughtfully into the fire, his strictly conscientious spirit was meditating what he ought to do with this communication of Thomas'.

"I don't think I ought to promise that," he said slowly.

Thomas looked really alarmed.

"I tell you, Paul, you must promise it. You don't know the train of arguments and bother of every kind you would bring down on my head; and I shan't go till the Spring gets up, anyhow. If you don't promise, I'll be off one day and let nobody know where I am going, and cheat you all that way. Promise me, Paul."

"Only on one condition," and Paul rose and laid his hand firmly on Thomas' shoulder, "and that is, that before making decided preparation for this step, you give due and proper notice to us all. On that condition I will not say a word now about what has just passed."

"Well then, I'll promise to tell you all the night before starting."

"I am in earnest, Thomas; proper notice, I said."

"There! proper notice then."

"You mean it, and will keep your word?"

"Of course I will; but it would be no kindness tormenting mother about it long beforehand."

With this assurance Paul was obliged to be satisfied; and a minute after, upon the entrance of his mother, Thomas assumed a perfectly different demeanour.

Mrs. Porter seated herself at her work, looked at Thomas and sighed heavily. The sigh acted contrarily on Thomas; he began vigorously poking the fire, and singing merrily as he did so. Then saying it was time to go, he kissed his mother and bade her a cheerful good-night, and they heard him still singing gaily to himself as he left the house.

Mrs. Porter sighed again: "How he can be so lighthearted, I'm sure I don't know," she said gloomily.

Paul made no answer; in his own mind he was wondering how such a shallow attempt at mirth, such palpable bravado, could ever for a moment be mistaken for genuine lightness of heart.

CHAPTER XII.

MARRIED BLISS.

A FEW days afterwards, Mr. Porter paid the desired visit to the Grove. He found his brother looking shattered and worn from recent illness, but there was a restless effort at sprightliness and gaiety of demeanour that puzzled but did not deceive Mr. Porter. Under that assumed cheerfulness he saw, or thought he saw, an altered and half-miserable man. There was an appearance too, throughout the house, of new arrangements and renovations ; the easy old-fashioned furniture had been replaced by new but less comfortable articles ; Mrs. Jenkins, with her time-honoured services, had been dismissed, and brisk, smart servants were stepping about in her stead ; and the changes altogether looked startling and incongruous. Something of this Mr. Thomas detected in his brother's critical gaze round the apartment.

"Ah, we have had a few changes. We have made considerable improvements, haven't we?" he said ; but there was a wry look about the corner of his mouth, that half belied the satisfaction he intended to manifest.

"Yes, you have made alterations, certainly." There was a half-curious expression on Mr. Porter's face as he spoke: he was wondering in his own mind how much *we* had had to do with the matter. And he was not altogether wrong. Blanche herself had designed the various renovations, and her mother, to whom her plans had been entrusted, had zealously carried out her daughter's wishes, adding a few improvements and ideas of her own at the same time; and for the person implied by *we*, remained only the doubtful honour of very considerably lightening his pocket to defray the necessary expenses incurred by all these changes, and the grace of almost unquestioning acquiescence.

But then when a bachelor—we won't say how much the shady side of sixty—marries a young and attractive-looking bride, he is apt to become so lost in the glory of the feat he has accomplished, as to be for the time being not quite so alive to pecuniary details. Besides, it may sometimes happen that the gentle creature, who in the days of honeyed courtship was so amiable and yielding, may in those after-days of married life display unmistakable talons beneath the velvety paws. So, with one reason and another, what is there for the bride-groom thus placed but acquiescence in his wife's doings? Mr. Thomas Porter would certainly have said such was the only course remaining to him, and so he put a good face on it all, by declaring to a share in the general proceedings.

But apart from everything else, Mr. Porter thought his brother looking considerably altered by the illness he had undergone.

"I am sorry to see you looking so ill," he said kindly.

Perhaps Mr. Thomas was not very used to sympathy, for the words drew from him quite a series of complaints and ailments. Then thinking he was making rather a miserable account for a bridegroom just returned from his honeymoon, he added by way of qualification,

"You see it was a cold, a thoroughly bad cold, and perhaps we went sight-seeing a little too much; but foreign ways and places don't suit when you are ill, they seem wretched and no comfort anywhere. I shall be all right now I am in England again, and back in my own home;" and he made a feint of leaning back in the formally modern chair, which seemed rather to repel than invite repose.

Blanche throughout the visit maintained an air of utter indifference to all surroundings. Finding himself alone with her for a few minutes, Mr. Porter expressed to her his concern at his brother's altered appearance.

"I consider," he said, "your husband is looking very ill."

"Oh, do you?" said Blanche, and the apathy of the tone caused Mr. Porter to look round at her with a searching expression; but Blanche made no response to the enquiring look; she had evidently given the subject all the consideration she thought it required of her.

Mr. Porter went home puzzled, and wondering to himself whether after all his brother's matrimonial experiences were altogether so enviable as they appeared. Perhaps he forgot that when a man has passed the greater part of his life in retired bachelor habits, and surrounded with special bachelor comforts, he is apt to feel almost keenly when these habits are unceremoniously broken into, and these comforts dexterously removed. Old household articles, which, from long association, seem like old valued friends, are not always easily relinquished.

Some experiences of this kind fell to the lot of Mr. Thomas Porter. Many fresh regulations were formed, and some items of comfort that had seemed downright essentials, were missing altogether. Mrs. Jenkins had humoured him even to a special spoon and fork, and a particular glass in which to mix his evening grog; but the new servants could not be brought to understand these distinctions; and his wife merely said with her usual quiet manner, "My dear, all the spoons and things are alike; they are all nice and new. What more do you want?" and Mr. Thomas could find no argument against the almost ironical indifference of his wife.

Then there was the little table, which in the days of privileged celibacy had always stood with the lamp on it at his elbow on winter evenings, and which had been so handy to place his book or paper on, or his breakfast cup of a morning, when that meal was quietly partaken of in the easy chair by the fire. Mr. Thomas looked round the room for the missing table in vain.

"Are you looking for anything?" said Blanche.

"Yes, my dear, I am looking for the little table."

"What little table do you mean?"

"My little table that always used to stand close to my chair."

"Do you mean that little old mahogany thing on casters?"

"Yes, that's the one," said her husband, with suddenly brightening countenance.

"Oh, mamma had that moved into one of the bed-rooms. She said it was not the thing for a sitting room, but would be very useful in a sick room, and that that was all it was fit for."

Mr. Thomas Porter shuddered; he had known something of sick-room experiences of late, and that his favourite table should be consigned to sick-room purposes only, sounded terribly ominous. He relinquished the subject with a profound sigh.

But the table was not the only loss. Where was the old-fashioned but luxurious easy chair, in which he had whiled away so many hours of undisturbed bachelor enjoyment? This too came under the head of articles missing. He wondered if this also was consigned to the regions of the bedrooms; if so, he resolved—the resolve was a daring one—to find it himself, and insist upon its re-instatement in its old quarters. Accordingly Blanche found him wandering through the bedrooms, and up and down stairs, in what seemed to her a perfectly objectless manner. Encountering him on the stairs, she stopped to speak to him.

"What do you want? Are you looking for anything?" she said.

"Yes, my dear, I—I—am looking for an easy chair."

Blanche stared at him.

"The easy chairs are downstairs," she said.

"Yes, my dear; but I want my chair, my own easy chair."

"I didn't know there was any difference in them. If you want one on purpose for yourself, I suppose you can take which you like best;" and Blanche made a movement to pass him. If the truth dawned on her mind, her impenetrable countenance did not betray it.

But Mr. Thomas, once the ice was broken, felt bolder, and stood his ground before her.

"I mean," he said, "the easy chair I used before I was married."

"That greasy old thing covered with American cloth?"

"Russian leather, my dear."

"Well, Russian leather then. Mamma said it was so old she could do nothing with it, so she changed it away for some of the new furniture."

Mr. Thomas' small blue eyes fairly scintillated with wrath.

"Then I shall have it back again. Whom did she exchange it with?"

"I'm sure I don't know; but it is of no use going after it; it would be re-stuffed and made all fresh most likely by this time, so it would not seem the same if you were to have it back. Let me come past you, please."

Mr. Thomas let his wife pass him without another word; Blanche's laconic indifference was more unanswerable than the most hot-headed opposition.

"Are you going out this morning?" said Blanche, half an hour later; "I am going for a ride, will you come too?"

"No, I prefer staying at home," was the curt reply.

He really did feel inclined to be a little sulky about that matter of the chair. Still, when his wife returned from her ride with bright eyes and glowing cheeks, and he reflected that all this beauty was his own by exclusive right; and also when later on in the day there arrived as the result of Blanche's morning drive, a beautifully finished and polished little walnut-wood table to take the place of the deposed favourite, why, if he was not only a contented, but exuberantly happy man, he certainly must have been of a most miserable and dissatisfied disposition. But perhaps the most sensible loss in the house was that of Mrs. Jenkins, and in this case the loss was hopeless; for on her dismissal from the Grove, her husband had accepted a situation with a farmer as overlooker on one of his off-hand farms, and so she had departed beyond recall. But there was one person who, by assiduous attentions, surely made up for all other lacking service, and that person was Mrs. Carter. And when shortly after his coming home, Mr. Thomas had a severe return of the cold which had so prostrated him abroad, Mrs. Carter tended him day and night with unwearying solicitude. If she was not duly appreciated, it was through no lack of energy on her part, but the sick man felt that the very fussiness and importunity of her attentions wearied and troubled him. If Mrs. Carter was not quite disinterested in her services, so long as the recipient of her favours was satisfied, perhaps it ought not to concern anyone else; but it must be confessed that just then anxiety was pressing upon Mrs. Carter's mind respecting a certain legal document, which, as she told Blanche, ought to be seen to and settled all right and square.

"I know," she continued, seeing no awakening of interest in Blanche's passive face, "that wives, and young wives especially, don't think for themselves much about these things, but I standing by can see plainly for you; and you never know what may happen, and it ought all to be made as I say, right and square."

Making things right and square, with some people means seeing that all have their rightful due, but with others it means securing to self a preponderating share. Mrs. Carter seemed to incline to the latter view, for as soon as Mr. Thomas Porter was sufficiently convalescent, the said legal document was duly executed; and Mrs. Carter, the day it was finally concluded, seating herself in her daughter's apartment, with the air of a person who has fought a battle and come off victorious, said impressively,

"There, it is all settled right for you at last, child; it is all yours, and no one can take it from you. You are to be envied, I'm sure."

Blanche turned away with an almost weary face. That morning, walking through Clansford, she had met Mrs. Blake, and Oliver driving her; Mrs. Blake coldly recognized her, and Oliver only acknowledged her by a distant, almost haughty bow. A little further on, and a happy young mother in her cottage home was singing lovingly to her first-born. Blanche saw her plainly through the open door as she passed. The first scene had brought a lowering cloud on Blanche's brow, but the last brought hasty tears to her eyes, and she felt vaguely, as much as her self-sufficient nature could feel, that somehow she had done something which, though indirectly, lowered her in the esteem of worthy people, and yet she had lost all the sweet, pure joys, which early wifehood ought to know.

Mrs. Carter noticed her daughter's look, and varied her tactics.

"I do say, Blanche, that you've got a husband in a thousand; a most liberal, compliable man, and it is your duty to study him in every way. Very liberal; I don't know what Phil would have done just now but for his help, and now to have settled every penny on you; I do say he is most liberal and compliable."

Blanche did not contradict the statement. Perhaps could Mrs. Carter just then have looked into the inner thoughts and intents of the man she had been lauding, she would not have considered him quite so compliable after all. Not that in the main Mr. Thomas Porter objected to what he had just done; and had he been in robust health, or had been asked in the first flush of married happiness whether a wife was entitled to her husband's possessions, he would undoubtedly have answered in the affirmative; but somehow during that last term of sickness, strange fancies and thoughts had come to him. Visions of days long past; of meetings with his brother and his family; of selecting a tiny baby and promising to make him his heir; of after days when the promise was again and again reiterated, till he seemed virtually to have adopted a son and heir, and it was generally supposed he had done so. And now by this last act of his he had cut the son and heir adrift, and dashed his expectations to the ground. Whether he ought still to remember his former agreement, or whether he ought to cede everything to the lately-married wife, was a matter upon which he never could decide. At this point his thoughts always strayed into inextricable confusion.

At last a prominent idea formed itself: the wife should have all her due, but something was yet to be done for the disappointed heir. But this part of his cogitations he by no means confided to Mrs. Carter. He knew too well the tenor of that lady's opinions; besides, a sick man does feel helplessly in the power of his nurse;

and so he formed a little plan in his own mind which wanted only opportunity and time to accomplish. Arrived at this point, he grew, as Mrs. Carter said, compliable. He even did most liberally extricate her scape-grace son from impending difficulties, though qualified by the positive assurance that such help would never again be repeated; and then he made quite a show of compliance, and invited Mrs. Carter herself to read the legal document, and see for herself that everything was right and as it should be, and all the while secret intrigue was working in his bosom.

But like a weak nature with a weak purpose, when the time came for the execution of his little plans, he almost lacked the necessary energy. Twice he let some trivial obstacle deter him. At last came a day when he arose fully determined to carry out his idea; but even then he betrayed such nervous anxiety, that had there been grounds for suspicion, he would most certainly have been suspected. The first part of the act was to get Blanche to go out, if possible, to spend the day with her mother, and he manifested such zealous concern that she should not let such a lovely morning go by, and yet so persistently refused to accompany her, that a suspicious person would at once have divined that something out of the usual way was premeditated. As soon as his wife was fairly off for a long country ramble, being the utmost to which he could persuade her, he ordered the close carriage and horses to be brought for his own use immediately. He then drove in the direction of Elmsbridge, and when on the outskirts of the place he ordered the man to stop, and complaining of feeling cold, told him to drive slowly for a mile in another direction, and then return and meet him at the same place, as he wished to walk a little while. The man stared, but so far obeyed as to set off in the direction indicated. Then Mr. Thomas walked at the utmost of his speed down through a little seldom-frequented lane, leading to the lower end of Elmsbridge street. At that end of the street lived his family solicitor, and to his office Mr. Thomas directed his steps. When his interview was over, he walked quickly back again by the same solitary route by which he had come, leaving Mr. Monson, who had been friend and legal adviser to the family for many years, in a state of wonderment, why a codicil of a few lines only should seem to so worry and nervously excite his client.

Blanche's country ramble not being quite the length that had been prescribed for her, she reached home first, and was naturally surprised to see her husband, who had so persistently wished to stop at home, come riding up in his close carriage. She looked her surprise as he entered.

"I changed my mind, my dear; the morning was so lovely."

"But why did you go in the close carriage?"

Mr. Thomas coughed.

"I—I wished to do so," he said.

"Oh, of course, as you like, only one of the horses is lame; I suppose, though, you knew that."

"I don't think this morning's exertions have hurt him, my dear. And where have you been walking?"

"Only through the woods," said Blanche, as she rose to go upstairs to remove her walking things. She did wonder a little at her husband's conduct and manner, but supposing it was only his peculiar way, gave herself no further concern or trouble about the matter.

CHAPTER XIII.

SYDNEY.

SYDNEY had for some time discovered that he had committed an error in introducing his brother Thomas into the Elmsbridge business, and could not be blind to various little delinquencies on his part; but Sydney chose to consider that his brother, being a wronged individual, was therefore less accountable than other people, and carelessly passed by failures of duty, which as master he ought to have sternly reproved. Moreover, his father had warned him against Philip Carter, yet on several occasions he allowed him to come and spend long evenings with Thomas. He excused it all under the plea, that Thomas appeared still to wish for his company, and Sydney did not see how any direct harm could come of spending an evening with him now and then. Besides, Philip could be an agreeable companion, and could wear almost a righteous aspect if required. In fact, Sydney was just as vague and impractical as ever. He attended to the business through principle and a good conscience; for, whatever his faults, dishonesty, falseness, or deceit never ranked among them; and Mr. Harrows was fully aware of his good qualities, and spoke of him as a young man who might be trusted. Sydney took his life much in the same unquestioning way that a man eats a dinner, about the provision of which he has had neither thought nor concern. His father wished him to go into business, and into business he went. Still there were times when, hidden away in his desk, were stray sketches, short stanzas, that would rather have betokened the artist than the man of business. Yet Sydney was in no way discontented with his lot, but he liked to diversify it by these chance pleasures, which to some would have been innocent recreation, but to him made life full of dreams and strange imaginings.

Then for a time his dormant soul flashed up within him. He was earnestly, devotedly in love; but even then it was love full of romantic tenderness. To him the object of his love seemed almost more than mortal. The ideal of all womanly grace, all womanly beauty, to him were concentrated in the merry, lively girl who had won his heart; and Alice Wilturn would have felt almost dismayed, could she have seen the halo of perfection with which her presence was always surrounded. The passion, so far from dispelling life's illusions, only increased them tenfold. Now down at Elmsbridge, something of the old artistic pursuits had again revived. A young artist had lately settled there, and he and Sydney became fast friends; and so it happened that on several occasions, as soon as ever business was over, Thomas and Philip could if they chose have it all to themselves, while Sydney was immersed in the beauties of imaginary scenes or far-away views and pictures, as portrayed by the facile pencil of his new friend. Thus one evening Philip Carter found Thomas alone in the little private room at the back of the shop, and volunteered to stay awhile with him. Sydney had gone out hastily that evening, and as a result of the new ideas engrossing his mind, had carelessly left his keys dangling in his table-desk. Philip's quick eye soon detected them, and Thomas, thinking Philip had been silent some time, looking suddenly round, saw him with the desk open, alternately peering at the papers inside, and the general manner of the key and lock.

"What are you doing there?" said Thomas hastily.

Philip quietly closed the desk.

"Nothing," he said, "that there's any harm in. If the governor leaves his affairs open, he must expect people to peep in at them."

"You had no right to look," said Thomas quickly, as he walked across to the desk, locked it, and put the keys in his pocket.

"Then you won't go with me to-morrow?" said Philip after a pause.

"No, I've no money for going out."

Philip whistled.

"If that's all, we can shake hands; and what is more, that honoured individual, your uncle, won't come down with another stiver."

"He can do what he likes with his own money, I suppose," said Thomas sullenly.

Philip saw Thomas was in no amiable mood; he sat quietly thinking for a few minutes, then he said,

"I say, old man, you seem flat and out of spirits. You're bored to death at this stupid business all day long; come with me to Martin's for an hour or two."

Martin was one of Philip's most chosen associates,

and was of that hospitable kind, that Thomas seldom entered his house to come out of it again a properly sober individual. Had Sydney been at his post, the temptation would not have been proposed in his presence; but there was no Sydney to restrain, and so after a moment's inward conflict, Thomas yielded, and the two set off in the direction of Martin's house.

It was ten o'clock when Sydney returned; the rule was for the whole establishment to be in by that hour, and Sydney came panting in, conscious of being himself late. He inquired for Thomas, and learned that he and Philip Carter had gone out together; that afterwards Philip had again come in and stayed some time, apparently waiting for Thomas, and neither of them had been in since. Sydney waited; an hour passed and no Thomas returned. Meanwhile Sydney had discovered the loss of the keys. Conscious that the day's entries were not completed, he had turned at once to the desk, and found it locked and the keys removed. It was considerably past eleven, and there came a low knocking at the door of the private entrance. Sydney went to open the door; as he did so, a form was pushed into his arms—the form of his brother helplessly intoxicated. With some difficulty Sydney got him inside; that feat accomplished, he sped hastily back to the front door. Some strange man had deposited Thomas in his arms, but he had caught sight of a face he knew too well lurking round, and smiling quietly to himself at the mischief. That person was now walking slowly down the street; Sydney flew after him, and Philip Carter started as he felt a hand violently grasp his shoulder.

"Well, what now?" he said.

"This—that with my consent you never set foot over my threshold again, sir."

The two men stood close by one of the lamps, and Philip looked with genuine surprise on the face before him. Could this be the gentle, apathetic Sydney—this man, with flashing dark eyes, and every feature of his sensitive, handsome face, quivering with indignant wrath and scorn?

"All right," he said; "only don't nip my shoulder quite off."

"I scorn to touch you," said Sydney, suddenly springing back; "you are a mean, wretched, disgraceful villain; and if ever you come into my house again, you do it at your peril."

Philip's face grew white and contracted.

"Do you know," he said, "that this is rank insult, for which the law could punish you?"

"It is my opinion that if the law had its rightful power over you, you would not be walking about free and at liberty," said Sydney quietly.

Philip Carter placed himself before Sydney in menacing attitude.

"Retract your words, or you will not come past me," he said, his dark, evil face working with undisguised anger.

"As you like;" and Sydney with one well-directed blow sent Philip sprawling into the street, and walked away towards his home.

Philip soon recovered himself.

"You have insulted and assaulted me," he bawled; "but there is law, and you shall pay for it."

Sydney merely turned, snapped his fingers at him

derisively, and then went on. Philip stood watching him, his teeth clenched with rage. He had been meditating a dark project that evening, and somewhere down deep in his heart had been a kind of latent feeling of honour that spoke, though faintly, against injuring a man who had always behaved to him generously and unsuspiciously; but now that man had become a deadly enemy, whose insults called loudly to be revenged.

Sydney found his keys in Thomas' pocket, but so powerful was the potion he had taken, that no connected account could he give of how they came into his possession. When he could recall his senses a little, he remembered distinctly how he had taken them from the desk, but the time at Martin's, and the latter part of the evening, seemed an entire blank; and when Sydney haughtily and with flushed brow spoke in no gentle terms, Thomas folded his arms on the table, and laying his head down on them, seemed completely bowed down with misery. There was something almost inexplicable in his manner. At last, one evening he said suddenly to Sydney,

"Did you tell father about the other night?"

Sydney had not done so; some lofty feelings of honour and delicacy having restrained him. He replied in the negative.

"I'm glad you didn't," said Thomas, and he had evidently something further to say. "Sydney," he said, after a considerable pause, "it was not drink that night; I was drugged."

Sydney started back from him. Was his mind going, or was he inventing vain excuses?

"You may look, Sydney," continued Thomas; "I

know how much I took. I could not remember anything at first, but I can now, and I say I was drugged."

Sydney felt too puzzled to reply, and Thomas continued for days wretched, morose, and taciturn. So a month passed by, and then one evening when Sydney returned home, he found Philip Carter had been inquiring for Thomas, and finding him not at home had gone in and waited for him quite half-an-hour, and finally had gone away without seeing him.

Sydney was annoyed at what he considered Philip's audacity; but two mornings later arrived a letter for Thomas from Philip, informing him that he was suddenly leaving home; that he had braved Sydney to call and give Thomas a parting word. Philip further stated that having lately received a letter from his cousin abroad, he was going out to join him; that he thought it useless to urge Thomas to go with him, owing to the breach that had lately occurred, so he was writing him a farewell, promising to write again and tell him how he prospered, and adding that Thomas could then follow him if he chose.

This letter considerably lightened Sydney's mind. If Philip was gone, then the chief danger for Thomas was over. Could he have seen the events immediately to follow, he would not have so complacently congratulated himself. The morning following the arrival of that letter, in the county town about five miles from Elmsbridge, in a private room of the bank belonging to Messrs. Rivers, Brown, and Co., the bank where Sydney kept his banking account, two men were seated in close conversation. The previous day a cheque, apparently written by Sydney, had been cashed for £350. There were suspicions attending that cheque; the clerk who cashed it, had almost immediately afterwards felt an uneasy conviction in his own mind that all was not quite right concerning it. The cheque was signed as all Sydney's business cheques were signed, with his own and Mr. Harrows' signatures, and it was also to all appearance Sydney's handwriting; but the man who tendered it seemed confused and awkward in manner. This, added to the fact that the clerk, directly after his departure, felt convinced that he had formerly seen the man elsewhere, and that he had then been pointed out to him as a loose, disreputable character, caused a strong suspicion in his mind. Besides, Sydney had the day before been in the bank transacting business; and so all things considered, the clerk spoke to Mr. Rivers on the subject.

Mr. Rivers hesitated what course to pursue, but when the morning after—by one of those coincidences that do sometimes occur in life—Frank Harrows, Mr. Harrows' eldest son, passing through to Elmsbridge, called at the bank on his way, Mr. Rivers at once signified to him his desire to speak to him in private, and immediately laid the matter before him. Frank Harrows soon proved himself equal to the occasion. Scarcely turned two-and-twenty, his firmly-knit figure, and settled expression of countenance, might have indicated him several years older. He had been quietly with Mr. Rivers going over the banking accounts, and comparing the writing on the last cheque with previous ones; but not a feature of his imperturbable face betrayed the conclusion he might be arriving at in his own mind. Mr. Frank Harrows was one of those individuals who, either through education or a natural turn to scepticism, complacently adopt a universal disbelief in the good faith and probity of the whole human race. If Sydney, or some one in Sydney's name, were juggling and seeking to defraud, it was no matter of surprise, but a very probable event. Had anyone proved to him that the grey-haired, christian gentleman sitting opposite him had defrauded his neighbours, he would have owned to the probability of the statement without any apparent demur. But Mr. Rivers was differently constituted; suspicion alone of evil was grievous to him.

"I hope," he said, "that when you see Mr. Sydney Porter, he will explain all to your satisfaction; I think you said you had great trust in him?"

"I said my father had," replied Frank drily.

Mr. Rivers thought the words implied a lack of confidence on Frank's part, but he was mistaken. Frank had personally no reasons whatever for suspecting Sydney; he only classed him in with the other human beings, of whom neither truth nor honesty were of necessity to be expected.

Arriving at Elmsbridge, without delay he asked Sydney for a few words alone with him, and Sydney at once led the way to the little room at the back of the shop. Frank Harrows made no unnecessary parley.

"I want to speak to you about this cheque," he said, laying it quietly before Sydney.

Some men so placed would have said the words with a perceptible tremor of voice or change of countenance, but Mr. Frank Harrows was subject to no such failings.

"I know nothing about it: it is no cheque of mine," replied Sydney, hastily glancing at the paper before him,

Perhaps this was about the answer Frank Harrows expected.

"Will you try and explain a little about it?" he said.

"I cannot explain; I know nothing about it; but I can at once refer you to my books," and Sydney produced the identical bunch of keys that he had once with such culpable carelessness left hanging in his desk.

Frank Harrows took them and opened the desk, Sydney standing by his side. Very quietly Frank Harrows took up the ledger, opened it, and then for once in his life with something like surprise, glanced up hastily at Sydney; and Sydney looking down, with a dismayed consternation he could never afterwards express, saw that leaf after leaf of the entries had been deliberately cut away, thus leaving no trace of the proceedings. Then the two men looked at one another: Frank Harrows had recovered his equanimity, and the expression of his face merely said,

"I suppose you will deny all knowledge of this also?" and Sydney looked and felt like a man brought suddenly into doubt of his own identity.

"What can it mean?" he stammered.

Frank Harrows closed the desk without a word.

"May I trouble you to ring the bell," he said quietly.

Sydney paused; his perceptions, fully awakened, were too quick not to perceive the distrust and suspicion lurking in Frank Harrows' reserved manner.

"You do not attach the guilt of this in any way to me?" he said, hurriedly. "I am as ignorant as you of who has thus tampered with my affairs."

Frank Harrows made no answer, save by a visible compression of his lips.

"Do you take me for a thief or a swindler, sir?" said Sydney, with a flash of the spirit that had astonished Philip Carter.

"Unless you can more satisfactorily explain yourself, I am afraid I must in some measure regard you in that light. Will you please to ring the bell?"

"Why do you wish it rung?"

"I am going to telegraph to Mr. Harrows, my father, for further advice."

"I will telegraph for you."

"Then you oblige me to say that under the circumstances I must forbid you to leave this room for the present."

A moment more, and Sydney gave the bell such an impulsive pull, that it fairly startled those who heard it.

As the messenger was being despatched with the telegram, Sydney called him back.

"Ask Mr. Thomas to come here at once."

"Mr. Thomas is not within, sir."

Sydney turned round impatiently; whenever was Thomas ready or available in time of need? Taking a piece of paper he hastily wrote on it a few lines, and having handed it to Frank Harrows for inspection, put it in an envelope.

"See this is sent to my father at Clansford at once," he said.

So the time passed on; Frank Harrows busying himself with the desk, and such of its contents as were undemolished; while Sydney, proudly indignant, yet feeling as though he must be dreaming, and that this could be no hideous reality, forbore to utter another word in his own defence. Then after about an hour Thomas suddenly entered.

"Do you wish your brother to be informed of this matter?" asked Frank Harrows.

"Certainly," replied Sydney.

Then in a few words Thomas was informed of the whole affair. At first he spoke out vehemently and indignantly, then suddenly his manner changed; he became cowed and agitated, and spoke in a confused, hurried way, and finally collapsed into a troubled silence. Sydney and Frank both noticed the change of demeanour. To the latter it was only an evidence of guilt; to Sydney it was distressing and perplexing in the extreme: and when, as the time passed, he saw Thomas grow restless and terribly disquieted in manner, and noticed the trouble and apprehension depicted on his countenance, Sydney felt himself overpowered with a vague, indefinite terror and dread.

The messenger despatched to Clansford found Mr. Porter out, and so long a time elapsed before it was discovered where he had gone, that it happened that he and Mr. Harrows, who had hastened down at once in answer to his son's telegram, met together in Elmsbridge street. The presence of both was required, but further than that they could not tell. Certainly not from his father did Frank Harrows derive his sceptical disposition; Mr. Harrows' whole face beamed with kindly benevolence and goodness. That eldest son of his, with his unbending materialistic views, was often an enigma to him; and Frank was daily coming more and more to the conclusion, that his father was undoubtedly shamefully deceived and imposed upon.

It was a curious trio the two men confronted: Thomas with his furtively agitated face; Sydney looking perplexed and distressed ; and Frank with all the calm imperturbability of a self-righteous nature, which has discovered what it always expected to discover, guilt and deceit in others.

In a few words the two new-comers were made acquainted with the principal facts. Mr. Harrow laid his hand gently on Sydney's shoulder.

"Well, what do you say to it all, my boy?" he said kindly.

"Of course you can explain that this is no doing of yours, Sydney!" said Mr. Porter, conscious of the integrity of his son.

"I can only repeat what I have before said, that I am ignorant of the whole matter," said Sydney.

"I am afraid simple ignorance will not avail you much," said Frank cynically.

"Do you take my son for a rogue, sir?" said Mr. Porter, hotly.

Frank Harrows made no reply; but at that moment Thomas half rose from his seat as though to speak, and then re-seated himself. Then passing his hand hurriedly across his brow, he rose and came up to the table. Putting both hands on it, he said,

"I may as well say it; it will have to come out sooner or later. I wouldn't say it before you came, father, but I may as well say it now; and after all, my name is not so white that I need be too afraid lest I should blacken it. I have not done it myself, and Sydney is as innocent as a babe; but I think I know who has done all the mischief. Don't you know too, Sydney? It is"—then he paused, as though his lips refused to utter the confession he had been bracing himself to make.

"Who is it?" said Mr. Harrows.

"It is—it is—I must say it out, father. It is Philip Carter who is at the bottom of it, and who has done it all."

For a few minutes silence followed the avowal. Frank Harrows was the first to speak.

"And who is Philip Carter?" he asked quietly.

"A young man against whom I have repeatedly warned my son," said Mr. Porter. He did not say sons; never for a moment did a doubt of Sydney's integrity in any manner cross his mind.

"Yes, I know that, father," said Thomas quickly; "but as I said just now, it is Philip Carter who has done all the mischief."

"Can you give us any evidence in proof of what you say?" asked Frank Harrows.

Thomas hesitated.

"Yes," he said, slowly, "I can do so, or of course I should not have spoken thus. About a month ago Philip Carter was in here, in this room, and I found him with Sydney's desk open, and he was looking into Sydney's papers, etc. I did not think about it at the time, but it is all plain to me now."

"You came in and found him at the desk?" asked Mr. Harrows.

"No, not exactly so; I was in the room here with him. I had not for a few minutes been particularly noticing him; when I looked round he had got the desk open, and was peeping inside."

"Your brother kept his desk unlocked, then?" said Frank.

"No," stammered Thomas, "but he—he found the keys."

Sydney stepped forward. "I must take the blame here, and I will do so, he said. I went out that evening and neglected to lock the desk, leaving the keys hanging in it."

Thomas looked relieved by the admission. Frank Harrows slightly elevated his eyebrows.

"And because," he said, "Philip Carter got a five-minutes' peep at your brother's papers, you choose to assert that he has done all the rest—forged his name, and destroyed his accounts?"

"No, not through that alone. I may as well make a clean breast of it; as I said at the beginning, it won't make me so much blacker. I went out with him that evening to a friend's house, and I don't quite remember what took place—I must own to it, father, I was overtaken by my old fault—but as I told Sydney afterwards, I believe it was something more than ordinary drink: I believe I was drugged. During the evening Philip Carter came in here again, professedly looking for me. I believe now he came in to do what mischief he could. He had left me at his friend's house, so he certainly was not looking for me. Then he came in again an evening or two ago, but Sydney and I were both out. He has written to me since, telling me he came in to bid me farewell before going abroad; but I believe—I feel I could swear it—that that evening, as I and Sydney walked down Elmsbridge street, I saw Philip standing in an archway. I did not speak, for he and Sydney had quarrelled, and I knew Sydney would not care to speak to him, but I feel sure I was not mistaken. If so, he knew before he came in that we were both out, and the mischief was done then, and that other evening when he came in before."

"That evening, when you were not quite in a state to note what was passing around you?" said Frank.

Thomas' face flushed scarlet.

"As you will," he said quickly; then added more quietly, "but there, I have told you all this as best I can. All these different points have kept flashing into my mind while I have been sitting thinking it all over this morning, and I think I am right in my suspicions."

"It is Philip Carter's doing, there's not a doubt of it," said Mr. Porter, righteous wrath gleaming from his countenance.

"We must find this Philip Carter up," said Mr. Harrows.

"There's the mischief," said Thomas; "he's off. He wrote to me from London: I can show you his letter;" and taking an envelope from his pocket, he laid it down before Mr. Harrows.

"He gives no address or real trace of himself from this," said Mr. Harrows. "This letter gives but a slight clue. What do you think, Frank?"

"I think, sir, that till stronger evidence can be adduced, we must continue to look to Mr. Sydney Porter for explanation."

"What do you really mean, sir?" said Mr. Porter hastily.

"I mean, sir, that the cheque and the destroyed accounts seem to indicate but one thing—intentional fraud, with a view to abscond with the proceeds. The accounts having been thus tampered with, how are we to know what sums may or may not have been fraudulently obtained? The proofs for or against are destroyed."

Mr. Porter stared blankly at Frank Harrows, then at

his sons. Was it of Sydney—Sydney, who had always been so tractable, who had never given him a moment's uneasiness, for whose honesty he would have vouched with his life—that such hard things were now said? He crossed sorrowfully over to where Sydney was standing.

"I warned you against that man," he said; "why did you ever let him come here at all?"

"It is my fault," said Thomas. "It is all through me—things always are. He came to see me, not Sydney."

"Sydney, Sydney, my boy, I can't stand it. If you had kept clear of that man, this would never have happened. But this is too much, to hear you are a thief, Sydney."

Mr. Porter sat down in the nearest chair, and every feature of his stern, square face relaxed into an expression of blank, dismayed sorrow. Sydney in all his life had never seen his father look like that before.

At the side of the room was a small window looking out into a narrow lane or alley running past the side of the house. Sydney walked to the window, and stood looking out. At a window in the opposite side, two little children peeped with merry faces over the wire blind; then a woman carrying a heavy bundle passed down the lane; then a boy ran by, gaily whistling as he ran: but Sydney, full of his own bitter reflections, neither saw nor heard any of these things.

Mr. Harrows, looking at his old friend Mr. Porter, felt grieved as he saw the pitiful expression of his face. After all, he had sons of his own, some quite young, sons whose future was yet to be determined; and who could tell the weal or woe those young lives might bring? So stepping up to Mr. Porter's side, he said,

"It seems to me, the first thing to be done is to endeavour to find out the whereabouts of this young man, Philip Carter. Has he any friends who might be likely to give us his address?"

"His parents live not far from me at Clansford," said Mr. Porter. "They, I should think, would know where he is at present."

After a few minutes' consultation, there appeared no better plan than to go to Mr. Carter himself. Accordingly Mr. Harrows and Mr. Porter departed on their errand. They found Mr. Carter standing at the door of his house, evidently about to enter. Driving up to where he was standing, they alighted to speak to him.

Neither Mr. Harrows nor Mr. Porter were skilled diplomatists, or men likely to disguise an important question under an unimportant manner; therefore Mr. Carter, turning full upon them his keen, restless dark eyes, at once perceived that his son's address was thus suddenly wanted for no pleasant or agreeable reasons. Still he spoke the truth when he said, "I have no more knowledge than you where he is gone."

"Try and remember. Don't you know at all where he is?"

"No, I do not."

"Have you any reason to suppose your son is gone, or going abroad?" asked Mr. Harrows.

"He may be; he said something of the kind some little time back."

"Read that," said Mr. Harrows, producing the letter Thomas had given him.

Q

Mr. Carter glanced through it. "It may be so," he said, "but I cannot tell."

The apathetic tone roused Mr. Porter's ire.

"It may be to your advantage to think where he is," he said. "Your son's name is connected with an unpleasant affair; would you rather we saw him privately and let him speak for himself, or shall we use other means to find him?"

His son's delinquencies did not seem much to affect Mr. Carter.

"You must use what means you like," he said; and his face grew obdurate and hard, as visions of his son, probably embarrassed with debt and consequent difficulties, rose up before him.

"And you cannot tell us where he is?"

"No, I cannot. It is no unfrequent thing for him to be from home, and we do not know where he has gone. When he left a few days ago, he said he would write before long, but we have not heard from him since."

It was evident the man was speaking the truth, but Mr. Harrows made one more effort.

"You may save your son, by telling us where he is now."

Mr. Carter gave an impatient stamp.

"I tell you, I cannot," he said. "And what do you mean? from what could I save him?"

"From arrest for forgery and burglary."

Mr. Carter's whole diminutive frame quivered with suppressed wrath. He hastily turned away his face and he uttered his son's name, but he uttered it with a curse. Turning round again and looking at Mr. Harrows, he said bitterly,

"Sir, I hope you will never know the pain of having a bad son: but I can tell you nothing more. I can neither save nor harm him, for I do not know at all where he is; and if I could save him, I don't know I would."

Turning hastily, his face full of bitterness and ire, he let himself into his house, leaving the two men outside feeling that they were labouring in vain.

There was only Blanche—but Mr. Porter remembered that morning, for he had been at the Grove when Sydney's messenger went for him, that she had spoken of her brother, and wondered where he had gone, and if he would be away long. So there was nothing for them but to return to Elmsbridge.

Meanwhile Sydney had been a prey to melancholy reflections. "You are a thief, Sydney," rang in his ears. Not that there was the slightest truth in the accusation: no positive sinning anywhere; all the fault seemed of the negative kind. In that sudden retrospect, Sydney seemed to awaken to the guilt of half doing what ought to be well and thoroughly done. The vast responsibilities of life seemed suddenly rising up before him. How had he met them? There had been trust for another in the daily work and business he had undertaken; and he had done it monotonously, as a thing coming in his way to be done, not as a part of a life's work for which he must be accountable. There had been evil in the world; evil close to him, and he had winked at it and parleyed with it, and suffered it to enter his domains, till at last it had tainted and ruined him. There had been a desolate, weary heart in his home, a desultory, wavering life. He had not striven to comfort the one, or direct the other; but had allowed

the pernicious friendship of a wicked man to exist under
his very eyes, as a means of help and consolation.   All
this kept vaguely running through Sydney's mind, till
how real, intensely real, seemed the life over whose
duties he had slurred, and with which he had trifled and
speculated upon, and lived out as in a dream.

His reverie was cut short by the return of Mr. Harrows
and his father.   Mr. Harrows beckoned him aside, and
the three went into another room by themselves and shut
the door.   It seemed a long interview to Frank Harrows
and Thomas ; at last they returned.   Mr. Harrows went
up to his son.

"We have decided that you remain here for the
present, Frank."

"Certainly, sir; and you will of course take proper
proceedings."

Mr. Harrows smiled.   " There will be no proceedings,
Frank, at present.   As far as my confidence is concerned
in our young friend here," looking at Sydney, "I feel I
could still allow him to remain at his post.   But this he
himself refuses to do ; his intention for the present being
to devote all his energies to track and bring to justice
the real criminal ; till then at least, he relinquishes his
duties here.   Mr. Porter has made himself answerable
for the appearance of his son, should his presence at any
time be required."

"But, sir, the money! the loss!"

"There will be no loss to me, Frank."

" I hardly see how you can know what you have lost,"
said Frank, looking towards the rifled ledger.

"Frank, I am satisfied.   After all, our returns will
shew in a measure about that."

"But what guarantee have you?"

"Mr. Porter has seen to that," replied Mr. Harrows, laying his hand on his pocket as he spoke.

Frank made no reply, but his face grew full of contempt and suppressed indignation.

At that moment Sydney stepped forward, and laying his hands on the desk, looked across it intently into Frank's face. They were a striking contrast; Frank with his short, compactly moulded frame, and stern implacable face; and Sydney with his tall, lithe figure, looking down at him with a face white from suppressed emotion, with lips slightly tremulous, and dark, glistening eyes.

"Listen," he said, "all of you, as I once more solemnly and earnestly declare that of this crime I am altogether innocent. I have discharged my duties here honestly, thoroughly honestly; but I take great blame to myself for negligence and carelessness. Had I kept all evil acquaintances at arm's length, and been diligent as I have been honest, this would never have happened. But all this is over now—" he pushed back the hair from his forehead, and slightly raised his head as he spoke— "I have trifled, but I shall trifle no longer. I have a purpose in life now, to find the man who has done this wrong, and to clear my own good name. Your father shall lose nothing: as far as money goes he shall be repaid; but his noble trust in me, his generous forbearance, I can never repay."

Frank was not quite adamant; it was impossible to watch Sydney's earnest face and doubt him, so for once in his life he was silent through not having anything appropriate to say.

Mr. Harrows turned fussily round: "We are old friends, Mr. Porter and I, Frank," he said; "very old friends."

CHAPTER XIV.

A PURPOSE IN LIFE.

A LITTLE later in the afternoon, Sydney hurried off to the bank to interrogate the clerk, but the young man could throw no further light upon it all. Some time back the man, who he believed to be the same that had tendered the cheque, had crossed his path in London. He had been warned against him then as a blackleg and a villain. The name he went by then he believed was Smith. Nothing further could he tell. He owned he should never have connected the two, but that the manner of the man excited his suspicions, and looking closely at him, he fancied he had seen his face before. The remembrance puzzled him, but immediately that he thought he had identified him, he spoke to Mr. Rivers on the matter. It was a peculiar face, and he thought he was not mistaken, but further information he could not give.

Little hope did all this afford: so many people rejoiced in the name of Smith, that the name alone was no clue whatever. Sydney got the best description of him the clerk could furnish, and took his departure. He had promised to go home round by Clansford, to let his father know the result of his undertaking.

The early dusk of the spring evening was just beginning to close over the silent country, when, as he rode along, turning a corner suddenly he came upon two people walking quietly together, and those two were Paul and Eleanore. Paul had gone out that afternoon for one of those long country rambles, which he said put new life into him; he had stayed at a friend's house on his way home, and was now returning, when, meeting with Eleanore, the two walked on together. All this Sydney did not know. That Paul was ignorant of that day's events, and that his appearance was a surprise, he gathered from his half-startled look as he stopped to speak. He merely told Paul he was going to Clansford to see his father on important business, and hastened on; but in those few minutes there had come to Sydney, with his newly-awakened perceptions, a sudden instinctive revelation. A few days back that revelation, had it come to him, would only have called up a dreamy smile; now it smote upon his soul with sudden anguish. Might not this late trouble—he well knew Paul's intense fastidiousness—drift between those two lives? And besides, might it not prove an obstacle and barrier to Paul's future career? Sydney could not say, but before his mind's eye rose up another mental vision, of a little brother who, in his childish simplicity and love, had once striven to help and cheer a startled soul, trembling on the very verge of an unknown land, to which it seemed fast drifting. Then still thinking of Paul— how earnestly and zealously had he answered to the voice within his soul, how diligently followed his calling. Had he, Sydney, bestowed upon his life and its purposes one-half the zeal that Paul had expended upon his, what might not have been the result? And now, all the shame and reproach, however undeserved, might go far to blight and hinder a pure and earnest life.

In few words Sydney told his father the result of his inquiries at the bank, and bidding him and his mother a hasty farewell, hurried back to Elmsbridge to be in readiness to depart for London on the morrow. He found Thomas moody, sullen, and downcast. He could give but little light upon where Philip's quarters in London might be: he gave Sydney a description, as far as he could, of some of Philip's boon companions, but none of them seemed in any way to answer to the appearance of the man who took the cheque.

"I have my views and plans," said Sydney. "I would take you with me if I thought you would be of any use."

"I should be no good; I never was to anyone yet," was the disconsolate answer.

"You will be at home, I suppose, for a time?" said Sydney.

Thomas growled something almost inaudibly, and rose to leave the room. In a minute he returned.

"Good-night, Sydney," he said, holding out his hand; "I am sorry, truly sorry, to have seemed to bring all this trouble upon you. Good-night, Sydney; remember I am sorry, very sorry;" after which he went away.

In the midst of Sydney's plans, there was one terrible duty uppermost: Mr. Wilturn must be informed of the matter, whatever the result. He would go and see him, and tell him; but here again his impractical tendencies hindered the right course. No, he would not go, he would write: and write he did; just one of those letters that sensitive people in dire trouble so often do write—a letter full of reserved emotion.   He told the truth—told it implacably, quietly, holding in stern restraint the feelings that would keep mutinously rising within him. It was an unwise step; for while it would have been almost impossible to have looked into Sydney's earnest face without believing him, it was very possible to read the constrained, formal letter, full of its mental reservation, and begin to doubt the probity and honour of the man who wrote it.

Mr. Wilturn was a man accounted great in philosophical research, but he had not philosophy enough to detect the anguish the letter concealed.

"He says there has been a forgery, and the ledger has been rifled," he said to his wife.   "They charge him with fraud, I suppose; and really, my dear, it looks very like it.   He says a mere nothing for himself, just a few words at the end about justice and rights, but nothing to clear himself whatever.   After all, he was a stranger to us, and Alice may think herself lucky to have done with him."

In consequence, as answer to his letter, Sydney received a few formal lines from Mr. Wilturn, informing him that the acquaintance between him and his daughter must from that time cease.   Sydney obtained an interview with Mr. Wilturn, but that gentleman had become settled in his convictions, and gave him no quarter. But for one thing, Sydney would have gone hastily away; he could yet stoop to plead for a last farewell to Alice.   This was at last accorded, on the condition that he saw her in the presence of her parents.

"Sir," said Sydney, with a sudden ominous flash of

his eye, "cannot you trust me not to extort promise or confession from your daughter? I wish to see her merely to relinquish her, and bid her farewell."

"Then you can do that in the presence of her mother and myself. You can come to-night; we shall be by ourselves."

"I will come," said Sydney; and not trusting himself to speak another word, he walked hurriedly away from Mr. Wilturn's office.

That evening, in a certain house in the suburbs, standing back behind its prettily-cultivated garden, in the drawing room, in the presence of Mr. and Mrs. Wilturn, Sydney took his formal farewell. It was a curious scene; Sydney spoke briefly, quietly. Going up to Alice, as she sat with downcast eyes, he said,

"I have come at the request of your father to bid you good-bye, Alice."

Mrs. Wilturn coughed and fidgeted on her chair; she had pleaded with her husband for five minutes for them. "Let them have just five minutes alone; he cannot say much harm in five minutes. Let them have so long together before they part; I won't ask any longer," she had urged. But Mr. Wilturn was inexorable: "In our presence, or not at all," he said.

Sydney paused, but Alice never looked up.

"I bid you good-bye," he continued, "till your father thinks me worthy of you."

"No, not exactly so," interrupted Mr. Wilturn. "There is to be no reservation; you give up my daughter unconditionally."

Sydney looked quickly round, but it was Alice's father, and the indignant words died on his lips.

"Yes, unconditionally, sir," he said, quietly and proudly. "Unconditionally, Alice, I give you up. You are free as ever you were in your life. Good-bye, Alice."

She placed her hand silently in his, but still she never looked at him. Sydney held her hand lingeringly in his own. He would give her up, but he must have one look before he went.

"Good-bye, Alice," he said again in a lower voice.

She understood him and looked up, but the glance was so hurried that Sydney could not rightly read its meaning. Another minute and he was gone, but as he turned to leave, Alice escaped by a side door from the room. Sydney went out of the house with a desolate heart. Half way through the garden some one hastily called his name, and then a small hand was laid on his arm, and a face looked wistfully up into his.

"Oh, Alice!" he said, instinctively drawing her nearer to him.

"Sydney," she said, hiding her face on his shoulder, "have you really given me up?"

"Alice, you know I have."

"Then I won't give you up, Sydney. Father has no right to control me; mother has no right; nobody has. Do you understand me?"

"Of course I do, darling," said Sydney, though hardly comprehending the exact drift of her words.

"When shall it be then, Sydney?"

"When shall what be, dear?"

"Oh, Sydney," she said, suddenly looking up at him, "you don't understand; you don't see, that I will leave father, mother, home, everything, for your sake; will run away with you anywhere, anyhow, so they don't separate us."

This was the ideal of all womanly perfection, proposing to run away with the lover who had just formally abandoned her. If any man's eyes were doomed to be rudely opened, surely Sydney's were; and yet, owing to perverse human nature, never had the form at his side seemed half so dear to him as then. Finding he did not answer:

"Shall I, Sydney?" she asked, with averted face.

"No, my darling;" and the voice was full of sorrowful firmness.

Alice sprang suddenly back.

"I see how it is," she said, "you don't really care for me; you wish to give me up, and this is how you do it."

"Alice, you know me better. Child, it is because I love you so much, I will not let you do this thing; because I love you so much I have done as I have. But though I have given up all lawful right to you, Alice, I will never give up loving you. If we have patience it will all come right yet, and I will love you and wait for you, though I love and wait all my life long."

"And I will wait for you, Sydney," she said, clinging to him again. "I'll never marry anyone but you; no one shall ever make me—no one."

"And you will trust and wait till I am proved worthy of you, Alice?"

"You are worthy," she sobbed. "Why did you tell them about it all, and separate us thus?"

"Because I love you so much: because you are so good and pure, that I felt you must never marry a man who had even the shadow of a suspicion upon his name, however undeserved that suspicion might be."

"And we part now for long, long years!" she wailed.

Sydney could not help it: by way of comfort, he stooped and pressed, what Mr. Wilturn would have deemed forbidden, kisses upon the face nestling close to him. Then there was a hurried adieu, and Sydney found himself on the outer side of the iron garden gate; but even then their hands sought each other in another farewell clasp, and Sydney saw a flushed, troubled face striving to keep back its passionate tears, and heard a small foot kicking imperiously against the separating iron bars,—and then he was walking alone his sorrowful way.

Alice sped back to the house, and to the solitude of her own room. When two hours later she rejoined her parents, Mr. Wilturn laid his hand approvingly on her head, and gently stroked her hair, as he said,

"My little daughter, I mean to say, has behaved like a Briton."

Alice winced; but when a minute later her father repeated the action, as he said,

"Like a Briton, my dear, I say; and I am proud of you. You have done most sensibly in giving the young man up," she sprang suddenly to her feet before him, as with flashing eyes she said,

"But I have not given him up; I will never give him up. We have promised not to write to each other, or try to see each other, and we will keep our word; but we shall never give up loving one another—never, all our life long:" and clasping her hands over her brow, she fled from the presence of her astonished father.

Mr. Wilturn's philosophy again failed him, and had not been powerful enough to fathom aright the workings and depths of the young heart that had so long pulsated in the very shadow of his home.

Meanwhile Sydney passed back to a life full of such intensity of purpose and aim, as he would not at one time have deemed possible.

CHAPTER XV.

BLANCHE'S SECRET.

IN the meantime, from Clansford came news by no means encouraging: another person had chosen to voluntarily banish himself.

When Mr. Porter, that afternoon, had bidden adieu to Mr. Harrows, he found Thomas loitering at the door, uncertainty of action depicted on his countenance. Mr. Porter gave hasty expression to his thoughts, as he informed his son, that from henceforth he must make his own way; that he had helped him for the last time, and would not allow him to be at home eating the bread of idleness. Mr. Porter never intended literally denying to Thomas for a time the shelter of a home, he only thought by thus speaking to stir him up to independent action. But Thomas appeared to take the words literally enough, for the next day he took his departure, posting, as he went through Elmsbridge, a letter to his mother, in which he bade her good-bye.

"When he came again," he said, "perhaps his father would think him worthy of being received; but now he was going away to do just what he found to do—anything, so that he was no further trouble to his friends; anywhere, away from Clansford and familiar faces."

The letter ended with a few kind remembrances to Paul, and a strain of subdued misery ran through it all. Mr. Porter grew exasperated.

"It was the most foolish thing possible to go away just then in that absurd fashion. People would soon be saying their minds about it; but then it was just like Thomas, to be as foolish as possible."

All this and more he said, and his face grew hard and lined, while his wife wept over the letter, and Paul sorrowed over it all in vain.

And the one person who might have given tangible help, was wearily oppressed with her secret knowledge. Letters at the Grove were delivered early, that being the first house on the postman's rounds; and one morning, as Mr. Thomas Porter was finishing his morning toilet, he heard the usual sharp ring of the bell, and then saw the postman with his quick, official step departing from the house. When a little later he went downstairs, he found his wife sitting at the breakfast table. She looked pale, and her lips were compressed, while her eyes had an absent expression as though thinking over scenes far away. But her husband did not note all this; his eyes were busily scanning the breakfast table: he was expecting an important letter, referring to certain money matters in which he had just been engaged, and he looked round quickly, thinking to see the anticipated document.

"Any letters, my dear?" he asked, still looking round.

To his surprise, Blanche, after a moment's pause, merely said the one word "No." Then the hot colour flushing into her cheeks, with an alacrity unusual with her, she began busying herself with the breakfast cups. She

R

felt her husband's small eyes were persistently fixed upon her.

"No letters!" he said. "I saw the postman go away."

Blanche had recovered from her momentary confusion. Looking up at him, the old smile came to her face as she said,

"There were no letters, only a sort of begging thing for me."

"Where is it, my dear?" Mr. Thomas seemed to have an undiminished curiosity upon the subject.

Blanche's brow slightly contracted.

"I haven't got it," she said. "I—" there was no friendly fire upon which it would have been so natural to have carelessly thrown it, so she hesitated—"it was no good to me, so I threw it away somewhere."

Mr. Thomas looked more puzzled than satisfied: not that he had any reason to suppose he was to see every bit or scrap of writing that came to his wife by post, or that he had any reason for persistently asking about a simple begging effusion. But those who play sly little games on others, are apt to imagine that other people are doing the same by them.

From that time Blanche seemed like a person opprest with a secret knowledge. Her reserve grew more intense, and towards her husband at times her manner became almost timid and restrained, and varied with that kind of compunctious attention, that we feel due to anyone whom directly or indirectly we have wronged; and if any of her husband's family came, as a rule she escaped as soon as possible from their presence. One evening, feeling the quiet monotony of the house beyond endurance, Blanche put on her hat and walked down to her mother's. Coming back, she suddenly came face to face with Paul; she would have avoided him if she could, but the meeting was too sudden. After shaking hands with him, she seemed anxious to pass on.

"I have been down to see father and mother," she said, "and I stayed chatting longer than I ought to have done. It is getting quite late."

She would have passed him, but Paul was standing directly in her path. Looking straight at her with his clear, grey eyes:

"Have they heard anything further about your brother?" he said.

"No, nothing whatever," replied Blanche hurriedly. "I will bid you good-night, Paul; I am in haste to get home."

"One minute, Blanche. Do you know where he is?"

The directness of the question staggered Blanche; her face flushed crimson, and then grew suddenly pale.

"No," she said, "of course I do not;" but she looked down at the ground as she spoke. "What right have you to ask me?"

"Only this; one of my brothers is disgraced and reproached, the other a hapless exile or wanderer, and this is to be laid to some one's door. This is why I ask."

Blanche's face was very white, and her lips had a perceptible tremor. Suddenly lifting her luminous, dark eyes full to Paul's face, she said,

"Paul, I have a right to ask you, after what you asked me just now, Have you heard anything further from Thomas?"

"No; but we have little cause to suppose he is doing any good for himself."

"Why not?"

"An utterly miserable man is almost sure to go down in the world, Blanche, and seldom does anything good or successful."

Blanche looked at him for a moment with a strange light in her deeply dark eyes. She seemed about to say something, and then hesitated; then she compressed her lips tightly and looked away from him. Another moment, and her usual expression of indifference to all things surrounding, crept over her face.

"I am very sorry, Paul," she said quietly; "perhaps it will all come right one day. Good-night, Paul," and she glided past him, and went on her way alone.

After that Blanche went out but little, and by way of diversion occupied herself at home with tasks of intricate needlework; but not unfrequently her husband, coming suddenly upon her, found her with her hands folded listlessly in her lap, and her eyes full of that far-away look they had worn that morning she received the noted begging epistle. And so time passed on, and there came directed to Philip Carter an American letter from his cousin, inviting Philip to join him, and alluding to a previous invitation in a former letter. Mrs. Carter shewed the letter in triumph; thus far her son's word had appeared to be correct, that if he had not gone out to his cousin, he had had the invitation to do so. Then very shorly after this, Mr. Carter was taken suddenly ill and died; and people said that then the truant son, if any where within hearing of the event, would return. But people were wrong in their surmises. No Philip appeared; but something far stranger than his appearance would have been, happened—Mr. Harrows received from an unknown source, the £350 in full; also a letter emphatically asserting the innocence of Sydney, and urging upon Mr. Harrows, that as the money was thus fully restored, to let the matter drop. The letter further added, that it was the fact of knowing the innocent to be wrongfully accused that had led the writer to make this full and ample restitution. Mr. Harrows was puzzled. Under the circumstances, it was most improbable that Sydney had sent the money, and from what he had heard of Philip, he did not believe, that unless goaded by fear or some equally potent reason, he would ever feel himself called upon to make restitution of any kind.

As soon as possible Mr. Harrows went to Sydney; he found him dejected and utterly cast down. Had Mr. Harrows for a moment harboured the thought, that Sydney in a moment of romantic zeal had sent the money, his manner would at once have dispelled such an idea. Sydney had cause for dejection. That letter from abroad had puzzled him; and besides, Sydney had from the first taken the whole matter into his own hands, and had solemnly pledged himself—if possible within a stated time—to bring the real culprit to light. But Sydney's means were limited; his father had told him at once that no help was to be expected from him. So time had passed; and what with employing secret agents, going hither and thither himself, and working out this plan and that plan, according as the least suspicion of a clue to the affair led him, Sydney had exhausted all available funds, if that promise to Mr. Harrows, which was a kind of hostage, was to be fulfilled. Lastly, he had with difficulty obtained a common-place clerkship, for which he gained but commonplace pay; yet out of that small sum his one idea and resolve was to spare something towards once again prosecuting his search and enquiries. He entered into Mr. Harrows' account, and all its details, with an avidity that would formerly have been simply astonishing in Sydney.

"I don't think Philip can have sent it," he said, and then buried his face in his hands and sat deeply thinking. He sat thus so long, that at last Mr. Harrows went quietly up to him.

"Sydney," he said, "when you first came to me in London I took a fancy to you, and being the son of my very old friend, I felt a kind of right in you, and I think we were friends from the first. Let me speak as a friend now. I think you must be mistaken in your ideas about Philip Carter; I fancy you must have had somewhere some other enemy whom you have overlooked. Whoever it may be, he appears to have come round to his senses. I am repaid fully, and in no way can I tell, as I have before told you, that there was any other loss beside the £350. My returns were quite satisfactory. Now take my advice; put this thing away from you, and begin life again as though it had never happened. I have been repaid, what more is there to think about?"

Sydney suddenly raised his head.

"You would have been that anyhow, sir. I was in trust and was culpably careless, therefore it was only right that to me you should look for payment. That, however, is but a very small part of it all. I had, and still have, my honour to establish; and you do not know, perhaps," he added bitterly, "all this has cost me."

Mr. Harrows did know better than Sydney expected.

"Yes," he said, "I know to what you refer." Then after a minute's pause, he said, "Sydney, I know Mr. Wilturn; I used to know him well. I could speak a word for you."

Sydney's face grew suddenly hot.

"Sir," he said quickly, "I suffer no one to speak for me there." Another moment he rose and stood by Mr. Harrows' side. "Forgive me," he said, "for speaking hastily. You are goodness and kindness personified; but you do not understand. I have a desperate work to do, but I will do it. I will track that man to the world's end, but I will find him. I am baffled and defeated now, but the time will come, and I will follow out my purposes though I die in the attempt."

"Well, well," said good Mr. Harrows, looking half startled at the set features and gleaming eyes of the man before him, "of course you know your own feelings best." And he took his leave, and went off wondering at the fixedness of purpose betrayed by the young man, who had always seemed to him so quiet and compliable. Little did he know that Sydney's spirit was, as it were, undergoing its birth-pangs, that under that compliable quiet nature was hidden a vast power of thought and action, and that out of the fierce anguish would yet appear a humbled, but resolute, purified soul.

CHAPTER XVI.

THE SHADOW BETWEEN THEM.

TO Paul it was a curious summer. The early spring had been ushered in with, to him, a month of intense happiness. One happy month spent by the sea. The secret of the happiness lay in the company in which it was passed. Mrs. Grattan had said just before his departure, "Eleanore and I are going for a spring trip somewhere: we may as well choose the same place you have done; we shall often meet, and it will be pleasanter for us all."

This was the keynote to the after blissful hours. As Mrs. Grattan had said, they met often, met daily; and Paul carried home with him strangely happy memories of that visit to the sea. The sea, that never before seemed quite so enchanting in its changeful beauty and mysterious voices. For the sea is full of voices. To the disappointed, melancholy soul, every billow breaking on the sands is full of responsive moans and lamentations. To the young, happy heart, the waves utter silvery music as they ripple gently over the shingly beach: but to the young heart in the first flush of youth, the sea speaks with an enthralling tone. Then, with the prosaic world behind us, we listen enchanted to its magic whisperings,

which sound like happy prophecies; and catching the
wild restless spirit of the stirring sea, nothing is then too
wonderful to do, nothing too vast to achieve, no blessing
to the utmost limit of all earthly desire so blissful but
that it may possibly, nay probably, be ours.

How it was that under the entrancing influence Paul
yet spoke not out the inspired language of his soul, he
could not tell. Perhaps he feared to break the spell, or
else some subtle feeling restrained the words fluttering
on his tongue. Anyhow Paul went home in happy
dreamland; and then soon after his return came the
trouble at Elmsbridge. Mrs. Grattan spoke to him, and
Paul to her made no secret of the details; but even then
Sydney's surmises were correct—the first chill of a
shadow came creeping up into his life. Then after
Thomas' prolonged absence, when people said hard
things—people who, not knowing the true statements of
the case, gave out exaggerated false ones—then Paul for
the first time fully realized the gulf that opened between
him and his soul's desires. Not that Mrs. Grattan in so
many words said that she gave credence to the rumours,
she was too kind and true a gentlewoman for that; but
her silence, and the very expression of her countenance,
betrayed her sentiments. And Paul felt as though a
chill hand was suddenly laid upon the fervour of his
soul; and the gulf was destined to grow wider. Towards the end of the summer another rumour arose—
Eleanore Grattan had become a grand heiress. From a
distant relative with whom she had had but little connection, she had inherited an immense fortune. Paul
heard of it, and a sickening kind of fear crept over his
heart. Then the time came when he knew the truth

fully: Mrs. Grattan spoke to him about it herself, and Paul did what would have been expected of any other intimate friend, congratulated Eleanore upon her good fortune. But the congratulation was in words only; his tone and manner were full of conscious, icy restraint. Had it only been Kitty Chignall—pretty, merry Kitty—how warmly would Paul have expressed the pleasure he would really have felt; but now he only said, very quietly, without the least shade of demonstration,

"Mrs. Grattan has been speaking to me of your late good fortune, Eleanore: I wish you with it every happiness."

Eleanore looked at him, her brow slightly contracted.

"Thank you," she said; and Paul sat quietly down again, as though he thought he had done all that could possibly be required of him. Whether she was most mystified or pained by his manner, Eleanore could not tell.

Thus the time went on, and the summer passed away. It seemed a long summer to Paul; not that he was spending it in that idleness which, more than any kind of work, makes the hours lag along. A gentleman in the neighbourhood had requested as a favour that Paul would allow his son, who through delicacy of health was detained from school, to study and read with him a few hours daily. Paul gladly consented, and then other results followed, and Paul had other pupils; and so every day brought with it its own interests and duties, duties that must of necessity be performed, but which were neither heavy nor irksome. Then Paul spent his spare hours in much thought and study, reading many books that a more active life would not have found leisure to peruse. Still there are some people, who if they have once decided on a fixed and definite course, seem to feel that all time is as good as lost, however well or nobly it may be spent, that is apart from the career they desire to pursue. So Paul yearned after his old hopes and desires; and soon after that evening, when he formally offered Eleanore his congratulations, his expectations seemed about to be realized, in the shape of a curacy in a small seaport town in the south of England. Paul was considerably stronger, and more than a year had elapsed since he made that first attempt which had ended in such unmitigated failure. Dr. Miller put in his opinion.

"I know Rixham," he said, "it would be just the place for you."

So the thing was soon settled, and then when it was all fully decided, there arose in Paul's path, what comes in the path of many men and women—duty inexorable, inflexible. Many are no strangers to duty thus sternly arrayed, duty which requires entire self-abnegation, utter renunciation of some most cherished hope or desire; only some people, when duty thus presents itself, make a show of acknowledging it, shake hands with it, grin piteously at it, and are all the while effectually wriggling their way past it. But Paul had not this power of evasion: in whatever garb the right appeared, it was right still. Perhaps some people in his position would have seen no such unpalatable object as duty just then in their path; but Paul, with his fastidious sense of honour, and as he was a true man, and a proudly sensitive one also, acknowledged the duty before him, and meekly bowed his head to its iron mandate.

A glorious light had been flashing into and illumina-
ting all his life; not suddenly, the light had long been
there, but of late it had broadened and brightened in
splendour—and now it must all be over. The dream
must be ended; the shining light was behind him, only
grey clouds before. Sydney's fears were realized on
one point fully. Whatever Paul had hoped or desired,
he would hope and desire no longer. So again and
again he told himself plainly, though often in vain.
"Time will alter things," said Hope's siren voice; "you
may keep the love alive in your heart, till the proud
time comes when all will acknowledge you fully and in
every way worthy of her." Yes, it might come: Paul
realized the delightful thought; but he had no right to
dwell upon that now; as things were, there seemed only
one course—to banish all the fond hopes and lingering
dreams out of his heart, without any thought whatever of
the future lying beyond.

So close upon the time of his leaving Clansford, he
went to bid Mrs. Grattan and Eleanore good-bye. It
was a curious meeting, full of restraint it seemed to Paul,
though he was only vaguely conscious that the restrained
moral atmosphere was really owing to himself alone.
But then when a young man chooses to sit in formal
attitude, with compressed lips, pale features, and half-
absent, half-melancholy expression, and carefully speaks
as restrainedly as possible, it is hardly to be expected
that he will draw forth much spontaneous vivacity or
conviviality from the friends thus animated by his
presence. The fact was, Paul was performing his duty,
but performing it with a degree of grimness that was
really unnecessary. Yet as he sat there, kept floating

through his mind memories of happy hours those three had passed together: those two young lives under the friendly shelter of that older but most essentially vigorous life. They had talked freely, pleasantly in those old days, and now the sunlight had all fled; they might have been three old people, all of them with their faces to the shadows, and the light and spring of life far back in the long buried past. But at last the farewell visit was over.

"Shall we see you again soon at Clansford?" asked Mrs. Grattan as he rose to leave.

"I hardly think so. After my long holiday, I shall be sparing about giving myself another. I was forced by circumstances into this," he added with a forlorn attempt at a smile.

He went to Mrs. Grattan first, shook hands with her and bade her good-bye; then going up to Eleanore he quietly bade her good-bye also. Eleanore looked up at him, her passionate, dark blue eyes suddenly full of mute, earnest questioning; but the grey eyes into which she looked revealed nothing, and withdrawing her hand, with lowered eyelids, she quietly bade him good-bye.

Mrs. Grattan sat watching that farewell. The way two people shake hands and take leave of each other, sometimes, to a careful observer, reveals a whole page of their history; and Mrs. Grattan saw something unusual in this farewell, something that perplexed and troubled her. Soon after Paul's departure, she called Eleanore to her.

"Paul does not seem at all himself to-night, Eleanore. Do you know what troubles him?"

"How should I, grandmamma?"

The answer was evasive, and Eleanore's face seemed purposely averted.

"Eleanore," said Mrs. Grattan in lowered tones.

"You have not grieved him in any way—not trifled with him, Eleanore?"

Eleanore's face was still averted, but Mrs. Grattan caught something of its deepening colour; then she looked fully round as she said,

"Grandmamma, did I ever trifle with anyone? And I should not trifle with Paul."

"Still, he seems changed. Tell me, Eleanore, do you know the cause?"

A slight tremor passed through Eleanore's frame; then once more she looked round with her peerless blue eyes full into Mrs. Grattan's face.

"No, grandmamma."

Mrs. Grattan for a moment made no answer, then she laid her hand softly on Eleanore's head as she knelt before her.

"Forgive me, my love; but I am not often mistaken. I had my fancies, Eleanore, I have them still; but his manner puzzled me. He must, I think, be laying that affair of his brother's too keenly to heart."

"I think that is it, grandmamma."

Eleanore spoke coldly, as though it had been some one they had been discussing in whom she had little or no interest. She would have risen, but Mrs. Grattan suddenly laid both hands upon her shoulders.

"Eleanore," she said, "my own good Eleanore, my very good child all these many years, you must not now look cold and hard with a pain your grandmother must not share."

Again for a moment Eleanore averted her face; there was one quick, irrepressible sob, then she rose to her feet. There were tears on her dark eyelashes, but a smile on her lips, as she stooped and kissed the face that had been everything to her all her life.

"I have you, grandmamma, dear. We have always been so happy together, we will be so still."

Then she went silently from the room, and though between those two that one subject was never renewed, there was henceforth perfect comprehension and understanding between them. Eleanore went out of the house into the still, quiet garden. It was September, and the last shades of evening fell quietly on all around. Past the soft even lawn, on through the darker shubberies she went, to the gate leading to the road down which Paul had just passed.

Meanwhile Paul, as he walked along, had become full of miserable reflections. Have you ever parted from dear friends, and afterwards blamed yourself for the prosaic way in which thoughtlessly you parted from them? Loving words and thoughts spring to your lips, and you long to hurry back, if possible, by a more demonstrative manner to make some atonement for your coolness. All this and much more Paul endured. He had done just what he had told himself he ought to do, he had acquitted himself admirably; yet his soul was full of self-reproaches. He had parted from two kind, good friends, coldly, formally, without one word expressive of a sense of their kindliness. To Mrs. Grattan surely something was due. From her first acquaintance with him, till now, she had been his constant unvarying friend. How keenly he remembered it all: when she first came to Clansford, she had walked up to his house seeking his company; and all through these years those two had been his very dear and faithful friends; and now because in his own mind he had raised a separating barrier, he must treat them icily, coldly, restrainedly,—and why? why should he? He had settled that question for himself; but Eleanore—she must think him altered, strange, and as a friend, nothing more, be grieved and hurt by it.

Then Paul found himself wafting off into fond memories of beaming smiles and happy glances, of a something that had seemed more than this very common-place friendship; and then a wild wish took possession of his soul. Why had he not, in that last blissful spring, why had he not spoken then? He would have known then—and oh! the delight that memory might have been. Ah, it might have been! it might have been! It had been in his power to speak, and he had kept silence; now it was past recall, but it might have been! It might have been! Paul did not realize the full temptation of the words—it might have been. Life is full of them; they are the ringing knell of many lives, and yet there is only one way—to do as Paul did. He battled furiously with the rebellious thought, then laid it down at rest for ever, on the bosom of the Omnipotent love that had led and guided him all his life. But for this one faithful resting place, surely at times we should go mad with the anguish of the cry—It might have been.

Then Paul came back to the other thought: he had exceeded himself, he had not done justice to old kind-nesses; and hardly knowing the exact thing he meant to do, he retraced his steps towards Mrs. Grattan's.

Just before coming to the house was a bend in the road, and Paul, walking slowly round this corner, suddenly looked up, and saw a still figure leaning with folded arms over the gate leading into the road : some one with pale face and downcast eyes ; then, as Paul looked, she raised her head. Each saw the other ; there was nothing for Paul but to advance.

"Are you coming back for anything?" said Eleanore, half pushing open the gate as she spoke.

"Yes, I was coming back again to speak to Mrs. Grattan, to say I am afraid I never thanked her, nor you either, for all your kindness and friendliness through all these years. Will you tell her this, and thank her for me?"

Eleanore's face was pale, as, hardly raising her eyes, she said,

"Would you like to see her again yourself?"

"No, I will not disturb her by going in again, if you will kindly tell her this for me." Then there was silence, till Paul, extending one hand over the gate, said, "Good-bye again, Eleanore."

What was it in the tone—the words were nothing—or was it her own quick, sensitive, passionate nature that made her do it, Eleanore could not have told ; but suddenly she took his hand in both of hers, and raising her gleaming eyes straight to his face,

"Good-bye, Paul," she said; "may you be always happy—always very happy!"

Then swiftly as a flash of light she turned from him, and sped quickly back through the garden paths, in the fast waning light, leaving Paul standing gazing after her like a man in a dream. Well was it for him she turned

S

and fled : that one clasp of Eleanore's hand had undone it all. Duty might be trumpeting her awful voice in his very ear, pointing before his eyes with her stern, inexorable hand, he would neither have heard nor seen her; another moment and he must have spoken, though it had been to his life-long shame and reproach. He must, he would have told her all, and then—but no, she was gone, he knew she would not return again ; but that one act had told volumes ; and whether he was most pleased or tormented during his homeward walk, it would be difficult to say.

Paul met Eleanore no more before leaving Clansford. It was an altered home he left : on Mr. Porter's face were new furrows and harder lines, and he had the appearance of a man perplexed and troubled in mind; and Mrs. Porter had that look of habitual mourning, which most surely breaks the sorrowing heart. Her favourite son was gone, and whither? In vain she appealed to her husband as to Thomas' probable fate.

"Where you find one of them, there you'll find the other," he said. "That's my opinion, he and Philip are together; I've told you so before."

At that she only said mournfully,

"It is hard, very hard; I am his mother. He was my favourite son, and I may never see him again; my own child—it is hard, very hard."

CHAPTER XVII.

PHILIP CARTER'S FORTUNES.

SYDNEY had at last come to a settled conviction that Philip had really gone abroad to his cousin, and that the last letter had only been as a blind. So settled this conviction became, that he had determined himself to follow him, when to his utter surprise, the man he was seeking suddenly reappeared at his old home at Clansford. Immediately Sydney altered his plans. All thoughts of openly denouncing or proceeding against Philip had been laid aside: there had never in reality seemed sufficient grounds for such a course, but Sydney's mind and purposes were as firm as ever. His one idea was to track Philip's course, to watch his companions and pursuits, and so to yet find a clue to the mystery that had clouded and darkened his life. He seemed nearer that point than ever. He had those he could depend upon who would warn him of Philip's departure from Clansford, then his own course was clear—to track and follow him. From this purpose Sydney never swerved.

Meanwhile at Clansford Philip was pursuing his fortunes rather under difficulties. Except from his widowed mother, he really met with no welcome at all. Whether

Blanche received him with most seeming dread or aversion, it would have been hard to say. Very quietly he told his tale: he had written home a little while after leaving, and receiving no reply had concluded that they did not care to hear about him, and had resolved to keep silence till they should relent. He had been working for an honest livelihood, and hearing one day of his father's death had at once returned. This and much more he poured into Mr. Thomas Porter's ears; that gentleman only looked grimly sceptical: Blanche's face grew very white and contracted as she listened.

One day, Philip going to the Grove, at the door of the house met two ladies coming out; their pony carriage was standing waiting for them there. Philip recognised Eleanore and Mrs. Grattan, and stepped forward to assist them in entering the carriage; as he did so, his eyes rested on Eleanore's face with undisguised surprise and admiration. He had never known her intimately, of late years had seen a mere nothing of her, and he now for the first time became conscious that she had developed into a singularly graceful and beautiful woman. Going indoors, he stood dreamily watching the carriage as it rolled away.

"And that is Eleanore Grattan," he said slowly.

"Yes," said Blanche.

"Do they often come here to see you?"

"Not very often."

Blanche spoke truly: very seldom indeed, and then in the most formal manner was she visited by Mrs. Grattan or Eleanore. The reason of their call that day had been a charitable object for which Eleanore had undertaken to collect.

"She has grown really beautiful!" said Philip again. "She has lately come in for a large fortune, I heard the other day. Is that true, Blanche?"

"I believe so; but Eleanore Grattan is nothing to you, and never will be, Philip."

Philip scowled darkly at her.

"How do you know that? What do you mean?" he asked fiercely.

"Hush!" said Blanche, as looking up she saw her husband crossing the hall, and her face settled down into its usual impenetrable expression.

A few days later Philip again saw Eleanore; she passed him in Clansford street, walking quite close to where he was standing. She did not appear to notice him. Philip was doubtful whether she would have acknowledged him had she observed him, and the feeling stung and troubled him. He was well aware that he dare not venture on an acquaintance with either her or Mrs. Grattan. He felt Blanche had spoken truly. Eleanore Grattan was nothing to him, surely. And yet a little later it seemed as if circumstances were going to be specially kind, in giving him one of those rare chances that hardly come once in a whole lifetime.

When Eleanore as a child had stayed with Kitty Chignall, the two had taken long country rides together on horseback, and Eleanore had promised to become an excellent horsewoman. Mrs. Grattan had not altogether encouraged her in this; still she saw nothing against Eleanore occasionally riding about Clansford, and thus Eleanore had in a measure kept up the old custom. So one afternoon Mrs. Grattan particularly wanting to send a message to Mrs. Blake, who

lived about two miles distant, Eleanore proposed riding
over with the message herself.

"If you like, dear," said Mrs. Grattan; "if you think
Peggy is quite safe."

"I am not afraid, grandmamma. We have had her
now nearly a year, and I have seen nothing wrong in her
yet."

"It is a safe piece of road, certainly," said Mrs.
Grattan, and offered no further opposition.

Eleanore reached Mrs. Blake's safely, and was within
half a mile of home, riding along at a brisk canter,
when suddenly up a side road came several huntsmen, attended by a pack of hounds. Had Eleanore
been a minute or two earlier or later, she might have
escaped the danger; as it was, the dogs ran suddenly
across the road, almost under her pony's feet. Peggy
seemed instantly imbued with extreme excitement and
terror. Eleanore did her best to control her in vain; a
few minutes later Peggy and her mistress were going
down the road at a headlong rate. Eleanore had
known what quick riding meant; she and Kitty had run
races together in the old days, but never before had she
felt so rapid a movement as this. Two huntsmen reined
up their horses, and looked after her. A little further
down, the road curved round a corner, and just beyond
was a steep, precipitous hill. Would the pony attempt
the descent at that flying pace? The men looked at
each other: to follow her was useless. Then the younger
of the two leaped quickly over the low fence, and rode
swiftly across the field in the direction of the hill. If he
could reach the brow of the hill first, he could save her.
Eleanore was conscious of her danger. At the corner

she passed some one, who, looking up, made a futile effort to stop her. Eleanore scarcely saw his face, most certainly did not recognize him; but Philip Carter saw and recognized her, and the danger to which she was speeding.

The huntsman, true to his purpose, reached the hill first; as he descended into the road, Eleanore was but a few paces distant. He was just in time then, but it seemed as though he only saved her from one danger to precipitate her into another more terrible still. On the right-hand side of the road was a piece of waste land, and at the edge of that a low fence, beneath which, on the other side, lay a low, deep piece of water. Anyone sinking to its muddy, miry bottom would have but poor chance of escape.

At sight of the huntsman the pony slackened, stopped, then instantly swerving round, darted across the piece of waste land at full speed. Eleanore knew what lay beyond the fence, and the huntsman knew. Philip Carter, who had hurried up with dim hopes of succour, knew also. Eleanore felt a kind of dizzy terror creep over her; almost unconsciously she sought to liberate herself from the saddle. Had Peggy gone straight across the piece of ground, help might have been vain; but taking a slanting direction, the man coming up the road had a bare chance of reaching the fence before her. Would he reach it? The huntsman held his breath as he looked. Yes, just as the pony gained the dangerous spot, and was evidently prepared to take the fatal leap, Philip laid a firm hand upon its bridle. So sudden was the act that he forced the pony back upon its haunches; but in that moment Eleanore slipped quietly from the saddle to the ground. Half numb with terror she saw Philip using all his strength to hold and quiet the fractious Peggy. Then the voice of the huntsman said in her ear,

"I rode across the field to stop you going down the hill, but this gentleman "—looking at Philip—"has saved you from something worse than that."

With a shudder Eleanore realized her full danger, and at the moment recognized the man who had thus opportunely saved her. Then seeing that Peggy had become quiet, and consented to stand still, and that he could be of no further assistance, once more congratulating Eleanore upon her escape, the young huntsman re-mounted his horse and rode away to rejoin his companions.

"You will not attempt to get on this animal again?" said Philip. "You must allow me to lead it safely home for you."

Eleanore did not quite know how she thanked him: people do not always know what they say under such circumstances; but Philip felt that for once fortune had been most exceedingly kind to him.

What could Mrs. Grattan do but thank him? Had it been a highwayman who had thus saved her child, she would have expressed herself warmly grateful to him. And when Philip dared to come again and yet again, at first with ostensible enquiries after Eleanore's health, what could either of them do but receive him hospitably and civilly?

To Philip these visits were full of a new and growing fascination. Had anyone suggested to him the idea of falling in love, he would have laughed in his face; he had had too many passages of that kind in his life, he would have told you. Truly he had played out pretty little scenes with women, who had about as much heart to lose as he had himself, and whose sensibilities were as blunt as his own; but to be in the intimate society of a refined and noble-minded woman, was a new experience to him. For the first time his dark, sinister soul felt a vague craving after something higher, purer, nobler than himself. Every turn of Eleanore's stately head, the changeful light of her dark blue eyes, haunted him afterwards, as visions of beauty will sometimes flash upon and illumine the most depraved minds. The fascination grew and fashioned itself into a daring purpose; and Eleanore was one day startled and utterly surprised by a letter from Philip, asking her to be his wife. It was a letter adorned with that special attempt at saintliness, with which hypocritical sinners are at times wont to gloss over and round their sentences.

Eleanore was grieved and astonished. Three words only told all the expression of her soul. "How dare he?" she said, and her eyes gleamed with sudden indignation. But the letter, such as it was, must be answered; and Eleanore's reply, in its primitive formality, might have emanated from Mrs. Grattan herself. Therefore, perhaps Philip was to be pardoned when, with a vanity sometimes peculiar to the circumstances, he persuaded himself into the belief, that that lady had had more than her due share in the proceedings. In a few words, that Eleanore had been influenced and advised. If he could only see Eleanore apart from that old wrinkled duenna, he told himself—and the chance came sooner than he expected.

Not far from Mrs. Grattan's was a thick wood, through

which was a walk, that in summer was exceedingly pleasant, under the green swaying branches. Through this wood, even in winter, Blanche, who when she went out seemed especially to desire to see no human face, often took her solitary way. Eleanore one afternoon soon after that letter to Philip, walked through this wood to visit an old woman who lived on the opposite side of it. Coming home, she had reached the centre of the wood, when hearing footsteps evidently coming swiftly after her, she turned and came face to face with Philip Carter. He came up and spoke to her, and then walked on by her side. Did he mean to accompany her? She was asking herself this, and how she could best escape from him, when he said,

" I have been wanting to speak to you, Miss Grattan. I wrote to you a few days ago."

" Yes ; I answered the letter."

" I know you did, but that did not satisfy me. I have been wanting to speak to you ever since, to plead my own cause in person. Sometimes ladies in writing such letters are apt to be a little influenced or advised."

" I have been neither. I wrote what I felt. If you refer to Mrs. Grattan, she saw the letter, as she has seen almost every letter I have written from childhood ; but she neither influenced nor advised me."

There was an ominous flash of Eleanore's eyes from under their dark eyelashes, that ought to have given Philip warning, but he was in no mind to be warned. Thinking Eleanore looked as though she intended to pass him, he planted himself full in her path. Eleanore saw then that there was no evading him, that nothing remained for her but to stop and hear him out.

"No, I did not mean that exactly," he said; "but I want you to listen to me,—to believe me when I tell you how much and sincerely I care for you, Eleanore."

"Miss Grattan, please."

Philip drove his heel down firmly into the loose, loamy soil.

"Miss Grattan," he said, "I want you to believe me. I still fear you have been in some way prejudiced—have heard things against me."

"What are you afraid I should have heard?"

"Nothing—not anything—I mean there is really nothing to hear; but there are few men but have enemies, and I have some just now who are saying things not altogether neighbourly; perhaps you may have heard of them."

"Look me in the face, and tell me those things are not true."

"Miss Grattan, you surprise and distress me."

"If you were my brother, or most intimate friend, I should say the same."

Philip tried to do as she asked, but it requires a high degree of consummate art to be able to look in an honest face and deliberately speak a lie. Philip's eyes were full of a perverted expression, and his features grew white and distorted. He looked something like Blanche did that morning when persistently questioned about the begging letter.

"No," he said, "they are not true." Then gathering strength from the assertion, he added, "No, I may have been a little wild and heedless, like a good many; but my hands on the whole are as clean as other people's. I know there are some who delight to injure me;

some who even say I am a party to the absence of
Thomas Porter, and that I know where he is."

"Do you know where he is?"

"No, I do not."

He looked her full in the face as he spoke, and
Eleanore noticing the difference of look and expression,
instinctively felt that he told her the truth.

"Now, Miss Grattan, are you satisfied? Now will
you hear me? I do not wish to refer to it, but do you
think I would have done what I did the other day for
just any one?"

Something very like a smile parted Eleanore's lips.

"No, I do not think you would have done it for just
any one."

Again Philip ground his heel into the earth.

"You do not quite understand me. Of course I would
have done my best to save any human being, but I
would have risked my own life to save yours. Miss
Grattan, I have proffered to you my love, and you treat
me with aversion and scorn, as though I were a scoundrel
or a dog."

A faint shade of something like compassion stole up
into Eleanore's face, and softened for a moment the
gleaming light of her eyes.

"Why do you persist in this?" she said. "I have
nothing more to say to you; nothing different to what
I said in my letter. Let me come past you, please."

The shadow was still in her eyes: Philip caught at
the stray expression.

"No," he said, "you shall not come past me till you
have heard all I have to say, and till you speak otherwise to me."

The soft light faded from Eleanore's eyes.

"How dare you thus force your presence upon me?"

"How dare I! I heard that Miss Grattan had of late become very rich and very proud."

"I am not proud of my riches, they are the last things on earth I should be proud of; but every honourable woman, though she be the poorest girl in all England, has a right to say to a dissolute, dissipated man, who proffers to her his love, 'How dare you!' You surely do not wish me to say more!"

She would have stepped past him, but with a dark frown on his face, he suddenly laid an iron grasp upon her arm.

"No," he said, "I am stronger than you; and I tell you, you shall not leave me thus, not till you can speak to me differently to this."

Eleanore looked at him, her fearless blue eyes flashed and blazed upon him, and under the power of her gaze, unconsciously he loosened his hold. By a slight movement she freed herself, and then looking him full in the face, she said,

"Mr. Carter, hear me once and for all. You saved me from a horrible death, I don't deny it: because of that we tolerated you, and you presumed upon our kindness; but I tell you, I would rather now be lying down in that deep, miry, muddy pool, where my friends should never find me—never look upon my face again—I would rather be lying there, than be your wife."

She turned and walked away from him. Philip stood looking after her, much as he had looked after Sydney that night in Elmsbridge street; looking after her with a dark, passionate face, as she walked away, an unprotected woman in that lonely wood, yet her innate purity and dignity encircling her as with invisible armour; and he, with only his evil passions and his brute strength, dared not, and knew that he dare not, attempt to follow her.

CHAPTER XVIII.

ON THE TRACK.

PHILIP CARTER left Clansford as he had come, suddenly. From Clansford he went to London, leaving behind him one at least at Clansford, who knew he had no settled purposes, no honest calling to which to return, and that certain illicit courses were the only profession to which he had allied himself. And all this Blanche bore in silence; the one great terror of her life being, that disgrace should be, though indirectly, one day through her connections brought upon her husband's name. There was a feeling, half pity, half pride, which made such a thought torture to her. She breathed more freely when Philip had fairly departed.

From London Philip went down to Bath to visit an old acquaintance there. A man got into the same train, and the adjoining carriage to the one Philip entered; that man lodged close to the house where Philip stayed, and secretly tracked his course when abroad. But little good did Sydney reap for his pains; wherever Philip's accomplice might be, he certainly did not appear to be there. Back to London Sydney followed him, and one day, walking along absorbed in his own reflections, he came into sudden and violent contact with a man coming from the opposite direction.

"Bless me!" said a cheery voice, "I haven't got so much breath in my body that I can afford to have it knocked out of me in this fashion."

Sydney looked into the face before him; surely he remembered those merry blue eyes, that open brow, over which the brown hair had still such a persistent inclination to fall in a wavy curl.

"Why," he said, looking intently at him, "it is Chrissie Brown."

"Aye, to be sure, old friend; and you are Sydney Porter. I didn't know you just for a moment, but I recognize you plainly enough now."

He shook hands heartily with Sydney as he spoke, and pressed him to accept an invitation to see him at his own house.

"I have a little nest of my own now. Come and see me in it, will you?"

"I heard you were married," said Sydney. "I will come and see you perhaps some day."

"Come to-morrow; any time you like. The morning will be sure to find me at home, if you won't mind my receiving you in my studio."

Sydney half promised; and the next morning finding himself in the vicinity of Chrissie's house, resolved to do as his friend had desired him. Chrissie was at home, and Sydney, according to orders, was shown at once to him in his studio. Sydney, in a vague kind of way, had always imagined that art was a pursuit that might be followed apart from laborious exertion. The Elmsbridge artist had rather helped to confirm these notions; and

Sydney's own attempts, never having got beyond stray
sketches, vague, half-finished pictures, he concluded that
all art was conducted on the same desultory principles.
But around Chrissie there were on every side very evident tokens of labour and toil. Chrissie himself was
simply immersed in work. He rose and welcomed
Sydney cordially.

"If you don't object," he said, "I have a few finishing
touches just to put here; but you won't interrupt me.
I can work and talk both at once." Then hastily clear-
ing an old lounge chair, that had been made the temporary receptacle of a huge portfolio: "If you don't
mind sitting down here, and can make yourself comfortable, I shall be glad of your company."

Sydney sat down as desired, and looked quietly round.

"You seem busy here," he said.

"Yes, I'm always busy. Getting up the ladder, you
know, you must keep at it; but I'm pushing up pretty
well. I have stuck to this sort of thing, you see, ever
since I was a boy. Would you have recognized me
yesterday if I had simply passed you by?"

"I hardly know; you have not much altered."

"So people tell me." Chrissie looked suddenly at
Sydney; he could not tell him he was not altered, but
wisely kept silence on that point. "I might have known
you," he said, "because I seldom forget an old face.
You left school before I did, but I remember you well.
And that reminds me: I thought the other day I was
going to drop upon another old acquaintance. Two
men were talking in the street close beside me; I felt
certain I recognised the voice of one of them, as a voice
that had once been very familiar; but turning and looking

T

full into his face, I saw a perfect stranger. Not till I got home did I remember whose voice that was."

. "Whose was it?"

. "You remember John Wicks?"

. "Yes, quite well."

"Then you know the very peculiar drawling kind of voice he had; it flashed upon me all at once afterwards, the voice was just like John Wicks'. Not that I should have renewed an acquaintance with him; he and I had more battles than any other boys in the school. Somehow I never could keep my hands off Master Johnny. You weren't there when there was that row about the caricature. He wanted us to lie about it, and say we didn't know where Master Theo was that night. Oh, I remember Mr. Johnny!"

Sydney sat quietly listening, then there was silence. Chrissie was again working diligently, when he became suddenly startled by Sydney standing at his elbow with white, intent face.

"Tell me, who was with this John Wicks?"

"A young man, rather tall and dark, not pleasant looking, with a long grey overcoat on, and a white scarf round his throat."

"Yes, yes; and John Wicks—he was rather dark and tall too. It was, it was he, at last!"

. Chrissie looked half bewildered into his friend's excited countenance.

"But I thought I told you it was not John Wicks. The voice was like his, I said. The man I looked round at was certainly not John Wicks."

. Sydney's countenance fell.

. "What was he like?" he said.

"Oh, he was light, his hair given to be red, and with reddish beard. The voice was like his, that was all."

Sydney returned to his seat, but in vain from that time Chrissie endeavoured to entertain him; he answered in a dull, absent manner, and somewhat suddenly rose to take his leave.

"Come and have an evening with me to-morrow," said Chrissie, kindly.

Sydney shook his head.

"I am afraid to promise," he said.

Chrissie looked intently in his face.

"Things are not going quite right, are they?" he said, kindly. "Could an old friend be of any help, Sydney?"

Chrissie had heard something he thought of troubles, pecuniary he fancied they were, having been connected with Sydney. A friend of the Wilturns had told him so much; also of the sundered engagement. This, as he looked into Sydney's troubled face, prompted the enquiry. Sydney's face slightly flushed.

"No," he said, "you cannot help me." Then he turned and looked eagerly at Chrissie. "Yes, you can," he said: "find me John Wicks."

Chrissie stared.

"My dear fellow, I don't know where he may be any more than you do. He may not even now be in existence."

"I believe he is," said Sydney impressively.

Chrissie felt half inclined to doubt his friend's sanity.

"If he is, and I meet him, I will not fail to let you know," he said kindly, as he bade Sydney good-bye.

All that day Sydney's mind kept constantly going back·

to that one centre—John Wicks. The man to whom Chrissie had seen him talking answered exactly to the description of Philip Carter; and yet why should he suppose that he and John Wicks were connected? and after all it was not John Wicks, only some one who spoke like him. But a vague kind of idea haunted Sydney all day, and coloured his dreams at night. It was still John Wicks. Once he was menacing him, then gibing at him, and then he was back again in the old days at Doctor Edwards', and John Wicks was putting on his head a huge red wig, and just as the boys were shouting with laughter, Doctor Edwards entered. He looked sternly round, and as the boys suppressed their mirth, John Wicks slunk away from Doctor Edwards' gaze. In this state of confused ideas, Sydney awoke.

The next evening, Chrissie Brown was wondering if his friend would avail himself of his invitation, when that friend was in reality placed in a dangerously critical position. Through one of the busy thoroughfares, up one street, down another, walked a man in a long grey overcoat; and behind him, just so as to keep him well in view, came Sydney. On they went. The grey coat vanished round the corner down a quiet street; still Sydney followed. It was a very quiet street, and the man in front walked briskly on; Sydney quickened his pace also. He had reached the middle of the street, which was but poorly lighted, when at its darkest point there came suddenly a stealthy step behind him, and the next moment, over Sydney's unconscious head, an arm was raised that might have for ever ended all his worldly plans and aims, but a very simple event stayed the assassin's arm. Just as the weapon in his hand was about to descend, a door close to him opened, and a woman stepped out into the lonely street. The man's arm swerved, and the blow, intended for his victim's head, came down instead with terrible force on his shoulder. The blow was such as to send Sydney reeling to the ground. The last thing he saw was the grey coat fast speeding on in front. For a moment consciousness failed, and when coming to himself he looked up, a strange woman was wringing her hands over him, and by her screams for help, attracting round her a motley crowd. A tardy policeman was the last to appear on the scene; but the woman could give but little evidence. Just as she opened her door and stepped out into the street, a man struck the gentleman down, right at her feet.

"What sort of a man was he?"

The woman, confused and nervous, could not tell; the street was not very light, but she fancied he looked rather tall.

"Was he dark or light?"

Again she faltered. She thought he was rather light; had rather light hair and beard.

"Would she know him again?"

No, she was certain she should not; and this was all that could be elicited concerning the attack.

If Sydney's assailant intended dealing him a death-blow, he was certainly defeated in his object; but if he thought by a timely stroke to place Sydney, for the time being, *hors de combat*, his plan succeeded admirably; for from the effects of that attack, Sydney lay weak and ill long enough for fifty Philip Carters, and as many accomplices, to have escaped clean out of the kingdom.

Then one day, while lying in a half-dosing, half-delirious state, there came or seemed to come to him a bright vision, a happy dream. All at once he seemed conscious of another presence in that room, of the glimmer of a light dress, the sound of a low, half-tremulous voice, of tearful eyes looking tenderly down upon him, and then a kiss imprinted half-timidly upon his brow, and the vision vanished. Perhaps that kiss broke the spell, or woke up his slumbering faculties. Was he awake or asleep? He lay dreamily debating the matter with himself, then raising his head, he looked anxiously round. If he expected still to see Alice Wilturn watching him, he was doomed to disappointment. The room looked in its usual order, and the nurse his mother had engaged was sitting by his side, looking straight before her, with half-vacant gaze, as though the exterior of her only was awake. As Sydney raised himself to make sure if any other person was present, she turned quickly to him with suddenly awakened expression of countenance :

"Do you want anything, sir?" she asked.

"No, only I thought—Has anyone been in here, nurse?"

"Your mother came up not long ago and looked at you."

There was a shade of reserve in her tone, on her face a glimmer of a smile, that did not escape Sydney.

"I don't mean my mother. Has anyone else been in?"

"Whoever should ha' been, sir?"

Sydney lay back wearily.

"Perhaps I was only dreaming, then," he said sadly.

"Aye, aye; you've been dreaming, sir, no doubt."

Sydney passed his hand to his brow; the action recalled forcibly the last act of that fancied scene. Again he raised his head:

"Nurse, I thought some one came in—a lady with a light dress." The woman did not answer, but began fussily arranging the clothes. "Nurse, tell me; I must know," he said, looking at her with feverishly anxious eyes.

"Aye, well then, I think it was a light dress she had on."

"Then some one has been?"

"Just for a minute or two, some one came up."

"And came close to the bed and looked at me?"

"Yes."

"And stooped and kissed me?"

"Aye, to be sure."

Sydney laid his head back again quietly on his pillow. The weary, distracted look faded away from his face, a smile peaceful as an infant's crept over his lips, and a soft, dreamless sleep soothed and renovated his soul. Twice Mrs. Porter stole to the bedroom door, and the nurse motioned her back; and when later Mrs. Porter expressed to the nurse her regret that she had informed Sydney of Alice's visit, and feared it might agitate him, she replied, by way of vindication,

"He would know, ma'am, and I always makes it a rule not to cross or contradict 'im; and after all, I always do find that for a sick person, there's no medicine half so good as telling 'em something they likes to hear."

Mrs. Porter looked doubtful.

"It was a risk," she said.

"A risk that's doing him no harm, ma'am; he's been sleeping like a baby ever since."

So far the nurse's opinion seemed correct, and Sydney speedily recovered; and by way of thoroughly establishing his health, went down to Rixham to join Paul. The sea breezes, the change of air and scene, and Paul's busy life among his humble friends, seemed to open a new sphere of life to Sydney, and the utter quiet of the place soothed and comforted his spirit. Then a third person joined them. Flashing into their midst like a gleam of sunshine came Chrissie Brown, just for two or three days' relaxation, as he said: but those few days were full of new life. Some people seem born of the shade, others of sunshine; Chrissie was among the latter, and it was impossible to be long in his company without catching some stray beams of illumination. Paul had done his best to cheer and divert Sydney, but these few days of Chrissie's enlivening presence did more towards the desired end, than all the previous visit had done.

Soon after Chrissie left Rixham, it seemed as if fortune was inclined to show kindness to Sydney; for about a week later he received a letter offering to him a situation of considerable pecuniary advantages. Sydney inferred rightly the person to whom the offer was chiefly owing. During his few days' stay, Chrissie had not failed to discover how affairs were, and on his return to town, an opportunity arising, he had used what influence he possessed in his friend's behalf.

Then it seemed as though one of those periods had arrived, in which the past claims to be forgotten. Such periods do sometimes come in life. In this way old family feuds are often suddenly passed over, simply because the people most concerned get weary of them ; and some new page opening in life, they seem willing that the old history should be sealed up and left to perish. So it seemed as if a new start, a fresh epoch, was opening for Sydney, and as though, could he himself have accepted the notion, the past might have been allowed to die away of itself. Something of this Paul vaguely hinted. Sydney replied :

"Yes, it seems one of those things doomed to end in a blank, for which nothing further remains."

"For which nothing remains but faith," said Paul slowly.

Sydney looked quickly at him, but Paul had spoken the words more to himself than to Sydney. They were words, however, that sank deep into the soul that heard them. How much faith, Sydney asked himself, had there been at all in the matter ? There had been obstinate resolve, inflexible determination, but of faith—faith as a quiet confidence in a Power higher than his own, a child-like confiding belief and trust—of all this Sydney felt there had been absolutely nothing. To that holy trust, which is the key-note to the soul's true repose, Sydney felt himself a stranger. The idea took possession of his mind ; he carried it back with him to London, into the midst of new and engrossing duties. It was a simple seed, sown as it seemed by the wayside, yet quietly developing into precious fruit.

CHAPTER XIX.

THE RETURN HOME.

SHORTLY after this, other events occurred at Clansford. Mr. Thomas Porter was taken seriously ill; so ill that all hopes of his life were relinquished. Then, late one afternoon, some one walked quietly back into Clansford; some one to whom all the place was most painfully familiar, but yet who walked almost with timidity up to his father's house and quietly entered.

Mrs. Porter was sitting musing dreamily by the fire, for the afternoon was chilly. She was thinking of her husband's brother lying dangerously ill, then of the absent son, and as though her thoughts were but the advanced shadows of his presence, at the same moment she noticed a step in the hall—not her husband's, but a half-cautious, half-diffident step. Wondering whose step it might be, she rose and threw open the door. Before her stood a young man, with anxious, haggard face, and shabby, much-worn clothes; but at sight of him the mother's heart uttered a glad, sudden cry, and the next moment she threw herself into Thomas' arms. Then she looked at him long and eagerly.

"Oh, Thomas!" she said; "where have you come from? Why didn't you let us know you were coming?"

"I hardly knew it myself, till just before I started."

He tried to speak cheerfully, but the worn, weary look did not escape his mother's notice. She drew him into the room, close by the cheerful fire, and seated herself by him.

"Thomas," she said, "where have you been all this long while?"

"Sometimes at one place, mother; sometimes at another. I did think of going over to America, but I didn't manage it. I have been at Liverpool the last few months."

Thomas sat looking for a few minutes silently into the fire. He could not tell his mother all; that he had been ill, at death's door, destitute, starving, with even his clothes pawned. No, he could not tell her this.

"Why didn't you write to us, Thomas?"

"I hadn't much to write about. I thought I would wait till I could send you good news."

"But what have you been doing all this while?"

"Not very much; I got some sort of situation at last."

He paused; again he did not like to tell the whole truth, that the situation only consisted of common porter to a Liverpool house of business. Mrs. Porter laid her hand on his knee; looking up earnestly at him, she said,

"And you have come back now to keep with us, Thomas?"

"No, mother, I cannot do that. I can never live at or near Clansford again."

"Oh, Thomas!"

"I cannot help it, mother; I am only come back to say good-bye. I could not go away without that."

"Where are you going?"

"To America, if I can anyhow manage it. Some more that I know at Liverpool are going. I shall have better days there, mother, and altogether reform and retrieve myself, and come home with a fortune."

He tried to smile, but Mrs. Porter looked tearfully at him.

"Oh," she said, "to think you have only just come to say this; and you have been away so long and have never written, and people have been saying hard things of you because of it."

A slight colour rose into Thomas' face.

"I thought perhaps they might. I never thought about anything when I first went away, but afterwards it did come into my mind, and I felt it didn't much matter. Better say bad of me than of Sydney. It doesn't much matter what people say of me."

He tried to speak indifferently, but Mrs. Porter, suddenly sinking down by his side, wound her arms round him, and laying her head down on his knees, wept bitterly. The fitful firelight flickered over Thomas' face, every feature of which worked painfully. He had persuaded, or rather hardened, himself into the belief, that he was the good-for-nothing he often styled himself, and as a consequence nothing at all to anyone; but his mother's tears broke the spell. She had never held much power over her children; perhaps in all his former life, she had never exercised over Thomas such powerful influence. Those tears woke up strange thoughts within him.

"Don't, mother," he said hastily, "I'm not worth it; I'm not worth crying over."

"You are worth everything to me," she sobbed.

For a moment a strange mist gathered before Thomas' eyes. Reprobate he might be, but one heart still cherished and clung to him; his mother was weeping over him, then he must be worth something still. Thomas never forgot those tears. Afterwards, in a strange land, in times of temptation, their memory acted on him like a restraining charm.

For a few minutes Mrs. Porter sobbed quietly, and Thomas, whose nature was always open to softening influences, poured out voluble promises of rare amendment in times to come; and his mother listened and wept. She dared not take much comfort from his words, even she could not be blind to the instability of his promises; but after a time she stayed her tears, and sitting by his side, the two talked quietly together,—of Philip Carter, their conviction of his guilt, and the seeming impossibility of bringing it home to him; of Paul, of Sydney—and then in the midst of it, the front door opened and shut with the quick bang with which the master of the house generally closed it, and Mrs. Porter, rising hurriedly, went out into the hall to meet her husband. She had a feeling of dread as to how he might receive Thomas, but at the news of his arrival Mr. Porter looked complacently satisfied.

"It's my opinion," he said, "he has come home just at the right time. Did he know his uncle was ill?"

"No; his coming just at this time was accidental. How is your brother?"

"Bad, very bad; not likely to live through the

night. But I've been down to Elmsbridge, and met with Monson. He wanted, of course, to know about my brother, and when he heard how ill he was, he began asking after our Thomas, if we knew where he was, etc. Then he told me something "—Mr. Porter lowered his tone and bent his head towards his wife—"Thomas has got some kind of interest after all in his uncle's will."

Mrs. Porter clasped her hands with a suppressed joyful exclamation.

"I don't know what," continued Mr. Porter, "and you can't get anything out of a lawyer. If it's much, sometimes they'll make nothing of it; and if it's only a little, they'll make out a great deal: but, anyhow, there's something. Where is Thomas?"

"In there."

Mrs. Porter pointed to the room she had just quitted, a strange throb of joy in her heart, one of those illusionary flashes of hope that only dazzle and beguile. If this was really so, what might not Thomas yet do and become? and for a moment it seemed possible that one of earth's very crooked things might yet be made straight.

Mr. Porter had not exaggerated his brother's danger: the next morning all the blinds at the Grove were closely drawn, and Blanche, in comparatively early womanhood, was a widow.

If Mrs. Carter had been officious about her son-in-law's wedding arrangements, she was equally so about his funeral. The few days following his death found her busily employed arranging matters incidental to such a period. Blanche remained passive, willing that her mother should undertake for her; till, finding that

Mrs. Carter was making arrangements for the day of the funeral on a most ostentatious scale, she stoutly set up her opinion against it.

"Mother," she said, "I cannot have all this show and parade; it is uncalled for, and I do not wish it."

"You leave all to me, Blanche; I know what is proper."

"I wish everything proper, but none of this outside show. I say plainly, I will not have it."

"Well, I never! I should have thought you would have paid the last respect in your power by giving him a noble funeral. He has been a good husband to you, Blanche; you ought not to grudge him the last respect you can show him."

A bright colour rose into Blanche's cheeks.

"Mother, you don't understand," she said; "he himself would not wish it:" and as she spoke, Blanche thought of the still white face upstairs, of the utter dislike he had always shown for all demonstration or show of any kind; and then instinctively of the sort of hollow mockery his last few years must have been to him; and now they would carry the sham even to the grave. How offensive all the pomp and splendour would be to him, could his wishes really be consulted. All this passed swiftly through her mind, but at this point Mrs. Carter broke in upon her meditations:

"How do you know what he would wish? and after all, it isn't so much that, as it's what people will say about it."

"Yes, that's just it." And Blanche spoke with sudden energy: "Haven't they had enough to talk about as it is? Hasn't there been show and sham enough already?

I will have everything good and plain, but there shall be no fuss, no show; I could not bear it. People shall have no more to talk about him one way or the other."

Blanche laid her head down on the sofa cushions, and to her mother's surprise wept more violently than she ever remembered seeing her do all her life before.

"There, there, you are a little over-wrought and over-come," said Mrs. Carter. "Leave things to me; I know best."

Blanche raised her white, quivering face.

"No, mother, in this thing I must have my will," she said.

Mrs. Carter was in the end obliged to yield. The coffin was as she had said, noble—Blanche wished that; but all further attempts of a demonstrative nature were abandoned. Everything was quiet and simple, just as Blanche said, so that people could not talk about it.

The day of the funeral came. When Mrs. Carter for the first time heard of the existence of the codicil, the thought flashed through her mind that Blanche was not altogether wrong in her wish to restrain all outward display. She remonstrated against the idea of Thomas and his father remaining to hear the will read; but upon Mr. Monson giving it as his opinion that it would be most politic and satisfactory for them to do so,—having a blind dread of all lawyers and lawyers' notions—she yielded to his advice.

People assembled together to listen to the last wishes of a deceased person, form not uncommonly singular groups, and the little party gathered together to hear the will of the late Mr. Thomas Porter, proved no exception. Mrs. Carter looked nervously agitated; Mr.

Porter's face betrayed a sudden interest, and a half expectant light shone from his eyes; Blanche cowered down on a low seat behind her mother; and Thomas, with his hands folded quietly on the table before him, seemed the most unconscious and self-possessed of them all. Mr. Monson duly read the will through, which declared everything left absolutely to Blanche; then looking significantly across at Thomas, he read the codicil, whereby the late Mr. Porter bequeathed the sum of two hundred pounds to his nephew Thomas Porter.

Mr. Porter's face suddenly relaxed, the expectant light died away, and a dull, heavy expression crept over it in its stead. Save a slight flush rising for a moment to his face, Thomas showed no sign of pleasure or dissatisfaction. Mr. Monson looked round. Would anyone like to look at the will? Finding no affirmative reply, he folded it together and laying it by his side, placed his elbow upon it. No comments were made, no remarks uttered, and very shortly afterwards Mr. Porter and Thomas took their leave. With the utmost frigidity of manner Mr. Porter bade Blanche and her mother good-night. Thomas walked up to Mrs. Carter and extended his hand.

"Good-night, Mr. Thomas," she said; "I'm sure you feel pleased and honoured by your uncle's kind remembrance of you, under such altered circumstances too."

"Yes, it was very kind of him," said Thomas quietly.

"Ah, I knew you would think so."

Thomas did not answer, he was looking at Blanche, who with white face evidently winced under her mother's words, and clasped her hands tightly as though in actual pain.

U

"I must say good-night and good-bye too," said Thomas, after a moment's pause.

"Are you going away again, then?"

"Yes; I leave home in a day or two, and hope to leave England very shortly. I may not see you for a long time, perhaps never again."

"Oh, dear me! I'm sure I hope so. But good-bye, Mr. Thomas, and I'm sure I wish you well."

Mrs. Carter spoke volubly; she could afford to be gracious. Thomas was a safe friend at a distance.

"Thank you," said Thomas; "good-bye." Then he turned to Blanche: "Good-bye, Blanche," he said.

She put her hand into his, and Thomas felt it tremble. "Good-bye," she said; and he dropped her hand and turned quietly away.

Long after they were gone, Blanche still sat with white, averted face. An illusion seemed taking possession of her. The immediate past vanished or seemed only like a horrible dream, and it was that night again at Clansford, when the man who had just parted from her, had stood with her hand in his, passionately pleading, "It isn't true; say you do not mean it, Blanche."

Vividly it all rose before her, as though the scene had been only that evening enacted; and then slowly crept over her soul the dark shadow of the time lying in between; time, that was no fanciful vision, but a dire, dread reality. With a shudder she realized it all, and yet, as on that other night, from the depth of her soul went up a bitter yearning cry, which even while she uttered it, she felt by a strange intuition was doomed never to be answered—in this world.

CHAPTER XX.

A GRAY LIFE.

AFTER the funeral, Mrs. Carter took up her abode at the Grove with her daughter, and Clansford busied itself with conjectures as to what future course the two ladies would adopt, and how young Mrs. Porter would conduct herself now she had plenty of money all in her own right. But the two lived very quietly, and gave no occasion for remarks of any kind; and then just as the public mind had ceased to wonder any more about them at all, it became suddenly known that Mrs. Carter and her daughter were about to quit the Grove, and leave Clansford altogether. A sale of their household goods speedily followed, and to all inquirers Mrs. Carter gave the ambiguous reply that they were going to travel a little while. Her daughter was a widow certainly, but a young and attractive one, and Clansford was the last place she would ever think of settling in.

Considering that Blanche had passed her life hitherto apparently contentedly in that place, the statement sounded rather inconsistent; however, the two took their departure, and as they had but few intimate friends— none likely to become their correspondents—it seemed probable that from that time they would drop out of the annals of Clansford altogether.

Meanwhile Paul worked on steadily; he seldom came to Clansford, and then only on very short visits. So two more years passed. Never since that night of unsatisfactory parting had he seen Eleanore. But being at home for a day or two, one evening, walking down Clansford street, he passed by the house of a man named George Walsh, one of the factory hands. The man was well known to Paul, as a young man somewhat rough perhaps in his habits, but on the whole quiet and well conducted. Seeing him standing by the house, Paul was about to speak to him and pass on, but something in the utterly dejected, downcast manner of the man attracted his attention.

"I hope you are not any of you ill or in trouble," said Paul kindly, noticing the sorrowful way in which the man responded to his greeting.

"Perhaps you haven't heard, sir," he said slowly.

"I have only been home a day or two. Is it your wife ill?"

"My wife is getting on, sir,—getting on all right, save that she frets so; but it's the baby—we've lost the baby, sir." He paused for a moment, and then continued: "We've been married this three years—perhaps you mayn't remember, but this is our first, and now it is dead—born dead."

The man turned his face away as he spoke.

"I am very sorry," said Paul.

"Aye, sir, there are folks, neighbours too, who say we oughtn't to mind it; and go so far as to say that they wouldn't ha' cared if the like had happened to some of theirs. But they know nothing about it, sir; it's the first, you see, and I do think I could never feel about another as I do about this."

Again Paul expressed his sympathy.

"Would you like to see it, sir?" he said, turning quickly to Paul.

Paul complied with what was evidently a request, and followed the man into the house. A hush and quiet pervaded the whole cottage, so like the quiet of bereavement, that you might have imagined something more serious had happened than the advent of a little still-born baby. The nurse was stirring something over the fire as they entered; she rose with a quiet, subdued air, and went slowly upstairs. As they stood there, Paul distinctly heard a voice speaking from the upper room; a voice that suddenly thrilled through all his being. Only one person spoke in those tones, and that person was Eleanore. Even as he listened, he was aware she was coming down, and the next moment he stood face to face with her. They shook hands quietly as ordinary acquaintances; he asked after Mrs. Grattan, made a few common-place remarks, and then she went away. Paul stood looking wistfully after her. He almost started as George Walsh said, in a low tone,

"You'd like to see it now, sir?"

"Yes, please," said Paul; and the man left him and went upstairs. He was gone several minutes: Paul could hear the murmur of a faint voice speaking to him. At last he came down, bearing in his arms a very tiny coffin.

There were people who said it was absurd of George Walsh to get a coffin for a still-born baby; but some-

thing of the feeling that had prompted Mrs. Carter—
only it was very genuine in this case—to show tribute to
the dead, moved the poor father to procure a coffin for
his little firstborn son, though his eyes had never opened
to the light of this world. He placed the box on the
table before Paul, and turned away. Paul, looking
down, saw a tiny waxen form. The features were very
perfect, soft dark hair lay round the forehead, and the
eyebrows were delicately pencilled. The little face was
peaceful and quiet, as of a baby asleep, only with a certain look that no living baby ever wears. Paul glanced
from the face to a bunch of exquisite hot-house flowers,
lying lightly on the little bosom that had never drawn
living breath. George Walsh came and stood by him;
he was evidently choking back his tears.

"Do you see the flowers, sir?" he said.

"Yes, they are very lovely."

"She brought 'em, sir."

"Who?"

"Miss Grattan, sir. You saw her as she came down;
she had just brought 'em; and oh, sir, those flowers
have comforted my wife—they have! When I went up
just now, she was smiling almost like an infant herself.
'George,' she says, 'look at baby!' I did look at him.
'Who has done this?' I says. 'Oh,' she says, 'George,
Miss Grattan brought 'em; she brought 'em herself to
lay on baby. She sat down and talked so to me, and
then she laid the flowers on baby and kissed him. And
now, George, I feel so comforted. There's somebody as
don't think it's only a lump of clay that never ought to
be cared about. She thought enough about it to bring
the flowers on purpose for it; and now I feel as if I

could leave it all. Baby and the flowers look so happy together—so alike, somehow; I do feel I can leave it now, George.' And, sir, when I came out, she closed her eyes for sleep with a smile, looking more peaceful like than I've seen her look yet."

Paul for a moment did not speak; he felt that the flowers, not for the first time heavenly messengers, had done their work so well : then after a few minutes' kindly talk with George Walsh, he took his leave.

Paul left Clansford again without fortune giving him another meeting with Eleanore. Not long after his return to Rixham, he received a letter from his mother, in which she hinted something concerning Eleanore Grattan. Something that might mean Eleanore about to be married, or might mean but very little; one of those stray sentences people sometimes put in their correspondence, which help to fill up space, but from their vagueness make it difficult to determine how much or how little they mean. Paul puzzled over it in vain.

Shortly afterwards Theodore came to see him on one of his flying visits. Theodore never stayed long ; he had no time for visits, he said. It was a summer afternoon when he arrived. Anyone might have observed a certain restlessness about him, as of a man who has a particular declaration to make, and is uncertain how to begin. The house where Paul lodged stood a little back from the main street ; his sitting room was on the second floor at the back, and the window looked out on one side over the ever changeful sea, and the other to an open country bounded by gently undulating hills. This window was a favourite spot with Paul ; he never seemed to tire of looking at the sea ; and on hot afternoons or leisure hours, his eyes would keep constantly turning from the page before him, to the ocean's broad, open surface, continually chequered by the fleeting lights and shadows from the sky. To judge by Theodore's manner, he also found the window attractive; he stood silently looking out of it so long. He wanted to tell Paul something, and seemed to find it hard work to begin. Not a voluble person at any time, speaking of his own sentiments and feelings—these being just then somewhat new and strange to him—was a fresh experience altogether.

"When did you hear last from home?" he said.

"I heard from mother a week or so ago. Have you been at Clansford lately?"

"Yes, I have been there very often of late."

Had Paul been looking at Theodore, he might have noticed something unusual in his expression; but he was thinking in his own mind, if that was the case, then Theodore might know about the something his mother. mentioned in her letter. Innocently he opened the way for Theodore's avowal.

"Mother hinted at something in her letter that I didn't quite understand," he said; then after a moment's pause—"Have you been to Mrs. Grattan's lately?"

A broad smile broke over Theodore's face.

"Why, yes, of course I have. That's where I go when I am at Clansford. I have been wanting to tell you all about it, but I see mother has put you on the right scent."

Paul stood looking at Theodore with wide open eyes, and a vague fear and dread rising within him. Theodore was too relieved in mind at the way Paul had helped him out with his denouement to notice much his expression.

"Come, old fellow, congratulate away," he said.

"Congratulate you on what?"

"Why, on my engagement, to be sure."

Paul made no reply, he turned abruptly to the window. Far away as eye could see stretched the vast ocean, that had often seemed to him like a companion and friend; now beneath a gray sky, for the day was dull and cloudy, it lay gray, as his own life would be if this hope died wholly out of it. Theodore noticed his changed manner, and the change perplexed and troubled him. In a few moments Paul looked round; save a slight tremor about his mouth, he had regained his composure.

"Yes," he said, "I do congratulate you, Theodore; congratulate you very earnestly. I hope you will be very happy, you and your chosen wife."

Then he walked away to the bookcase, and began busying himself as though searching for some particular volume. Theodore stood looking at him, the half-pleased, half-restless look on his face had died away, and given place to one of undisguised trouble. He divined, or thought he did, the cause of Paul's manner, and it was an afflicting thought to him to find any approach to a rival in his brother. Some would have passed it over, as though failing to notice it; better diplomatists than Theodore might soon be found, but few so given to settle anything and everything openly and straightforwardly. He walked up to where Paul was standing. Laying his hand on his shoulder, he said,

"Paul, are you and I in the same boat?"

Paul laid down the book he had just taken in his hand.

"It cannot be helped if we are," he said ; "only there is this difference—I have never spoken a word of this to her. If mother had written a little plainer, I should have understood."

"I don't think mother really knew. It is only just settled."

"She did not speak positively; she only hinted—but there, we need say no more. Give me a little time, Theodore, and I will congratulate Eleanore as well as you."

"Congratulate Eleanore! What do you mean, Paul?"

"Didn't you just now say you were engaged to her?"

Theodore sprang back a step or two and looked fixedly at Paul.

"Engaged to Eleanore Grattan! Eleanore Grattan!" Then seeing Paul's brow slightly contract at the derogatory tone, he added, "No, no, Paul; I have no thoughts of Miss Grattan. It is Kitty Chignall. Haven't you heard that since her father's death, Kitty has made her home with Mrs. Grattan and Eleanore?"

"I think I did hear something of the kind," said Paul, abstractedly passing his hand over his brow.

"I thought so. Well, it is Miss Kitty who has done the mischief. As for Eleanore, I respect her exceedingly; but I should as soon think of marrying Mrs. Grattan, her grandmother, as marrying her. She is above me ; I don't aspire to her in any way, Paul."

"But it was Eleanore mother mentioned in her letter."

"What did she say?" Theodore asked the question earnestly.

"She hinted that Eleanore was engaged, or about to be engaged to some one. She did not speak plainly."

Theodore turned away with an uneasy expression that did not escape Paul.

"Theodore," he said, "she is not engaged to you; is she to anyone else? Tell me plainly; I would rather know."

"I really *know* but little; people are saying she is engaged, but Kitty even does not know. Eleanore likes keeping her own counsel."

"Who is it?"

"Sir William Harrell's second son. It would not be altogether unsuitable. He seems above her in rank, but he is only the second son, and Sir William is not rich; the Grattans are well descended, and Eleanore has a very large fortune."

"What sort of a man is he?" Paul asked the question with sudden intensity of tone.

"I don't know him. I hear him spoken of as a gentleman, and a worthy man; but if it is true, he may probably cross my path before long."

Just then there was a knock at the door; some one below was waiting to speak to Paul. He looked up with a suddenly startled expression.

"Theodore," he said, "upon all this you will be quiet and still."

"Still and quiet as the grave, Paul."

The subject was not reverted to again between them, and the next day Theodore went away.

That evening Paul walked a long way to see an old parishioner who was sick. Benjamin Watson had been in his time a brave seaman, a vigorous and courageous man; now old and infirm in body, his mind was clear and vigorous still. There was a simplicity of trust about him, a distinctness and positiveness of belief, that was cheering and comforting. He had drifted into that state of health, not uncommon to old age, when it was impossible to say how long his life might yet last; how long the time-enfeebled powers could still endure. Something of this was evident to his own mind, for when Paul enquired that evening especially after his health, he answered,

"Just waiting for a breeze, sir; that's what I am now. The port is right in sight, sir; the sails are all spread ready; only a breeze, sir, and the old ship would waft straight into port."

Benjamin spoke the words with a hearty, earnest tone, and Paul, looking into the old face beaming with honest desire, felt that his words were true and genuine. He smiled as he said,

· "I am not so old as you are, Benjamin; but when I get to port, I should like to hail it just in the same spirit you do."

"Aye, you are a young man, sir, and have most likely got a long voyage yet before you."

"Yes; and you have had your voyage, Benjamin, and have got through all its storms."

"Aye, sir, I have had my storms; it would be a comical thing if I hadn't—so long a voyage and no storms. I've known storms, sir, when the wind and the sea seemed like mad things, and we, poor men, like helpless babies, tossed about at their mercy; and I've known storms here, sir"—laying his hand on his heart—"storms, that threatened worse shipwreck than the

sea ever did; storms that seemed worse than any ever
met by sea or land. Yes, I've known storms, sir, and
I've known calm—calm that has sometimes seemed
worse than storm, when you would have given all the
world to be going, and there you were set fast, becalmed,
the waves just lap, lapping round you, and nothing for
it all, but to wait. Nobody used to ask why it all
was so impatiently as I did, aye, and fret over things
when they weren't to my mind, or so slow, so very slow
coming; but I learned the right way at last: and
now, looking back, I know it is faith we want, sir. I got
it at last: faith to trust our lives to God. Aye, we
always want faith; but there be some things in life
nothing but faith can bring a man through. I know
now, sir, faith makes life easy, death bright, and sends
the old ship in at last with flying colours."

Paul smiled; with that humility of mind peculiar to
him, he was doing what many a genuinely humble
teacher does, learning where he was professedly teaching.
He stayed some time longer with the old man, and then
walked home in the soft summer gloaming, choosing the
way by the seaside. It was one of those intensely still
evenings, that sometimes follow a close, sultry day.
The tide was low, only just turned; not rushing in with
loud noisy billows, but falling in small rippling waves,
creeping almost imperceptibly on. The sea beyond lay
calm almost like a lake. Perhaps in all nature there is
nothing so enlivening as a bold, stirring sea; nothing so
intensely quiet as its calm. Paul felt the utter stillness
oppressive—not a sound or breath broke the surrounding solitude; on one hand the gray lifeless sea, on the
other tall cliffs shutting out all sight or sound of life

beyond. Even the heavens above were dim with misty grayness. Instinctively Paul recalled old Benjamin's words about a sea, a life becalmed ; and then the thought flashed upon him as though by intuition, that was what his life was like now.

Ever since that conversation with Theodore, a cold chill had fallen over his soul. Hitherto, if days were dark, there had always been a rift in the clouds through which a stray beam of sunlight had fallen across his path, despite all his resolutions one happy thought that had kept up a glow of warmth and light within him. Now the clouds had closed together ; the gleam of light was gone. He felt it was so ; he was conscious of the gloom penetrating through every fibre of his being. Had it been some mighty affliction, he would have met it with more strength. Extreme adverses, intense calamities or trials, call forth all our powers of resistance or endurance ; but the chill, invisible touch of disappointment numbs and paralyses the soul. Just like that sea, just like the whole scene before him, seemed his life—gray, a gray life. Not a life without interests, without real solid joy. No life full of earnest effort for others' good, but must even in its own peace reap abundance of reward ; but it was still what he called it—a gray life, and his heart grew weary at the sight of it. Then again came the words, "Nothing but faith, sir. There be some things in life nothing but faith *can* bring a man through." The words seemed full of chiding and reproof. Faith—yes, perhaps Paul did not fully realize how much faith those simply gray lives require ; but he was slowly righting himself, learning a simple yet grand lesson, in that silent walk home. Not that the battle was then fought and over; again and again must turbulent thoughts be resisted and wrestled with, but he had got the right shield, the only shield that can ever be proof against the "fiery darts."

CHAPTER XXI.

PASSING AWAY.

TWO more months passed. In those days Paul laboured with unabating zeal, never suffering himself to be idle, scarcely to rest; but one evening, coming in after a long, wearying round of visits, he threw himself, utterly tired and worn out, upon the couch in his little sitting room. He had not lain there long when the landlady's little daughter tapped at the door.

"Please, sir, there's a man below wants to speak to you."

Paul raised his head wearily.

"Who is it?" he said.

"He didn't give his name, sir. He said he should like to speak to you; but if you were busy or engaged, it did not matter."

A temptation seized Paul: he was so tired, so unfit for anything but rest. Doubtless it was some unnecessary errand, that the man could just as well leave till the morrow. But the hesitation was only momentary; shaking off the slothful feeling, he said,

"I will come and speak to him directly. Where is he?"

"In the hall, sir; I left him just inside the door."

Paul went down, it was getting quite dusk; the long passage the girl designated hall, leading from the foot of the stairs to the front door, was almost dark, but at the farther end Paul could discern the outline of a man standing close against the wall. He walked down to him; then, finding the stranger did not speak,—

"You want to see me, I think," he said.

"Yes."

The voice sounded peculiar. A strange thrill, not exactly of recognition, passed through Paul's mind. The shadow of the half-open door so fell upon the man's figure, that Paul could not see his features distinctly; then he put out one hand and laying it on Paul's arm, opening the door with the other hand, he drew Paul out into the street. It was lighter there. Paul took one look at the face before him—a face haggard, ill, and worn, but recognizable enough to Paul; as he looked at him, he said—

"Thomas!"

"Yes, you're right, Paul. You know me, then?"

"Know you!" Paul looked hastily at the altered face, and did not wonder at the question. "Come in, come in," he said, and hurriedly conducting him down the long narrow hall, he led the way to his own sitting room. The little room was getting almost dark, but Paul, having procured a light, looked anxiously at the form before him. He saw a man dressed in shabby, very shabby clothes, the outline of his figure sharp and angular, every feature of his face drawn and pinched by illness or want. His brown hair fell low over his forehead, his beard looked untrimmed and shaggy, and his eyes scintillated with feverish fire.   X

"There's not much left of me to look at, is there?" he said, sinking wearily into the easy chair Paul placed for him.

"I am afraid you must have been very ill?" said Paul.

"Yes; ill, out of work and out of money, and all the rest of it. They told me there was just a chance if I could get home to England; but a doctor on board said my life was not worth a groat. I have come to you, Paul; I couldn't go to Clansford. After I found out where you lived, I went past this house twice before I could get up my heart to ring. I sent in a doubtful message; I half hoped you wouldn't come to see me, then I should have gone away somewhere, I suppose."

A sudden thrill of gratitude shot through Paul's soul. All his life long was he thankful that he had not yielded to that momentary temptation: had he done so, what might not have been the consequences?

"I am thankful you came," he said; "we will nurse you up, and do everything for you."

The sick man laid his head back wearily.

"I could get well here if anywhere, I fancy," he said. Then seeing Paul busy in preparations for his comfort: "Don't trouble yourself, Paul," he said. "I haven't been used to much of anything; a bit or a shake-down, just as I could get them."

He swallowed some of the refreshment set before him, and then leaning back in his chair, fell into a light doze, and a hectic flush stole up into his thin, sunken cheeks, and the low ominous cough smote upon Paul's heart like a prophetic knell. Seeing Thomas looked very jaded and worn, Paul persuaded him to go early·

to bed; and soon he was sleeping the dreamless sleep of the weary, while Paul kept up a restless vigil far through the soft summer night.

The next day Paul proposed writing to Clansford to his mother. Thomas gave a half-grumbling assent.

"Yes," he said, "write; of course they'll have to know it, but I can't go there, Paul. You understand; if you can't have me here I must go somewhere else, but not to Clansford."

Mr. and Mrs. Porter both came in answer to Paul's letter: both were shocked at the altered appearance of their son. The news from him during his absence had not been satisfactory. At first he had written more frequently; of late, but seldom. He was generally doing middling; always going to do better; but they were hardly prepared to see him quite in the condition in which he had returned at last. In reply to his mother's enquiries he said,

"I couldn't stand it. You see, mother, I had never been used to hard work, and folks must work for a living abroad as well as at home."

"But you had a little money to start with."

"It melted away somehow, I don't know exactly how; two hundred pounds don't go far; and then the work got too hard for me. Then I was ill, and kept getting worse, till at last I came home as my only possible chance."

Mrs. Porter listened with tearful eyes. Mr. Porter at once saw the truth.

"He is a doomed man," he said to his wife afterwards.

Mrs. Porter gave a half-audible sob.

"No, no, I hope not," she said. "We must get a doctor to him at once."

Mr. Porter shook his head. The doctor was sent for accordingly, but he only confirmed the opinion of the doctor Thomas had sailed home with. He was a candid man, given to speak plainly where occasion required. If he did not think it needful to tell all the truth to the sick man himself, he considered it his urgent duty to tell it to his friends.

"It is only a question of time," he said. "I cannot say how long he may live, but I do not think he will see November through. Still he may linger for a time; but it is folly to speak of recovery for a man in the last stages of consumption."

The truth soon became apparent to them all; still there were days when, with that illusionary hopefulness so peculiar to the disease, Thomas would seem to rally, and declare cheerfully that a little more of the fresh sea air, his mother's nursing, and Paul's company, would set him right again yet—words that only smote with a keener pain the hearts that loved him best. But the hopes vanished. Whether he read it directly from the looks and words of those around him, or from that voice within which gives instinctive warning that the time is growing short; when the soul, looking out with suddenly awakened vision, catches distinctly a glimmer of the dark, flowing river, and sights the faint outlines of a strange land lying beyond; certainly Thomas at last accepted the statement, and realized in the depth of his heart, that his life here, such as it was and had been, was speedily drawing to a close. Then with wistful eyes he watched Paul, hardly ever liking him to be absent; and though he spoke but little, he listened intently, his blue eyes full of appealing earnestness. And all the while Paul was thinking, "Oh, if he would only speak!" Till at last he said,

"Thomas, is there anyone you would like to speak to? Would you like Mr. Blake to come? Anyone you would wish to see, I will send for."

Thomas smiled.

"There's no one like you, Paul: I don't want anyone else," he said.

So the days passed by, and then perceptibly to all a change came over Thomas; the restless manner changed to calm, and a peace settled over him,—peace, quiet as the slumbers of a child. Very like a child Thomas seemed in those days. The self-seeking spirit, the waywardness, all seemed to have died away, while the natural sweetness of disposition revived, and he became humble, tractable as a little child. He spoke of his past now more freely; spoke of it quietly, penitently. Once he mentioned Blanche. Some allusion being made to the Carters, he asked what had become of Mrs. Carter and Blanche; but being told that they had left Clansford, and nothing further had been heard of them, he said no more on the subject.

Still Paul hungered for something more than this. He wanted the torn, disabled bark to be like Benjamin Watson, to go into harbour like a noble ship that had done valiant service, the torn sails all mended, and bright colours flying. Something of this Thomas gathered from him.

"Paul," he said, "I die humble, very, very penitent; but it is not for such as I have been to be full of joy and victory. I *can* believe," he added, with a suddenly brightening smile, "but it is not for me to triumph and rejoice."

Paul in his heart could not but admit the justice of this; still one prayerful hope remained—oh that the poor bark might yet drift into the haven on still waters at last!

Then they came to see him. All of them came; Oliver, and Susie, with her gentle, matronly ways, bringing with them their eldest son, a bright, joyous-hearted school boy; Sydney came, Theodore came, all of them feeling it was less a visit than a farewell.

The September, the mellow September days passed away, and October, with its bright, clear sunshine, and its richly-tinted woods, made the whole land full of gorgeous beauty; and then, when October was nearly over, the end came, peaceful, quiet, as Paul had prayed and desired. Thomas had then become very weak, so weak as to be unable to leave his bed, save for an hour or two daily; and the last week he had been weaker, worse than ever, and Mrs. Porter had kept in constant attendance upon him. Then came that last rallying, so often a sure prophecy of the rapidly-approaching end. Deluded by the apparent betterness, Mr. Porter, who had been summoned when he seemed so much worse, departed for Clansford, business affairs being pressing; and Mrs. Porter being worn out with nursing, Mrs. Gibbons, the landlady, who had done no inconsiderable share of service in the sick room, persuaded her to leave him.

"Most likely, ma'am," she said, "he will have a good night, so do you go to bed and try and get a little rest. You want it badly enough, I'm sure."

Mrs. Porter yielded, and Paul and Mrs. Gibbons watched that night by Thomas' side. He lay asleep, his lips half-parted by a happy smile. About the middle of the night he woke, and Paul, bending over him, caught the one word, "Pray." Paul knelt down by his bedside—it was the last prayer those two would ever pray together on earth. The lips of the sick man moved visibly, till when in conclusion Paul uttered the prayer so familiar yet so dear in life or death, at the words, "Forgive us our trespasses, as we forgive them that trespass against us," he said the words audibly after him. Then he lay back with closed eyes. In a few minutes he opened them, and looked earnestly at Paul. Paul bent over him, but the words were distinctly spoken,—

"If ever you see Blanche again, give her my dying love, and tell her I forgave her wholly."

It was a dying request, but Paul instinctively hesitated. Earnestly Thomas looked at him: "Promise me, Paul," he said; and Paul hesitated no longer.

"I do promise you," he said.

Then again Thomas slept, and even in that last peaceful sleep, came the final mysterious change. Paul had seen deathbeds before; he recognized the look; and Mrs. Gibbons took one glance, and laid her finger hurriedly on her lips. Going softly round to Paul, "I must call his mother," she said; but before his mother came, once Thomas opened his eyes and looked straight at Paul; a look that said more than words could ever utter: the look of the soul whose wings are fluttering their last against its prison bars: a look full of mysteries that could not be spoken; yet, as Paul afterwards thankfully remembered, a look pre-eminently full of love and peace and joy. Then the tired eyelids closed softly, never again to open in this life. He lay still, breathing faintly, peacefully, as Mrs. Gibbons and his mother entered. She bent eagerly over him:

"Speak to me; speak to me once more," she wailed.

"Hush! he seems sleeping," said Mrs. Gibbons, not knowing how best to comfort her.

Yes, sleeping a sleep, every breath of which was wafting the shattered bark nearer the desired haven. They watched him silently awhile; then over his face passed a strange, mysterious smile. Once more Mrs. Porter wailed out, "Oh, my child, speak to me; my child, my child!" But he heard her not. He had already passed the boundary line where earth's voices failed to reach him: his feet already touched the chill waters of the cold stream, and the first gleaming of eternity lay on his brow. Paul's last petition was abundantly answered— without a struggle, with only a passing sigh, even as they watched him, the spirit took its flight.

Morning broke fresh and glorious, and the fishermen passed out to their daily toil, but a tender, reverent hush pervaded their manner. The news had got afloat, and with sympathy in their hearts, they pointed towards the house whose blinds were drawn. "His brother is dead," they said, "died in the early morning;" and tears stood in their eyes; not tears for the dead man—of him they knew but little—but tears of loving sympathy for him who, in their own troubles, had come to them as a brother and friend.

CHAPTER XXII.

PAUL'S NEW FRIEND.

THEY buried Thomas at Clansford, and there were the usual condolences of friends, and then people went on their own way again, and the autumn passed away and winter followed. But as light and shade for ever chase one another in life's pathway, the next event that seemed likely to happen was Theodore's wedding. The time fixed for it was the middle of June. Spring had already set in bright and warm, and one very sunny day in the early part of May, a curious little procession was making its way up the street where Paul lodged, in the direction of his lodgings. Three or four stalwart men were supporting among them the body of an elderly man whom they had found lying at the farther end of the street, apparently in a fainting fit. They had managed to raise him up, when the discussion arose where they had better carry him. The doctor did not reside in the village; his house was fully two miles away. There were only two hired rooms, with "Doctor Marshall's surgery" written over them, where for two hours daily his assistant dispensed medical advice, etc., to the villagers: but the consulting hours for that day were over, and the men hesitated where to deposit their helpless burden. Then by common consent they agreed to take him to Paul.

"Aye, let's take him there. He'll know if anybody does what had best be done for him."

They had got close to Paul's door, when the sick man groaned slightly and opened his eyes.

"He be coming to hisself," said one of the men, looking down upon the sufferer, who, giving another loud groan, looked round at the strange faces peering into his. He raised himself slightly :—

"Let me down, can you?" he said.

The men obeyed, lowering him as gently as possible. The stranger looked curiously from one to the other.

"Where are you taking me?" he asked.

"To the parson's—at least, to our curate here, Mr. Porter."

"My good fellows, what I most want, I fear, is a doctor."

"There ain't no doctor within two miles; but here comes Mr. Porter hisself."

Paul just coming out of his lodgings, walked towards the group. Bowing courteously to the stranger, he inquired what was amiss.

"We was a-bringing him to you, sir," said one of the men; "we found him down at the bottom of the street, on the ground, as if he had fallen down in a fit. He is come to now a bit, and seems hurt somehow."

"I shall be very happy to do anything I can for you," said Paul.

"Thank you," said the old gentleman, his keen, dark eyes looking searchingly into Paul's face. "I believe you are the gentleman they were bringing me to? I will tell you about myself if I can, but I am in great pain. I had a bad fall down on the beach, and managed to get up as far as the street, when the pain got too much for me, and I suppose I fainted. As I tell these good men, it is a doctor I want. Is there any hotel or inn?"

"Yes, there's the 'Anchor' and the 'Black Boy,'" said one of the men. "The 'Anchor' is the best; the landlord is a bit of a rough 'un, but you'd be all right there."

A despairing look crept over the stranger's face.

"I am afraid that won't do," said Paul. "My rooms are close at hand; will you come in there till we can see what can be done?"

"You be a stranger, I reckon. No one you're stopping with about here?"

"No, I am quite a stranger." Then, despite his pain, a half-comical look crossed his face. "I suppose I must let them take me to your place, after all," he said, glancing at Paul.

Accordingly, by the help of the men, he was assisted up into Paul's sitting-room, and a messenger despatched for the doctor. He arrived quicker than might have been expected, the messenger having met with him at a house just outside the village. He soon pronounced his opinion. One of the stranger's knees had received a severe injury, for which the one great remedy was perfect rest.

"But I must get back to London to-night."

"It would be a very rash thing to do," said Doctor Marshall. "Any degree of attempting to use that leg, even jarring it violently, might bring on most serious consequences. Cannot you telegraph to your friends?"

"Oh, for the matter of that, I have no friends to alarm themselves. A lonely man has that advantage, doctor."

"Certainly, certainly. Then suppose you stay somewhere here just till you can get the better of it a little. Has Mrs. Gibbons any other rooms to let?" he asked, turning to Paul. Mrs. Gibbons was just then passing the sitting-room door. "Here, Mrs. Gibbons, could you give this gentleman a bed for a night or two?"

Mrs. Gibbons looked perturbed. She passed her hand to her cap, and from her cap to her apron, both signals of inward perplexity. Finally she beckoned Paul from the room.

"If I might ask you, sir, what had I better do? I've got other rooms, you know; but this very morning I had a letter from Mrs. Williams, the lady who comes down with her two little boys every summer. You remember her, sir; she came a month last summer. Well, you see, of course I must take her in. I shall give up my own room as 'tis; there's one more coming this year, so if I take the gentleman in he must turn out in a day or two's time. What must I do, sir? I am willing to do what I can, as anyone would be."

"I don't know," said Paul. "No one could make him so comfortable as you, Mrs. Gibbons."

"I'll do what I can, sir, if he don't mind the chance of turning out. Sitting room, you see, he wouldn't want. Will you tell the doctor just how it is?"

Paul stepped back and explained the matter to the best of his ability. The person about whom the discussion was taking place caught the tenor of the conversation.

"Is Mrs. Gibbons your landlady, and is it the woman who has been in once or twice?"

"Yes."

"Then I like the look of her. I feel among friends, somehow;" and he closed his eyes for a moment wearily. "If she will take me for a day or two, I will risk having to move. I like her face," he added half to himself. Not the first either who had found comfort and help written on Mrs. Gibbons' kindly face.

This settled the matter; and in due course of time the injured man was conveyed to the bedroom Mrs. Gibbons prepared for him. Paul stayed with him, and rendered what help lay in his power; then promising if at any time he could give assistance he would do so, thinking further attentions might seem intrusive, he withdrew.

The next morning Mrs. Gibbons lingered in Paul's room after removing the breakfast things.

"You say he is as well as you can expect," said Paul, who had already inquired after the new lodger, "Mr.— I don't know what his name is?"

"His name is Paul, sir."

"Paul! yes, but that would be his Christian name."

"No, it's his other name; he said so, sir."

"That's an odd name, certainly," said Paul half to himself.

"Yes, sir, that's what I thought; but it's no business of mine. I didn't ask him his name, but last night he fell a-talking about you, sir; he asked your name—your Christian and surname both. He asked all about you, sir, your father and mother; he said he used to know some one of the name of Porter a long while ago. So he chatted for some time; and this morning he says, 'Will you give my respects to Mr. Porter, and tell him that Mr. Paul'—that's the name he said, sir—'would like him, if he could find time, to sit with him a little while to-day.'"

"Certainly I will," said Paul.

Not only that day, but the next day, and the next, Paul passed some very pleasant time by the bedside of his new friend. He was evidently an elderly man, and his hair was quite grey; but there was a freshness and variety of expression in his vivacious dark eyes that made you forget all question of his age. He had been a great traveller, Paul found, and knew how to make the records of his travels both interesting and amusing. So the two became good friends. He explained he had come to Rixham in quest of some friends who used long back to live there, but found them all scattered and gone.

The fourth day Mrs. Gibbons' perplexity again revived.

"They're a-coming to-morrow, sir," she said to Paul. "I've just got a letter from Mrs. Williams; and now, sir, what had I better do? There's every bit of room in the house taken. I'd willingly give up my bit, but my husband and I now have only got not much more than a large cupboard to ourselves. I have been thinking, sir, if you wouldn't mind the liberty, there is that little tiny room next to yours. We did put a little bed up there, if you remember, once when we was so full, and your brother and another gentleman came."

"Oh, yes, I remember."

"I could make him a little bed in there, sir, if you wouldn't mind."

"No; I'll take the little bed, and he can have mine."

Mrs. Gibbons placed her back against the door.

"That you never shall, sir. I can't hear of your turning out of your bed, nohow, sir."

Paul laughed.

"I don't mind, I'm sure, Mrs. Gibbons: I believe I slept there one or two nights when the bed was there before. When your limbs and joints are all right, you can sleep anywhere; but a person in pain requires room to turn himself about. Put the little bed up, Mrs. Gibbons; I'll settle the rest."

Mrs. Gibbons did not dispute the point further, though her look hardly spoke satisfaction.

"Well, sir," she said, "I will say, if everyone was like you, there wouldn't be much quarrelling in the world about who should have the best things."

Mr. Paul expressed himself much as Mrs. Gibbons had done, and at first stoutly opposed the arrangement; but sick people are obliged to be over-ruled, and so that night saw him installed in Paul's room, and Paul himself occupied the small one adjoining. The room altogether seemed to the invalid far more comfortable than the one he had just vacated, and he awoke the next morning feeling more refreshed than he had done since the accident occurred. Paul came early to his bedside to inquire how he had passed the night.

"Right royally, young man; right royally," was the answer.

Paul smiled.

"I am glad to hear it," he said. "Shall I draw up the blind and let a little more daylight in?"

"Yes, please."

"It is another lovely morning," said Paul, as a glow of light and sunshine streamed into the room. "There, that will quite cheer you up," he added, walking back to the bedside.

"Yes, it's very bright, very cheering; and now, my young friend, what sort of a night have you had?"

"Very good, thank you."

"That's right. It is all very fine for me, having the best of everything, to have a good night. It is thanks to you and your kindness."

"You are very welcome; I am very glad to do it for you."

"Ah, you are a good lad, a very good lad." Then seeing Paul smile: "Ah, you may smile; you think yourself anything but a lad, I expect, now; but in some ways you are as simple as a child. You are a good lad, a very good lad."

He lay silent for a few minutes, and the quick, dark eyes grew full of a softened expression.

"I never said it before," he added, "I don't know whether I ever felt it; but looking at you, I feel as if I should have liked just such a son as you. I am a lonely man, you know, and never had wife or child. I was to have been married; twice was on the road to it. The first—well, perhaps she was too good for me; anyhow she passed early to that other world, where, when I meet her again, there'll be no more parting. That was the first time. The second—well, there are some people would make you believe there is no bad in the world, no women anyhow who are not good and noble and pure: but I say different; there are wicked women as well as wicked men; women who are bad and selfish and mercenary; there are some such, not many, perhaps just enough to show up the graces of their better sisters, and make them look all the lovelier by contrast. Well, that was the sort the second time, but I don't want to speak of her, evil is generally best not talked about. My eyes were opened in time; I escaped her, a woman who wanted my money, not me." He stopped suddenly, as a man who has made an unlucky admission, and looked curiously at Paul; but if Paul noticed the slip of the tongue he did not betray it, and the other continued: "I saw it in time, and it was all stopped. Since then I've been content with a solitary lot, and I have found kind friends in most places where I have gone; but I can't help thinking this morning, could it have been otherwise, I should have liked a son just like you."

"You are not like my father, then; he always so desired to have a daughter."

"Did he have one?"

"No; I've heard mother say he was bitterly disappointed though. He had one little sister, Selina, who died quite young; had he had a daughter, he wanted to have named it after her. I believe he was seriously disappointed when I made my appearance, and turned out to be only another boy."

"Why did they call you Paul?"

"I believe because they couldn't think of anything else for me. No, I am wrong; father gave me the name after an uncle of his, who was very early drowned at sea. Mother, I am sure, told me so once, but I don't know much about it. I suppose you think Paul Porter sounds rather odd?"

For a minute there was no answer; the face of Paul's

Y

listener was turned persistently away. At length he looked round.

"Yes, rather so; but then people have strange notions about names. There's Mrs. Gibbons, your good landlady, the least curious sort of woman as landlady that I ever saw, she could not resist saying to me the other day, 'Do you spell it with an *c*, sir?' 'Spell what?' I said. 'Your name, sir; don't you spell it with an *e* at the end?'"

"What did you say?" asked Paul.

"I said, 'My good woman, do you spell Gibbons so?' 'Why, no, sir,' she said; 'I'm sure I beg your pardon for the liberty I took, sir,' and went looking quite abashed from the room."

Perhaps it was the comfortable room, or Paul's and Mrs. Gibbons' kind attentions, but from the time of his removal the invalid began to mend. Still, it was fully three weeks before he was fairly on his feet again. That point being reached, he at once declared his intention of leaving.

"I have taken advantage of your kindness full long," he said. "All being well, I leave to-morrow."

In the afternoon, it being bright and sunny, he strayed down with Paul into the little garden at the back of the house, and sat awhile in the bright sunshine.

"I have just been settling accounts with good Mrs. Gibbons," he said; "but I feel as if the bill ought by rights to have proceeded from you. You have had for more than three weeks the trouble of a cripple thrust upon your care, and he an utter stranger to you."

"We did not seem strangers long; I think we have become very good friends."

"Yes, very good friends. I, for my part, have found a friend of whom I feel truly proud; but still I do feel some sort of recompense is due, and I don't know how to make it."

A slight colour rose to Paul's face.

"Pray do not speak of recompense of any kind," he said, half stiffly; then with a sudden smile he added, "When friends stay with us, we think their company recompense enough."

"Yes, yes, I believe you; still I wish—but there—rich or poor, you took me in without questioning."

"I never thought about it whether you were rich or poor," said Paul, with an amused smile.

"No, I know you didn't; but you don't know the world perhaps so well as I do. If you did, you would be aware that would be the first question of all."

Then he began feeling in his waistcoat pocket. Presently he drew out a rather large, very old-fashioned gold locket. He held it towards Paul.

"At least," he said, "let me give you this as a token of my affection and esteem. It was given to me long, long years ago, by a very dear relative and friend, who I believe would have given it to no one but me. I have kept and guarded it all these years. If I had had a son I should have given it to him as a kind of heirloom; but I want you to have it and keep it as a sort of bond between us. You may one day know me again by it."

Paul did not quite understand the significance of the last few words.

"If you really wish me to have it," he said doubtfully.

"You will pain me exceedingly if you do not take it."

"I will then, and will keep it always as you say, as a sort of keepsake."

Paul took it in his hands as he spoke; touching the spring, it flew open. Inside, on one side was a plait of soft fine hair, on the other the two letters "P. M." were plainly engraved. Paul did not ask any questions, but linked it carefully to his watch-chain.

"It will be quite safe there," he said.

"Yes, and will help to remind you of me. Excuse me," he added, after a slight pause, "but you were speaking the other day of your brother's coming wedding. When did you say it was to take place?"

"The twentieth of this month."

"The twentieth of June, and this is the fourth: rather more than a fortnight first, then?"

"Yes," said Paul, half wondering why the date could concern an utter stranger to Theodore.

The next morning Paul's visitor took his leave. He promised to write to Paul and tell him of his safe arrival in London. "And then," he added, "when my address becomes settled, you shall know of it." Paul thanked him, and accompanied him himself to the station. Arrived there, he seemed seized with a sudden fit of demonstrative affection. He took Paul's hands in both of his, and stood and shook them vigorously, while over and over again he thanked Paul for his kindness. Then when once in the train he was seized with another fit of demonstration; reaching both hands out of the carriage, he once more seized Paul's hands, and continued shaking them.

"Stand back from the train!" shouted an official's voice, but the shaking still continued.

"Stand back! I say, stand back!" shouted the warning voice; but not till the train was literally beginning to move, and he became suddenly aware that the process might be endangering Paul, did he let go his hands; and as long as Paul could see the carriage he was in, he was conscious that his strange old friend was still vigorously waving his hand in his direction.

Paul walked slowly home; at the door he met Mrs. Gibbons.

"Have you seen him off all right, sir?" she asked.

"Yes, all right and safe," said Paul; but Mrs. Gibbons still visibly lingered.

"Should you think, sir," she said, "he was a gentleman well off?"

"I never enquired; I did not think that was our business!"

"No, nor I either, sir; only I was just going to tell you, sir. He settled up all yesterday, paid me every penny owing; and then the last thing this morning before he went away, he drew me on one side, and 'Mrs. Gibbons,' he says, 'when strangers get taken in and treated well as I have been, there's something more due than just the charge. Will you accept this little present?' and he gave me this, sir," holding up to Paul's view, as she spoke, a five-pound note.

"Well, I'm glad of it; you've had extra trouble, certainly," said Paul. Still he walked away half wondering. He would hardly have expected this from the remarks of the day before, and he concluded he must have slightly misunderstood his old friend. It was as he had just said, no business of his, and he dismissed the subject from his mind.

CHAPTER XXIII.

THEODORE'S WEDDING, AND WHAT HAPPENED AT IT.

ON the 20th of June Theodore was married, and Paul went down to Clansford to be present at the ceremony. It was a quiet wedding, but like many such, more attractive perhaps than one aiming at more outside show. Kitty was a pretty bride, but then Kitty could hardly have been otherwise; but the one who by a beauty peculiarly her own eclipsed the others was Eleanore Grattan. She was very simply attired; still those who saw her thought they had never seen her look lovelier. One woman, a spectator, turning to a neighbour at her side, said,

"It's a pity it isn't Miss Grattan that's married; she makes even the bride herself look dull."

The wedding passed off pleasantly with its customary wedding breakfast, toasts, and congratulations, and the couple took their departure quietly. Theodore hated sensation, and he had not chosen a sensational bride.

It was a bright, sunshiny day, and the evening was soft and balmy. People strayed at will about the pretty garden, and the green scented shrubberries. Oliver and his wife sat hand in hand, thinking of and talking over their own wedding day, on that May-day that now seemed so many years back.

: ' The drawing-room at Mrs. Grattan's had on one side a large glass window opening to the ground, leading on to a covered walk just outside. Sweet-scented roses and flowering creepers grew round the pillars that supported the covering. Up and down that walk Paul and Eleanore slowly paced together. That day to Paul had been one of strangely mingled feelings. His eyes could not be shut to the beauty observed by eyes less enthralled than his. Only the night before, he and Theodore had sat up talking over many things far into the night, and just at the close of their conversation the old theme had been revived. Theodore attempted no concealment.

"I believe," he said, "it is all settled, Paul. He was there one day about a week ago, and stayed a long while. Eleanore promised Kitty she would tell her all when she came home from her honeymoon. But this much is quite clear, he himself evidently plainly desires making her his wife. You asked me, Paul; and if you are to meet to-morrow, it is best you should know the truth."

"Yes," said Paul, half wearily.

But there was one drop of consolation ; Sir William Harrell was ill, taken ill suddenly away from home, and his family had all been summoned to his bedside, his second son Edward among them. Therefore, however matters might stand, he would not form one of the wedding guests.

So to one of these two, walking to and fro in that covered walk that June evening, with the sweet, blushing roses nodding at them as they passed, the day had been full of strange bitterness. Paul had been righteously, dutifully striving to keep in abeyance his adoring soul; and even now that walk together seemed a stolen sweet. How it was they thus found themselves alone, perhaps they could neither of them have distinctly stated; drawn together probably by that subtle influence which attracts two harmonious souls. Paul talked restrainedly at first, then unconsciously they drifted into their old familiar friendship. Eleanore asked him about Rixham; what it was like. Did people visit there? And Paul began telling her about Mrs. Gibbons, and the only seaside visitors Rixham ever had; Mrs. Gibbons' summer lodgers; and so, quietly chatting, the time passed by, till in their walk a choice flowering plant caught Paul's attention.

"I never saw but one like that before," he said; "that was at my uncle Thomas' at the Grove. It was given to him by a great lover and cultivator of flowers. Did you get this one from there?"

"No, it came from Sir William Harrell's."

Eleanore half turned her head away as she spoke, and though she tried to say the words quite naturally, Paul thought he detected the colour rising in her averted face. He hesitated a moment, then he said,

"May I claim the privilege of a very old friend, Eleanore?"

"Yes; what for?"

"To congratulate you."

"Why do you congratulate me?"

"Upon your engagement with Sir William Harrell's son Edward."

Eleanore turned her face away again, but this time there was no mistaking the crimson flush that rapidly dyed her cheeks. For a minute or two she did not speak, then she said,

"Thank you;" and her voice was low and tremulous. After a pause she spoke again. "What makes you think this?"

"I was told so."

"Who told you?"

"Theodore."

Turning round, she looked into Paul's face; her own had become pale, its lines compressed.

"In other words, you mean to wish me joy."

"Yes, only I have always wished you that."

"Were you pleased to hear it?"

"Yes—no—I mean I was glad to hear him a man worthy of—I mean a man so well spoken of."

"Worthy of me, you were going to say."

"I trust he will be that."

The tones were low and kind, with just that mixture of pain that made them doubly tender. Eleanore looked at him, and a slight tremor passed over her lips; another moment and she grew calm and self-composed, and her eyes had a strange glitter in them as she said,

"And when may I claim the privilege of a very old friend, and congratulate you, Paul?"

"Me! I believe, placed as I am, I shall never marry."

"You do not think your Church enforces celibacy, I suppose?"

"No, only such a thing is not to be thought of at present. I must get beyond a country curacy first."

"Then it is only a lowly position deters you?"

Paul looked pained; the tone was almost cynical, the

conversation becoming more than he could bear. Looking very distressed, he said,

"Why do you ask me, Eleanore?"

"Only as a very privileged old friend."

"But it is needless; my circumstances and means are of course at present very limited, even if I had the desire, which I think I never shall have now."

"You are not quite a centenarian either. Well, if you escape all your life through the shafts of love, you will be a happy individual."

Paul looked half perplexed at her. She stood still and queenly before him, a white rose in her hand, the stem of which she was unconsciously twining round one of her fingers. There was a bright flush in her cheeks, but her eyes were downcast.

"It is hardly for you to say so," said Paul. "People going to marry generally hold a different opinion to that."

"But I am not going to marry."

"Eleanore!"

"Like you, I mean to remain single."

"But—but—"

"But as a very privileged old friend you jumped to your own conclusions. I am not engaged to Sir William's son; I never have been; I never shall be."

She looked at him as she spoke, and her eyes were worse tell-tales than her words. Paul suddenly moved a step nearer to her, hardly knowing what he was saying, lured on by that one fatal glance.

"Why not, Eleanore?" he said.

"Because a better man than he stands in the way."

Her eyes were again downcast as she spoke. Paul

retreated, and leaned against one of the pillars with a suddenly white face.

"Oh, E'eanore!" he said, "I didn't know of this." Seeing she did not answer: "Eleanore, can you pardon me?" he said.

"I am not angry with you."

"Nay, but I have pained you." In the midst of his own sudden misery, his first thought was of any pain he might, though inadvertently, have caused her. Eleanore did not speak; she lifted her eyes and looked, not at Paul, but far away over the garden, and the still quiet country beyond. So still she stood, she half startled him. He laid his hand gently on her arm. A slight tremor ran through her frame, the light and colour came back to her face. She seemed inclined to hurry away, but Paul stayed her. "Stop," he said; "say that I have not given you pain, you that I would not harm for all the world. I did not know of this other one."

She turned away her head; her voice was very low, but Paul caught every word.

"It does not matter, Paul," she said; "that other one is poor and proud. I shall never marry him; he will never ask me to be his wife."

Once more she looked at him. What in those eyes did Paul read, or think he did? A strange, wild thought, half hope, half fear, seized all his mind. He could not think aright, but his soul gave one great leap up to his lips. He took her hand in his; she did not seek to withdraw it.

"Eleanore," he said, "can you mean—do you mean? Oh, Eleanore! I seem to have loved you my whole life long: do you—can you mean?"

Looking with her blue eyes straight into his, she said, "I mean you, Paul."

A great joy, a dazzling light seemed all at once closing round Paul.

"Oh, Eleanore!" he said, and other words utterly failed. Was it a vision or a delusion? "Look at me, Eleanore," he said, "that I may know it is not a dream."

Again Eleanore lifted her eyes to his; those eyes that had first given him hope now made consummate his bliss.

When two people have loved one another for several years, without being able to reveal that love to each other, and at last the avowal does take place, it is only natural for them to wish to linger awhile in their newly-found joy and communion of soul. So the dusk began quietly to gather over the garden, and people in groups began to reunite in the drawing-room, when Eleanore and Paul, leaving the roses and the soft evening light behind them, stepped back through the glass window to help to entertain the other guests in proper prosaic fashion. At that moment a servant opened the door of the room and announced, "A lady wishes to speak to Mr. Sydney Porter."

"To me!" said Sydney, half rising. "Who is it?"

"She wouldn't send in her name. She wishes to speak to you alone, sir."

Sydney instantly rose and went out. Half-an-hour elapsed and he did not return; when at last he came back, he led in a tall lady in close black, with a thick black veil quite concealing her face. He placed a chair for her facing them; then she sat down, and there was silence. Sydney stooped towards her.

"Shall I speak for you?" he said.

The lady in reply threw back her veil, and disclosed a face well known to all—the face of their old acquaintance, Blanche.

"Why, it is my poor brother's wife!" said Mr. Porter.

Blanche looked at him and essayed to speak, but for a moment conflicting feelings prevented her. Then at length she said, speaking slowly,

"Yes, Mr. Porter; and I have come here to-night publicly to clear your son's name—your son Sydney. I intended first seeking him alone, but finding he was here, I thought it seemed only right to come and thus clear him before you all."

She drew from under her mantle a folded paper and opened it, but her hand trembled as she held it. Sydney took it from her.

"Who will read it for her?" he said. "You, Oliver?"

Oliver took the paper; it was the confession of an apparently dying man, and began—

"I, Philip Carter, believing my death draws near, solemnly declare that Sydney Porter is perfectly innocent about Mr. Harrows' £350 cheque."

Oliver read slowly. The first part of the statement was written in the shaky handwriting of the sick man himself; the latter part Blanche had written at his dictation, and it was signed with Philip's own signature. The declaration went on to say that he, Philip, had himself written that cheque and obtained the money; and explained that that evening Sydney left the keys in his desk was the first beginning of it all. It seemed, Philip said in his confession, like a temptation put in his way. He then confessed how that afterwards, taking

Thomas to his friend's house, he actually did drug the liquor he mixed for him, professedly to his friend Martin for the sake of a spree, but in reality to obtain possession of Sydney's keys; that having so done he went back, and opening the desk made himself master of how the cheques were signed, and all necessary items. When occasion required, he wrote the cheque about which Sydney had been blamed, and the night before his departure, seeing Sydney and Thomas both out, he had gone boldly through the shop inquiring for Thomas, and having previously procured a duplicate key to the desk, he cut the leaves of the ledger, thus hoping to cast upon Sydney the suspicion of having falsified his accounts, and then of having destroyed all proofs of wrong doing if inquired into. The name of the man who tendered the cheque for him he suppressed, as he said, through motives of honour. This was the sum and substance of it, and the confession, such as it was, was signed in Philip's sprawling, irregular handwriting. As Oliver ceased, utter silence followed. Mr. Porter was the first to speak.

"And your brother wrote this on his dying bed?" he said.

"No, not exactly; from that illness he afterwards recovered. He tried to make me give up the paper, and I made a pretence of destroying it, but in reality I kept it, intending one day to clear all up."

"Then he is still alive and unpunished?"

"No, he is dead."

"Well, well, I don't wish to speak too harshly, of course; but people who do such things ought to be punished."

. Blanche turned her dark, luminous eyes full upon Mr. Porter's face.

. "After that illness he took to habits of inveterate drinking, which brought their own punishment. He died of delirium tremens. You did not see his death-bed—I did."

Again silence fell over the little party. Oliver spoke next.

"That being the case," he said, "I hardly see the need of suppressing the name of the man who tendered the cheque. It cannot now harm your brother, and I think it ought to be known. Do you yourself know it?"

"Yes; and on condition that no measures are taken against him, I have told his name to your brother Sydney. The man's right name was John Wicks."

"You, Paul," said Sydney, "remember John Wicks at Doctor Edwards' better perhaps than I do?"

"Yes, I remember him; but where did Philip meet with him?"

"I don't know," said Blanche; "I believe he often went by an assumed name. I think Philip had not known him long when he tendered that cheque for him. Philip had to give him something to keep him quiet, and afterwards, under the name of Jones, he entered Mr. Harrows' service as the surest way of escaping detection. He disguised himself (for his hair was dark) with a light or red wig and whiskers. He kept with Mr. Harrows some time. It was he who struck Sydney down in the street that night. Philip found that Sydney was dodging and tracking him, and he and John Wicks concocted a plan to lead Sydney into a lonely street and then attack him. After that assault Philip went to

Germany; my mother and I afterwards joined him. John Wicks came to us while we were there, but had to leave in a hurry, owing to some fray he got into. He is now in England; I believe I can give you his,address, for since Philip's death he wrote to him, thinking he was still living." She took the paper from Oliver's hand as she spoke, and pencilling something on it, handed it to Sydney. "That is the address he gave in his letter," she said.

"One thing more," said Mr. Porter; "who sent that money back?"

"I did, at my father's death."

"But you did not know then?"

"No, not quite, but I almost knew; in my own mind I had no doubt; that is why I sent it, thinking it might take the blame off Sydney."

Blanche looked as if she would have risen, and then for the first time her listeners seemed fully to awake to the nature of her communication. Some one began congratulating Sydney upon being thus unexpectedly exonerated, and the example became contagious. Then Mr. Porter advancing to Blanche, said,

"And I think something is due to you for thus coming and speaking out about it. Of course it is right, only what ought to be; but still I feel you have done it well and nobly."

"I have only done what I felt it my duty to do. After having told Sydney, finding there were only near friends here to-night, I determined to speak out before you all."

"Yes, yes, quite right. And you are living in England now, I suppose, you and Mrs. Carter?"

"My mother is dead; has been dead a year."

Blanche spoke in that quiet, laconic tone, to some expressive of want of feeling; to others of deep sorrow, too deep for the balm of sympathy to heal.

"I am sorry to hear that," said Mr. Porter kindly. "May I ask you where you are now living?"

For a moment a bright colour surged up into Blanche's cheeks.

"Just for the present I am staying with an aunt, my Aunt Jemima; but I have been seeking, and I believe have now obtained, a situation as companion to an elderly lady."

Mr. Porter started back, then in a lower voice he said,

"But you don't mean to say—and such a handsome fortune too—you don't mean to say he made that off!"

"It cannot be helped now," said Blanche sadly. "I do not wish to speak evil of the dead, only so far as duty constrains me; and I am young and strong still, and hope to be able to make some sort of way for myself in the world."

Mr. Porter stood silent. Mentally he was saying, "Such a handsome fortune too! such a handsome fortune!" Then Blanche rose to depart.

"I think there is nothing further to be explained," she said.

Mr. Porter shook hands with her, Sydney also shook hands; Oliver, from the other end of the room, contented himself with a formal bow; but Paul crossed over from where he was sitting by Eleanore's side, and opening the door for Blanche, walked with her into the hall beyond. At the front door she would have bidden him good-bye, but Paul said quietly,

Z

"I have something I want to say to you; I will walk with you to the garden gate; some one may hear us here."

He walked with her in the soft twilight, through the silent shrubberies, down to the garden gate, where he had found Eleanore standing with folded arms, that night he had come back to offer some kind of thanks for the past kindness and friendship he had received. He did not tell her till they reached the gate, then he said,

"I have something more to tell you. I do not wish to give you further pain, for I am sure what you have done to-night must have cost you considerable effort; but I have a message I once promised to deliver to you should I ever meet you again. Doubtless you noticed some one absent from our midst to-night."

"Yes, yes," she said, with a sudden gasping of her breath; "I have heard of his death."

"He died whilst at my lodgings. I watched by him the night he died. The last words he ever spoke were of you, to send a message to you. 'If ever you see Blanche again,' he said, 'give her my dying love, and tell her I forgave her wholly.'"

Blanche had endured well thus far, but the simple message from the dead destroyed all her self-composure. Leaning against the gate, she sobbed with a vehemence that astonished Paul, accustomed as he had ever been to her laconic unconcern.

"Blanche," he said kindly, "this pains you now; afterwards, when you come to think about it, it may help and comfort you."

"Oh, Paul," she sobbed, "you don't understand; it comforts me now more than anything else on earth.

Paul, I have been punished, bitterly punished. I was young and—no I was not exactly young and foolish, I was not quite the sort for that; but I was young, and had no one to counsel me better. I found out my mistake too late, and then soon after that affair at Elmsbridge came a letter from Philip; though he made no downright admission, I knew from that letter he was guilty, and the whole burden of it seemed to settle down upon me. He was 'keeping dark,' he said. I knew what it all meant, and my wretchedness at times became more than I could bear. I never told anyone I received that letter, I hid it all; and then I seemed to be deceiving everyone, till even my husband, mild and quiet as he was, became a dread to me. I felt sometimes I would leave and run away, my misery was so great. When my father died, I sent the money to Mr. Harrows; I never gave mother any rest till it was done. She wouldn't believe it about Philip, but somehow I overruled her, and the money was sent. Since then, after my husband's death, my life has been one of wretchedness; scenes I need not mention I have had to witness; and, when all was over, I could only do one thing—what I have done to-night. Do you know what nerved me and gave me power?" She looked up into Paul's face with a sudden intensity, yet tenderness of expression. "I did it for *his* sake, to clear *his* brother. I don't know, Paul, otherwise I could have done it. But I have had my reward; your message has comforted me at last. To be loved and forgiven to the end! I shall never forget that." She turned away her head for a minute and wept silently, then she looked up and quietly drying her tears, she held out her hand, "Good-night, Paul," she said.

"Good-night, Blanche; and if ever at any time I can help you, I will do so."

"Thank you, Paul. Good-night, and may God bless you."

She spoke the words with quiet reverence. Paul held open the gate, and she passed out; and for a few minutes he stood looking after the solitary figure walking away in the quiet evening light.

Going back, Paul found them all busily engaged discussing the new intelligence. Mrs. Grattan herself had heard it all silently: sitting in her easy chair, she had heard it all through in silence. Not long after Paul returned, she called him to her; Eleanore was kneeling by her side. As she took his hand in hers, "God bless you, my son," she said gently; and Paul, looking from her to Eleanore, understood that one more heart had become a partaker of his joy.

CHAPTER XXIV.

A STRANGE VISITOR.

EARLY the next morning Sydney departed for London to show the document to Mr. Harrows. That gentleman behaved himself in truly demonstrative fashion.

"I knew it would come one day, my lad; I knew it would," he said, giving Sydney a series of vigorous slaps. But when he came to the part about John Wicks, his open-eyed resentment knew no bounds. "That fellow!" he said, "know him! know where he is! I should think I do. I got him his last place; he's in it now by my recommendation. The villain! the abominable wretch! That's how he hides, is it? Takes a respectable situation to brew more mischief! but I'll be even with him at last. We'll go straight down to Grimes and Son's, that's where he is; and we'll take his red wig off for him, that's what we'll do. And Frank—we must take him with us."

Pulling the bell vigorously, he demanded the presence of his son. Frank came immediately. In few words Mr. Harrows informed him of what had taken place, and of the proposed errand to Grimes and Son's.

"To think," he said, "that he should have been taking

us in like this, all this time! To think of it—I cannot make it out."

Frank smiled.

"You were always credulous, father," he said gently. Then with a conscious smile he turned to Sydney, as he said, "But I ought not to say a word; my suspicions once did you great injustice. I think mother is right; she says father and I want to be mixed up together."

"Ah, it wouldn't be amiss," said Mr. Harrows meditatively, as though such a process were really practicable. "But come with us now, Frank; we shall be none the worse for your head with us."

When Mr. Jones, alias John Wicks, was at first confronted with the evidence against him, he tried what a solemn show of innocence could effect; but the guilty are prone to be cowards; and Mr. Harrows, bethinking himself of an expedient, stepped cautiously behind him, and with one dexterous move dislodged the red wig. John Wicks clapped his hands to his head, but after the momentary scuffle that ensued, he found himself minus wig and whiskers, while he presented to view a crop of thickly springing, short, dark hair, and whiskers of the same colour, endeavouring to sprout also. The experiment had the desired effect; John Wicks saw it was useless contending further. On his knees he confessed his share of guilt; there, in the presence of Mr. Harrows and his present masters, and Sydney and Frank, he confessed and implored for mercy. He obtained grace to a certain degree. He was to make himself scarce, quitting England within a given time; and if found loitering about amongst honest people again, he should be openly exposed—if possible, punished.

As Sydney shook hands with Mr. Harrows at parting, the latter, after many expressive nudges and winks, gave him to understand that he wished him joy in one more quarter also.

"Let the old gentleman know all about it," he said; "and tell Alice, from me, that I think she is a brick for waiting as she has done."

Sydney thanked him, and a happy smile, that had long been a stranger to him, hovered round his lips as he walked away.

Light and shadow, sunshine and storm, blend and intermingle all through life, and something of the cloud appeared yet doomed to be in Paul's lot. Cloud enough it would have seemed to a man of grosser mould, to have blotted out the most celestial sunshine. The night after the wedding, coming home from spending the evening—where of course it was very natural he should have been spending it—at Mrs. Grattan's, he found his father and mother sitting together in gloomy consultation, the latter in tears. In answer to Paul's questioning look, Mr. Porter said,

"You may as well know it, my boy, it will have to come out sooner or later. I and your mother have just been talking it all over. Perhaps you may have known things have been going queerly of late—for the last few years, I may say—but I staved off the evil day somehow. It is no good blaming myself now; I'm not the first who, not content with the proceeds of a lawful calling, must needs dabble in speculations beyond their ken. That was the beginning—as I say, it's no good talking now—but things have got worse and worse, and now there's nothing, as I can see, but downright failure and bankruptcy before me."

Paul listened in pained surprise. He had fancied something of all this, but never imagined things to have arrived at such a crisis. After a few minutes,

"Did Theodore know of this?" he asked.

"Partly; I told him he didn't want to bother you about it. I don't know I should have told you now, but to-day I've had news—bad news, that threatens another serious loss, and brings me to a thorough standstill. The old factory must go into other hands, and the men find a new master."

The square, solid face relaxed, the corners of his mouth looked pitiful, like those of a child about to cry. Mrs. Porter wept softly to herself.

"I've brought up my children, that's one thing," continued Mr. Porter. "I've done my best to start them all honestly in life, but now in my old days it seems hard to come to failure and grief. Oliver is a good lad, he has helped and done his part—more than that too, I fancy—and now we must take what follows."

Then he sat looking with stolid, mournful gaze straight before him. Paul said and did all he could, but the circumstances were new and troubling to him. So the three sat there talking till eleven o'clock; then, as Mr. Porter after prosaic fashion observed, it was useless sitting up longer—lost money, like spilt milk, it was no use crying over; they all sought that one refuge for the weary heart as well as weary body, and went to bed, with what chances they might have of going to sleep also. Mrs. Porter lay awake, but her husband, with that peculiar stupor which often follows in the wake of sorrow, fell into a slight doze, which would soon have ended in a profound sleep, when he was startled by a sound—he could not at first have said what—something resembling a call it seemed.

"What was that?" said Mrs. Porter, giving her husband an emphatic nudge.

Mr. Porter roused himself and listened. Some one under the window was evidently calling his name. Now Mr. Porter's name was William, though he was seldom so designated. His wife, when their children were small, had been obliged to drop the appellation, substituting the term "father" instead. When speaking of him, she commonly said "my husband," and to the outside world he was simply "Mr. Porter," so that he was somewhat a stranger to the sound of his Christian name as applied to himself. But by that Christian name alone the person outside was calling him, only he pronounced it after a rather peculiar fashion, pronouncing the *i* softly, and laying particular stress on the last syllable, so that, thus rendered, the name sounded Weelly*um*.

As Mr. Porter and his wife listened, distinctly they heard the voice call "Weelly*um*."

"It's somebody calling you," said Mrs. Porter.

That was very evident, as the next moment there it came again, perhaps a little louder, "Weely*um*."

"Whoever can it be?" said Mrs. Porter.

"I don't know, I'm sure; nobody ever calls me like that;" and Mr. Porter got slowly out of bed and moved towards the window. Yet at the sound of that voice a strange thrill of something almost akin to recognition, though he had not the slightest idea of what or of whom, darted through his mind.

He went to the window; in the light of the soft summer night he could distinctly see the outline of a man standing below. "Weely*um*" again said the importunate voice. Seeing something tangible standing there, Mr. Porter threw up the window sash.

"Is it you, Weely*um?*" said the figure below.

"Yes, who are you?"

"Who am I? You don't know my voice, then?"

"Not at all. Who are you?"

"Then I'll tell you: I'm Paul Munro."

Mr. Porter stood and gazed out of the open window. For a moment he could not recall that name—just for a moment, then over his whole soul burst a horror of astonishment and dismay. He looked with terror-strained eyes at the individual below.

"Who did you say?"

"Paul Munro, your uncle."

Mr. Porter shut the window with a sudden bang. He was not a superstitious man, had never had a passing thought that there could really be such things as ghosts; but if this was no ghostly visitant, what on earth could it be? A man who had been dead more than half a lifetime! His hair began fairly to bristle, and his knees seemed to have a strange propensity to become hostile towards one another.

"What does he say?" said Mrs. Porter, who had been busy at the other end of the room getting a light. Seeing her husband's white, scared face, she uttered a faint little cry. "Whoever is it?" she said.

"A man who's been dead these forty years!"

Mrs. Porter staggered against the bed, and would probably have given another cry, but again the incorrigible voice without uttered its imperative call, "Weely*um.*" Meeting no response, "Weelly*um*" it said again.

Mr. Porter was half conscious of a hazy idea passing through his mind of having somewhere heard, that when ghostly visitations do take place, it is generally with some terribly definite end in view, therefore making it useless to dally with, or, in plain words, to try to put them off; as, if they have a message to convey, or a work to perform, they give the mortals honoured by their visits no rest till the said message be duly received, and the said work duly executed. Therefore, with a sort of numb feeling of going to his fate, Mr. Porter once more cautiously lifted the sash.

"What is it you want?" he asked, with a solemnity of tone that was almost sepulchral.

"I want you, Weelly*um.*"

Mr. Porter once more shut the window, and turned a horror-stricken face towards his wife.

"What is it?" she gasped.

"He says he wants *me.*"

"Wants you!" she almost shrieked.

"Yes; and the man has been dead these forty years."

"Weelly*um*, open the window."

Again Mr. Porter did as desired, and peered curiously out.

"Whence do you come?" he said, feeling instinctively that formality of expression was due to the ghostly presence, though his tone was somewhat marred by a sudden chattering of his teeth, and a restless movement of his lower jaw.

"Where do I come from? The railway station is the last place I came from. Bless me, man, do you take me for a ghost? Ha! ha! ha!"

The laugh was loud and cheery, and in the dim light

·Mr. Porter could distinctly see the little figure vigorously clapping his hips as he laughed. That a ghost should come and speak aloud, even desire you to open a window—well, these were items Mr. Porter under the circumstances might possibly have swallowed ; but that a ghost could stand and laugh and clap its sides was nowhere connected with ghosts or ghost-lore of any kind. A feeling that it must be flesh and blood after all standing down there talking to him, forced itself upon his mind.

"You are really Paul Munro, then?" he said slowly.

"Of course I am."

"But you have been dead these forty years!"

"No, not exactly ;" and again broke out through the still night the old reassuring laugh. "Is your son Paul at home?"

"Yes."

"Then call him ; he'll know me."

Paul had not yet undressed for bed ; the communications his father had made that night had not tended to feelings of repose, so he had sat by his window, thinking and pondering over what he had just heard, till the sound of a voice attracted his attention. At that moment he appeared at the door of his father's room.

"What is the matter?" he asked.

"There's some strange man outside," gasped Mrs. Porter.

"Yes, yes, Paul will know me," said the voice below.

Paul went hurriedly to the window.

"Why, Mr. Paul," he said, "is that you?"

"Ah, you know me, my boy ; run down and let me in, there's a good lad."

"Paul, what does this mean?" queried Mr. Porter

"It is a gentleman who came to me in my lodgings at Rixham, father. He and I were very good friends; I think I mentioned him in my letters home."

Paul had done just this, mentioned him, and since his return home other events had put his old friend quite out of his mind.

"He says he's Paul Munro," said Mr. Porter; "my uncle who was drowned at sea."

"He called himself when with me Mr. Paul."

"Well, go down and speak to him, anyhow."

Paul obeyed; and by the time he had got the hall door open and Mr. Paul Munro inside, his father and mother had made their way down into the hall also. The strange visitor was shaking Paul vigorously by the hand.

"Your son knows me," he said gleefully; "he and I are good friends. A few weeks back I was at Rixham, poking about after lost acquaintances, as lonely old men are apt to poke, and I met with an accident that might have been serious, and your good son here took me in, put me in his own bed, and treated me as though I had been his father. I soon found out who he was, but I didn't see fit to tell him my true name. I passed with him for Mr. Paul, but I heard all about you all; and now that I come in bodily form and declare myself, you take me for a ghost! Shake hands, Weelly*um*."

Mr. Porter did as desired.

"You really are my uncle Paul, after all?" he said.

"Of course I am. Pull out the locket, Paul."

Paul produced it. Tears glistened in Mr. Porter's eyes at the sight of the love-token he had given long, long years ago to the young man who, uncle to him though he was, was only two years his senior, and who had been to him as a brother. On one side of the locket lay the soft fair hair of the dead Selina, and on the opposite side the letters he himself had had engraved.

"Does that satisfy you?"

"Yes, fully," said Mr. Porter, grasping the hand he had never hoped to grasp again on earth. "But if I did take you for a ghost, I may be excused: you have been silent all these years."

"Ah, yes," and a slight shadow passed over Paul Munro's face. "I ought not to have done so; but I wrote, and I believe now the letter was lost. I had been shipwrecked; I found it was reported all hands had perished. I had escaped, and, as I say, I did write, and I believe the letter was lost. But fortune at that time was very changeable with me, and I was constantly moving from place to place, so I got used to the feeling of being forgotten by my friends. Then when I did think about it, I always put myself off with the notion that I should come home before long, but that time always seemed in the future. Had my parents been living, I should have been without excuse, but you "— looking at Mr. Porter—"always seemed the dearest, if not the nearest tie I had. Now I am grown grey and something over sixty years; and when I do come home you take me for a ghost! Ay, and it serves me right after all. But there, you are scarcely remembering your manners: I conclude the lady by your side is no other than your wife."

"My dear," said Mr. Porter, "this is my uncle, Paul Munro. You have heard me speak of him: the one Paul is named after, you know."

The two shook hands, but even at that moment Mrs. Porter grew suddenly aware of the incongruous figure she presented to a stranger. She had arrayed herself in a long dressing-gown, over which she had hastily thrown a shawl; but as her hand left Paul Munro's it glided instinctively to her head, as she suddenly remembered that all the front part of it was profusely adorned with curl papers. Mr. Munro noticed the action, and caught her apologetic glance:

"Don't name them, madam," he said, bowing low; "don't name them; they look very nice, and we will put off seeing the curls till to-morrow."

The general laugh that followed seemed to put matters on an easy footing at once. Mr. Munro looked half furtively round:

"I don't know," he said, "whether it seems very polite to come calling anyone up in this fashion; and, in fact, I intended coming earlier, but I made some mistake about the trains and got delayed, and"—laying his hand on Mr. Porter's shoulder—"to tell you the truth, I didn't quite know whether after all this long absence I could walk up in broad daylight and declare myself; and so the thought coming into my head, I surprised you all in this fashion: but I hope I have not caused you any serious alarm or disturbance."

Judging by the hearty manner in which Mr. Porter tried to satisfy his visitor on this point, you might have supposed he had forgotten the curious sensations with which his first appearance had inspired him.

Provision having been made for the stranger's refreshment and rest, the next best thing seemed once more to seek repose after this new and unlooked-for event;

further news and items being, like Mrs. Porter's curls, put off till the morrow.

The next morning Mr. Porter woke from light slumbers full of a strange mysterious jumble of days and scenes long passed by, to the unpleasant feeling that the whole thing must have been a vision or a dream. In the first half-dreamy moments of waking, he felt unable to discern between the fanciful and visionary, and what was really truth and reality. He appealed to his wife for help.

"Did it all really happen?" he said. "Did Paul Munro really come back here alive last night?"

"Come! of course he did. What can you be thinking about? I suppose you've been to sleep and forgotten all about it. You were frightened enough too last night at his coming. For my part I have not slept a wink. I've been lying awake all the night thinking about it; it all seems so strange."

Mr. Porter drew a sigh of relief. There could be no doubt about the truth of it all if his wife, as she declared, had been all the night lying awake thinking about it. Had it been possible for any doubts still to have remained, the cheery presence of Paul Munro himself, making that morning such an unexpected addition to their family circle, must have dispelled all such feelings; and under the influence of this new and most unlooked-for event, Mr. Porter lost for a time the harassing cares and troubles that of late had so oppressed and perplexed him.

Later in the day, Paul coming in, found his father and Mr. Munro sitting closely conversing together. As he entered, Mr. Munro looked up and beckoned him to them.

"Come here, my lad," he said, "your father and I have been having a long talk; now we will hear what you have to say to it all. You remember the conversation you and I had in Mrs. Gibbons' little garden? I wanted then to have rendered you some acknowledgment for all your kindness, but I found it wouldn't do: I began to understand pretty well the stuff you were made of. You didn't ask me if I was rich or poor, and I didn't see fit then to tell you; but the truth is, my lad, like many another lonely life, I have been almost more than successful, and have prospered in all I turned my hand to. I have come home with fortune to invest, and money more than I know how to dispose of, and your father and I have been talking matters over, and have come to the conclusion that it would be as well for him to take me in as a partner, a sort of sleeping partner, you know." He nudged Paul's arm expressively at this point. "The active part cannot be in better hands than your father's. What do you say to it, Paul?"

Paul glanced at his father's brightened face, from which half the furrows had disappeared, and in their stead was an expression of beaming happiness.

"Oh, sir," he said, "I don't know what I can say rightly; the proposal makes me, for my father's sake, so full of sudden happiness and joy."

"One thing I ask you, my lad,—never say that again."

"Say what?"

"What you said just now. Never call me that again; I will not be 'sir' to you. I wish you could call me a very near name; but if that cannot be, at least call me uncle."

Paul smiled.

A 2

"I thought you were going to lay down some terrible mandate," he said. "It seems easy enough to call you uncle: you and father seem exactly like brothers."

Paul was right, like brothers seemed the two sitting together there, talking over times so long since gone by; till they hardly knew whether they were not growing suddenly young again, in this gleaming flash of light that thus brightened the lives fast gliding into the shadows of evening. Light is always good, always precious; but perhaps we never so intensely realize its mysterious power and beauty as when, nearing the long shadows of night, and feeling that the day's glamour and brightness lie far away behind us, suddenly there comes with cheering power a gleam of light, bright almost as the morning beams, scattering the shadows and making the close of life luminous. Such experiences may not be common, and perhaps but few know the happiness of this late illumination, this light at eventide.

*   *   *   *   *   *

The next year two more weddings took place. Sydney and Alice were married in London.

"I knew it would one day have to come to this," Mr. Wilturn said to Sydney after the return of the party from church. "Ever since that time when you were ill, and Alice gave me and her mother no rest till we let her come to see you, I knew it would come to this sooner or later. She was only just to look at you, or if you recognized her, at the most just to speak to you; and then leave directly; but my wife, standing at the bed-room door, had to confess that Alice rather outstepped her orders, for she did not come away till she had stooped and kissed you."

"You must not blame that kiss, sir," said Sydney. "Only half conscious of it as I was, there was more healing for me in that kiss than in all the medicine in the world."

A little while afterwards Paul and Eleanore were married at Clansford. Paul had partly fulfilled his word of not marrying till he had got beyond a country curacy. The living at Rixham becoming vacant, Paul had been presented with it, to the intense delight of the people among whom he had laboured as curate.

After a short bridal tour, when he brought his wife to her new home, the road from the station to the parsonage was decorated and adorned as though a royal visit had been anticipated. Arches were raised, mottoes of welcome, flags and banners were hoisted on every side, and a glad people, who welcomed them with loud and hearty cheers, lined the way. The reception to Paul was unexpected and overwhelming.

"They must be doing it in honour of you, love," he said, glancing at Eleanore sitting by his side.

Just then a man close by the carriage distinctly uttered the words, "God bless you, sir; God bless you—ay, God bless you both!"

Eleanore smiled as she said, "No, dear, the welcome is not to a stranger but to an old friend, and to me for your sake."

Paul responded heartily to the friendly greetings, but as the carriage turned into the Parsonage gates, leaving the cheering and welcoming outside, he pressed both hands over his face, while tears born of a fount of unspeakable gratitude sprang suddenly to his eyes. Later in the day, when he and Eleanore were left at last to themselves, he said,

"Oh, to think that there have been times in my life, even in my life here, when I have mur—no, not exactly murmured either; but it was something very much akin to it—when I used to tell myself that life was gray and cheerless; and now—even if the last blissful joy had not been mine—only to think of the harvest of love and kindness all the time growing up around."

Time passed on, and at the Parsonage at Rixham was grouped one of those family gatherings that often follow a wedding and the settling of a bride and bridegroom in their new home. Mr. and Mrs. Porter, and all who formed the family circle—of course including Paul Munro—were assembled there. Mrs. Grattan, who—the Parsonage being large—had had a part of it devoted to her separate use, was present at the social gathering. Though now very advanced in years, her intellect was clear as ever, and there was still the same winning smile as she said,

"I have had one good child all these years; and now, in my old age, I have two good children to comfort me instead of one."

Such occasions are often marked by formal speeches, commonplace congratulations; but Mr. Porter, looking hastily back at the long years behind, and then at the glad circle surrounding him, felt he had something more than commonplace expressions to utter. And yet, even as he expressed his pleasure at seeing them all thus assembled, a shade crossed his face.

"No, not all here," he said; "one face is absent—one of our little circle gone on before."

Paul Munro rose in reply:

"I wish," he said, "that I had returned earlier, then I could have shared with you all in your sorrow as well as in your joy. Still, as it is, if I can feel my coming back helps to fill up any gap—not that I am thinking of substituting an old life for a young one—still, if I can feel my presence in any way cheering my friend and brother here"—laying his hand on Mr. Porter's shoulder as he spoke—"I shall not feel I have returned even now in vain."

Later in the evening Mr. and Mrs. Porter sat apart silently watching them all. At last their eyes rested lovingly upon Paul.

"Aye, wife," he said, "things have turned out better than we thought they would. There was a time when we feared our youngest lad would never be anything at all in this world. Even when he was born I was full of discontent; I wanted a daughter, and had only got a son, and that a feeble one. Yet he has grown up a good man, and a son to be proud of. Through all our ups and downs he has always seemed consistent and true. We named him, as it were, by chance; but a very holy man, a mighty preacher, once bore that name. We named him after a great example—named him right, wife, perhaps, after all."

Mr. Porter was not the only one that confessed to a thankful retrospect. Sydney, with Alice's hand in his, could bear now to think of the dark days he had once passed through. Sydney had learned hard lessons, but, like other lessons difficult to learn, he had learned them well; and the vague speculative dreamer had become a resolute, earnest man and Christian.

And Paul—but need there be further said of him? There are such lives as his, many such, scattered throughout the land : lives intent upon the good of others, especially of those committed to their care. Humble lives, perhaps, yet full of noble living, earnest striving : lives whose tender zeal for others must sooner or later bring its own harvest of reward. They are not always widely known ; you may not find them in the world's annals, but yet of such lives is there not a sure and lasting record? Yea, verily, and the record is on high.

JARROLD AND SONS, PRINTERS, NORWICH.

Jarrold & Sons' New Books, Season 1888.

3/6 BOOKS FOR PRESENTATION
PRIZES, &c.

Mabel Berrington's Faith, and other Stories. NEW BOOK. By MRS. H. B. PAULL. A Series of Eight Stories for the Young People of the Family, bearing upon Domestic or Family Life. Cloth, elegant. Frontispiece.

The Greatest is Charity. A Series of Eight Stories on the Attributes of Charity, described in the 4th, 5th, and 7th verses of the Thirteenth Chapter of St. Paul's First Epistle to the Corinthians. By MRS. HENRY B. PAULL. Frontispiece. Crown 8vo, cloth, elegant, 400 pages. (Or with Gilt Edges, 4s. 6d.)

By MRS. WALTER SEARLE.

Redcar Lee. A Tale. Frontispiece. Crown 8vo, cloth, gilt.

Sarah Deck's Victory. A Tale. Frontispiece. Crown 8vo, cloth, gilt.

Somebody and Nobody. A Tale. Frontispiece. Crown 8vo, cloth, gilt.

Paul Haddon. A Tale. Frontispiece. Crown 8vo, cloth, gilt. An excellent Book for Young Men.

Paul Porter and His Brothers. By P. A. BLYTH, Author of "Merry and Grave; or, What's in a Name?" Frontispiece. Crown 8vo, cloth, gilt.

The Mother of the Wesleys. By the REV. J. KIRK. Portrait, crown 8vo. Sixth edition. (Or with gilt edges, 4s. 6d.)

Ishmael: a Tale of Syrian Life. By MRS. J. B. WEBB, Author of "Naomi," &c. With Eight full-page Illustrations. Cloth, elegant.

Mother's Last Words. By MRS. SEWELL. With fourteen beautiful Illustrations, designed and etched on Copper. By A. D. L. Handsomely bound in cloth.

Our Home Work. A Book for Girls. By MRS. WIGLEY, late of the Normal College Schools, Cheltenham. With Recommendatory Note from the Authoress of "The Peep of Day," "Line upon Line," &c.

London: Jarrold & Sons, 3, Paternoster Buildings.

2/- BOOKS FOR PRESENTATION, PRIZES, &c.

Elegantly Bound in Cloth.

Black Beauty: The Autobiography of a Horse. By ANNA SEWELL. Frontispiece. 12mo, cloth.

The Uses and Abuses of Domestic Animals. Uniform with "Black Beauty." By WILLIAM SMITH. 19 Illustrations.

Patience Hart's First Experience in Service. By MRS. SEWELL, Author of "Mother's Last Words.' Frontispiece. Cloth.

Clean Money: How it was Made, and What it Accomplished; or, the Birthdays of Peter Conyer and Josiah Marten. By MRS CONRAN. Crown 8vo. Frontispiece.

The Myrtles of Merrystone Mill. By MISS ONLEY. Crown 8vo. Frontispiece.

Little Gladness. By NELLIE HELLIS, Author of "Little King Davie." Crown 8vo. Frontispiece.

Two Little Lives. By MISS D. RYLANDS, Author of "Alfred May," &c. Crown 8vo. Frontispiece.

The Mother's Crown Jewels. By MRS. C. BICKER-STETH WHEELER, Author of "Memorials of a Beloved Mother," &c. Crown 8vo, cloth. Frontispiece.

The Art of Thriving; or, Thrift Lessons in Familiar Letters. By JOHN T. WALTERS, M.A., Rector of Norton. Revised edition. Crown 8vo. Frontispiece.

Ballads for Children. Including "Mother's Last Words," "Our Father's Care," and "The Children of Summerbrook." By MRS. SEWELL. Coloured Frontispiece and Illustrations. Fcap. 8vo, cloth, bevelled boards.

London : Jarrold & Sons, 3, Paternoster Buildings.

1/6 BOOKS FOR PRESENTATION
PRIZES, &c.

Kitty and Her Queen. By MISS ONLEY. 8vo, cloth.

Fred Williams. A Tale for Boys. Frontispiece. Crown 8vo, cloth.

Under the Apple Tree: a Story of Unselfish Love. By DANIEL DARLINGHURST.

The Story of the Two Margarets. By EMMA MARSHALL, Author of "Katie's Work," "Rose Bryant," &c. Fcap. 8vo, cloth.

Free England; or, Old Stories of the English Parliament. By MISS H. E. BOOTH. 8vo, cloth.

Joe Jasper's Troubles, and other Stories. By the REV. CHARLES COURTENAY. 8vo, cloth. Twelve Illustrations.

The Flower Show at Fairley Court. By the REV. JAMES M. RUSSELL, Curate of the Abbey Church, Hexham.

The False Key, and other Stories. By J. W. KIRTON, LL.D., Author of "Buy Your Own Cherries."

The Squire's Hat, and other Stories. By the REV. JAMES M. RUSSELL, Curate of Abbey Church, Hexham. 12 Illustrations.

Plain Words on Temperance. Twenty-four Interesting Sketches. By the REV. CHARLES COURTENAY. Twenty-four Illustrations.

Gone to the Bottom. Twenty-four Interesting Sketches, and Twenty-four Illustrations.

Half-Hour Temperance Readings (Series I.) By the REV. CHARLES COURTENAY. 8vo, cloth. Twelve full-page Illustrations.

Half-Hour Temperance Readings. (Series II.) By various Popular Authors. 8vo, cloth. Twelve full-page Illustrations.

These books are eminently adapted for reading at Mothers' and Cottage Meetings.

London : Jarrold & Sons, 3, Paternoster Buildings.

1/- BOOKS FOR PRESENTATION, PRIZES, &c.

The following Series of Books are suitable for Sunday or Week-day reading, and are elegantly bound in cloth, with Frontispiece.

Cecil Arlington's Quest. By HARRIETT BOULTWOOD.

Little King Davie; or, "Kings and Priests unto God." By NELLIE HELLIS.

A Star in the Crown. A Story of Schoolboy Life. By DANIEL DARLINGHURST.

Roy's Life. By DANIEL DARLINGHURST.

The Boys of the Cross. By DANIEL DARLINGHURST.

Father's Benjamin. By P. A. BLYTH.

By MRS. H. B. PAULL.

Oakfield Lodge.	**Dora's Difficulty.**
Horace Carleton.	**Frank Merton's Conquest.**
School-day Memories.	
Ethel Seymour.	**Lost Half-Sovereign.**

Buy Your own Cherries! and other Tales. By J. W. KIRTON, LL.D.

Mother's Last Words, Our Father's Care, &c. By MRS. SEWELL.

The Royal Brothers. By AGNES STRICKLAND.

Guthred, the Widow's Slave. By AGNES STRICKLAND.

Katie's Work. By EMMA MARSHALL.

The Little Forester and His Friend. A Ballad. By MRS. SEWELL.

Stories from English History. By M. J. WILKIN.

Stories from Home Life. By MRS. BEIGHTON. Illustrated, 12mo, cloth.

Davie Blake, the Sailor. By MRS. SEWELL.

The Children of Summerbrook. By MRS. SEWELL.

London : Jarrold & Sons, 3, Paternoster Buildings.

9d. BOOKS FOR PRESENTATION,
PRIZES, &c.

The following Series of Books are suitable for Sunday or Week-day reading, uniformly and elegantly bound in cloth, with Frontispiece.

Just Saved. The Story of Tim's Troubles. By HARRIETT BOULTWOOD, Author of "Isidora," &c.

John Fenton, the Young Hero. By HARRIETT BOULTWOOD, Author of "Cecil Arlington's Quest," &c.

BY MRS. H. B. PAULL.

Mabel Berrington's Faith. "Let us not be weary in well-doing, for in due season we shall reap if we faint not."

Aunt Ellen's Success. "Whom the Lord loveth He chasteneth."

Constance Somerville. "Even a child is known by his doings, whether his work be pure and whether it be right."

The Vicar's Children. "In all thy ways acknowledge Him, and He will direct thy steps."

Horace Brereton's Discovery. "Set a watch, O Lord, before my mouth, keep the doors of my lips."

Walter Stanley's Essay. "Before honour is humility."

The Two Homes. "Let them learn first to show piety at home."

Philip Thornton's Legacy. "In everything give thanks."

London: Jarrold & Sons, 3, Paternoster Buildings.

Books for Presentation, Prizes, &c.

PUBLISHED AT 9d.

My Teacher's Gift. For Girls. Frontispiece, 18mo, cloth. A suitable Present for Sunday School Girls.

My Teacher's Gift. For Boys. Frontispiece, 18mo, cloth. A suitable Present for Sunday School Boys.

Tales of the Work-room. The Sisters. By Mrs. CURTIS. Frontispiece, 18mo, cloth.

Consideration; or, How we can Help One Another. By EMMA MARSHALL. Coloured Frontispiece, 18mo, cloth.

Lessons about God. For very Young Children. By SOPHIA SINNETT. Coloured Frontispiece, 18mo, cloth.

PUBLISHED AT 6d.

My Text Book. A Text of Scripture with Appropriate Poetry for Every Day in the Year. Cloth, gilt edges.

Whisperings of the Soul. Sacred Poems. By HARRIET ROBBERDS. Cloth, gilt edges.

The Morning Repast. Being Daily Meditations and Hymns for a Month. Cloth, gilt edges.

Elizabeth Fry's Text Book. Texts for Every Day in the Year. Principally Practical and Devotional. Cloth, gilt edges.

Hymns for Quiet Hours. By Mrs. TOMKINS. Cloth, gilt edges.

The Martyr's Tree. By Mrs. SEWELL. 12mo, cloth.

The Mother's Sabbath Month. Hymns and Meditations for a Mother during her Month of Convalescence. 12mo, cloth.

Roger Wright's Fortune. By A. B. K.

London: Jarrold & Sons, 3, Paternoster Buildings.

Books for Presentation, Prizes, &c.

PUBLISHED AT 6d.

THE "GILES'S TRIP" SERIES.

Giles's Trip to London. A Norfolk Labourer's First Peep at the World. (Or in cloth, 1s.)

Molly Miggs's Trip to the Seaside. A Country Woman's First Peep at the World. (Or in cloth, 1s.)

Johnny's Jaunt. A Day in the Life of a Suffolk Couple. (Or in cloth, 1s.)

Jack Jawkins's First Vote; and How He Won Polly Pawkins. (Or in cloth, 1s.)

The Cockneys in the Country. A Diverting Story, in which the tables are turned on the Londoners.

Daisy Dimple: Her Loves and Her Lovers.

Nobody's Boy. A Strange Discovery.

'Arry and 'Arriett at Yarmouth. A Tale about Norfolk Dumplings. **2d.**

Tom Todgers and His Christmas Party. By the Author of "Giles's Trip to London." **2d.**

Joe Jenkins on the Great Crisis. A Labourer's Views on Home Rule. **1d.**

London: Jarrold & Sons, 3, Paternoster Buildings.

Lightning Source UK Ltd.
Milton Keynes UK
UKHW030638240720
367095UK00006B/527